Young People, Drugs and Community Safety

Edited by
Alan Marlow and Geoffrey Pearson

Russell House Publishing

First published in 1999 by:
Russell House Publishing Ltd.
4 St. George's House
Uplyme Road
Lyme Regis
Dorset DT7 3LS

Tel. 01297-443948
Fax. 01297 442722
e-mail help@russelhouse.co.uk

British Library Cataloguing-in-publication Data:
A catalogue record for this book is available from the British Library.

ISBN: 1-898924-38-4

Typeset by The Hallamshire Press Limited, Sheffield.

Printed by Cromwell Press, Trowbridge.

Russell House Publishing
Is a group of social work, probation, education and community work practitioners working in collaboration with a professional publishing team. Our aim is to work closely with the field to produce innovative and valuable materials to help managers, trainers, practitioners and students. We are keen to receive feedback on publications and new ideas for future projects.

Contents

Contributors   v

Introduction
Joined-up Thinking: Youth and Drugs Policy at the Millennium   1
Alan Marlow

Section One: Drugs Policy in a New Era

Chapter 1
A View from Government   10
Rt.Hon. George Howarth MP

Chapter 2
Drug Policy Dilemmas: Partnership, Social Exclusion and Targeting Resources   14
Geoffrey Pearson

Chapter 3
Between Two Stools: Children, Drugs Policy and Professional Practice   24
Mike Ashton

Chapter 4
Dutch Drug Policy and Cannabis   51
I.P. Spruit and M.W. van Laar

Chapter 5
The Development of Drug Services in European Prisons, 1995–1998   59
Alex Stevens

Section Two: Research and Evaluation

Chapter 6
Young People, Drugs and Community Life: The Messages from the Research   69
Nigel South and David Teeman

Chapter 7
Youth, Minorities, Drugs and Policing: A Study of Stop and Search   81
Alan Marlow

Chapter 8
Project Evaluation: Problems and Pitfalls   90
Nick Tilley

Section Three: Into Practice

Chapter 9
Multi-impact Drugs Prevention in the Community   99
David Teeman, Nigel South and Sheila Henderson

Chapter 10
Homelessness, Drugs and Young People   109
Geoffrey Wade and Trudi Barnett

Chapter 11
Selling Sex, Doing Drugs and Keeping Safe   118
Jenny J. Pearce

Chapter 12
Poverty, Drugs and Youth Prostitution: A Case Study   127
Sarah Crosby and David Barrett

Chapter 13
Drugs, Young People and the Internet   134
Alan Dearling

Chapter 14
Drugs and Peer Education   145
Joan Bailey and Andrew Elvin

Chapter 15
Casing the Joint: An Evaluation of Two Drugs Education Projects 155
David Porteous

Notes on Contributors

Mike Ashton	Editor, *Drug and Alcohol Findings*
Joan Bailey	Youth Action Co-ordinator, 'Safer Luton Partnership'
David Barrett	Head, Dept. of Applied Social Studies, University of Luton
Trudi Barnett	Development Officer, Hertfordshire Health Action with the Homeless
Sarah Crosby	Service Manager, Manchester Action on Street Health
Alan Dearling	Research Fellow, Vauxhall Centre for the Study of Crime, University of Luton
Andrew Elvin	Co-ordinator, 'Safer Luton Partnership'
Sheila Henderson	Fellow, Health and Social Services Institute, University of Essex, Colchester
Rt.Hon. George Howarth MP	Home Office Minister
M.W. van Laar	Fellow of the Trimbos Institute, Utrecht, The Netherlands
Alan Marlow	Senior Development Fellow, Vauxhall Centre for the Study of Crime, University of Luton
Jenny J. Pearce	Principal Lecturer in Social Work, Middlesex University
Geoffrey Pearson	Wates Professor of Social Work, Goldsmiths College
David Porteous	Research Fellow, Vauxhall Centre for the Study of Crime, University of Luton
Nigel South	Professor of Sociology and Director of the Health and Social Services Institute, University of Essex, Colchester
I.P. Spruit	Fellow of the Trimbos Institute, Utrecht, The Netherlands
Alex Stevens	European Project Manager, Cranstoun Drug Services
David Teeman	Research Officer, Health and Social Services Institute, University of Essex
Nick Tilley	Professor of Sociology, Crime and Social Research Unit, Nottingham Trent University
Geoffrey Wade	Development Officer, Adams Integra, Community Development Consultants

Acknowledgements

The conference upon which this book is based was organised at the University of Luton in July 1998 by Alan Marlow, Geoffrey Pearson, David Barrett and John Pitts.

Chapters 4 and 5 of this book are reproduced by kind permission of *Social Work in Europe*.

Chapter 3 was originally published in *Drugs Forum Focus* under the title of *Between Stools: Children in Trouble with Drugs* and it is reproduced here by kind permission.

Introduction

Joined-up Thinking: Youth and Drugs Policy at the Millennium

Alan Marlow

With the election of a Labour government in 1997, drugs were moved to the centre of the political stage. Drugs policy was to be 'joined-up', in the sense that a holistic multi-agency approach was to be adopted. Intervention was to be 'evidence-based' and closely monitored to ensure that it constituted 'best value'. As with Community Safety Partnerships resulting from the Crime and Disorder Act, action to reduce harm caused by drug abuse was to be driven by strategic agendas defined by the setting of key objectives. Disputes over causal links between drug use and crime notwithstanding, it is clear that, at local level, the issues of crime, drugs and community safety are inextricably linked. In many areas of the United Kingdom, public consultation conducted to construct community safety strategies indicate significant public concern over the issue of young people and drugs. The political will underpinning the anti-drugs policy was signalled early in the life of the new government by the appointment of the Anti-drugs Co-ordinator to the Cabinet Office – the so-called 'Drugs Tsar'.

Young People and Drugs

Official and public concern over the issue of youth and drug misuse is not simply a 'moral panic'. The research evidence leaves little doubt that the use of illicit drugs by young people is widespread. In their authoritative study *Young People and Crime*, Graham and Bowling concluded:

> *Just under one in two males and just over one in four females had ever used controlled drugs, while one in three males and one in six females had done so in 1992. The most common were cannabis, LSD, amphetamines, magic mushroom and ecstasy. Use of heroin, crack and cocaine was rare. Most drug users did so relatively infrequently, but around one in three male and one in five female cannabis users did so once a week or more* (Graham and Bowling 1995 p 22)

At least at the 'soft' end of the drug spectrum, it is clear from this research, based on the self-report method, that larger proportions of the population of young people have experimented with drugs and that gender differentials in usage are narrowing. There is also a fluidity in the patterns of substance misuse, probably dictated by fashions and supply factors within drug markets. Parker et al. (1998) point to major heroin outbreaks in many areas of Britain in the mid 1980s. These involved a minority of 18–25 year olds, predominantly unemployed and living in deprived urban areas. Whilst these 'heavy end careers' continued:

> *the 1990s have been dominated by the extensive 'recreational' use of drugs like cannabis, amphetamines and ecstasy, particularly by youth populations.* (Parker et al. 1998 p.v)

Drawing on the results of an audit of local Drug Action Teams, Parker et al. reported a recent spread of 'new' heroin outbreaks amongst young people. The evidence is that the outbreak is supply led, in that the UK has seen a major illegal importation of heroin from South West Asia brought in via the Balkan route. Prices have fallen and purity is high. Whilst most new young users might be described as socially excluded, there are signs of a broader penetration amongst young people 'bonded' in education and work and coming from more affluent families. Moreover, the age of onset has been falling for all drug initiation (Parker et al. 1998).

This scenario is alarming, suggesting an intensification of the problems confronting health care agencies and an increase in drug-related criminal victimisation. A projection from a random sample of suspects arrested by the police suggests that over 60 per cent of suspected offenders have traces of illegal drugs in their urine (Bennett (1998) quoted in *Tackling Drugs Together* Cm 3945 p 18). The precise causal link between drug abuse and offending is fiercely argued. Some research suggests a progression from dependency to crime and other interpretations conclude that the use of illicit drugs and offending form part of an overall pattern of illegal activity. However, the correlation linking drug use and wider offending is persuasive. In a recent study, 664 habitual drug users surveyed committed 70,000 offences over a three month period (Gossop, M. (1996) quoted in *Tackling Drugs Together to Build a Better Britain* Cm 3945 p 18).

It is tempting, therefore, to draw conclusions from the evidence that predict a downward spiral, using the thesis of a hedonistic progression from soft to hard drugs with ever increasing numbers of young people becoming enmeshed as habitual users and all that this implies for their life chances. Parker et al. (1995) conclude that adolescents of the 1990s are growing up with this new level of availability and that the accessibility of drugs is a normal part of the leisure and pleasure landscape. Nevertheless, the picture may be less bleak. Drugs are a common feature of the social landscape of young people but patterns and customs of use tend to be more complex and should be analysed in the contexts in which they arise.

Shiner and Newburn (1999) challenge the notion of normalisation, which, they suggest, exaggerates levels of youthful drug use:

> *Any theory relating to the place and meaning of drug use in contemporary youth culture must take account of the fact that many young people do not use, and never have used, an illicit substance .* (Shiner and Newburn in South (1999) p 156)

These authors point to American parallels which tend to undermine the claim that increased drug use is an inevitable consequence of the structure of post-industrial societies. In both the USA and UK, restrictive attitudes are widespread amongst young people and drug use continues to be heavily rule governed. Such resistance could be a resource for preventative programmes. They add the cautionary note that:

much of what is being said about young people and drugs, including a great deal of academic discourse, has simply reinforced adult concerns about the problematic nature of youth. (Shiner and Newburn in South (1999) p 157)

Indeed, the comment might also be added that the tone of the government's plans for youth justice, which identify young people as a 'problem', lends some force to that observation.

Amongst drug users, there is little cultural heterogeneity. Indeed, it could be argued that the only common characteristic is the illegal nature of the substances they use. According to a quantitative and qualitative research monograph by Demos (Perri 6, Jupp, B., Perry, H., and Lasky, K. (1997)), drug use features in a wide range of youth sub-cultures in Britain, but its importance to any given sub-culture varies enormously. The authors found a distinct difference in outlook between problem users on one hand and recreational and non-users on the other. Judged by a number of variables, such as sociability, respect for families and what is described as 'puritanical outlook', those who had tried illicit drugs tended to be similar in perspective to those who had not. Recreational users were as likely as non-users to disapprove of behaviour they regarded as being 'out of control'. Attitudes and behaviours that reduced the potential harm of drugs were evident within the youth sub-cultures of the interviewees (Perri 6, Jupp, B., Perry, H., and Lasky, K. (1997)).

However, amongst interviewees in a relatively socially deprived area, fatalism and family and social breakdown did coincide with heightened drug use, which was often a substitute rather than a supplement to other, very limited, leisure activities. That conclusion is common to most commentators and researchers in the field. The effects and consequences of illicit drug use are most pernicious and 'embedded' for those whose life chances are already circumscribed. As Pearson (See Chapter 2 in this volume) puts it:

it is recognised throughout that the most serious drug-related problems are inter-woven with the question of social exclusion and hence broader socio-economic forces and policy considerations

In the context of social exclusion, drug abuse is just one manifestation of adverse social conditions and therefore a single focus on 'drugs' may be at best only partially successful and at worst a doomed strategy. From this analysis, inter-agency, 'broad spectrum' approaches, based upon rigorous locally based research, are a pre-condition for progress.

New Labour and New Responses

The Government published its ten-year strategy document *Tackling Drugs Together to Build a Better Britain* in April 1998. The strategy was developed by the UK Anti-drugs Co-ordinator, Keith Hellawell. The underlying principles are, in summary, as follows:

Integration. The Government recognises the links between drug misuse and other social problems and positive advances in remedies for other social ills may have similar consequences for drug-related harm.

Evidence. The strategy is to be based on accurate, independent research.

Joint Action. The evidence is that joint action - if managed effectively - has a far greater impact on the complex drugs problem than disparate activities.

Consistency of Action. The approach will be nationally co-ordinated with fairness and consistency.

Effective Communication. The messages must be clear and consistent. The constant theme must be that drug-taking can be harmful.

Accountability. Progress must be objectively assessed and the structures, resources and performance mechanisms exist solely for that purpose.

(*Tackling Drugs Together* Cm 3945 April 1998 p 11)

There are four aims to the strategy:

1. To help young people resist drug misuse in order to achieve their full potential in society
2. To protect communities from drug related anti-social and criminal behaviour
3. To enable people with drug problems to overcome them and live healthy and crime free lives
4. To stifle the availability of illegal drugs on our streets

The model adopted for community safety and youth justice is to be applied to the anti-drugs strategy - central co-ordination with devolved accountability for locally derived initiatives. Action is to be based upon 'key objectives' and performance indicators through which progress might be assessed.

The strategy will be co-ordinated and driven across government by the Cabinet Sub-Committee on Drug Misuse, to which the Anti-drugs Co-ordinator reports. In turn, the Co-ordinator will chair a new body, the UK Anti-drugs Strategic Steering Group. Delivery at local level will be through Drug Action Teams and their Reference Groups. The stress of the document is towards a more effective use of existing but poorly co-ordinated expenditure rather than an overall increase in resources. Agencies will be expected to direct resources from their budgets towards inter-agency work. In particular, there will be two key reforms:

1. Drug-related expenditure will shift over time away from reaction to the consequences of the drugs problem and towards positive investment in targeting and preventing drug use.

2. The bulk of targeted resources should be spent on collaborative projects which tackle high priority groups – in particular vulnerable young people, drug-related offenders and problem drug misusers. (Cm 3945 p 30)

This new emphasis makes sense, as research conducted by the RAND corporation, quoted by Geoffrey Pearson in Chapter 2, demonstrates, the cost-effectiveness of treatment programmes for harm reduction far outweighs the cost effectiveness of enforcement. Shifting the direction of resources will not be easy. As the document points out, 62 per cent of the total is spent on enforcement-related work, 'much of it reactive and not drug specific' (p30). However, the Home Secretary signalled how such a transfer might be achieved. In his Ministerial Priorities to the police service for 1999/2000, he set a performance indicator which relates to prevention through treatment

the number of offenders referred to and entering treatment programmes as a result of arrest referral schemes. (Home Office 1998)

In May 1999, following the publication of the Anti-drug Co-ordinator's first annual report, Dr Jack Cunningham, the Minister with co-ordinating responsibility, announced these ambitious targets:

- reducing the proportion of people under 25 reporting use of heroin in the last month and the previous year by 25% by 2005 and 50% by 2008
- reducing levels of repeat offending amongst drug misusing offenders by 50% by 2008 and 25% by 2005
- increasing the participation of problem drug misusers including prisoners, in drug treatment programmes which have a positive impact on health and crime by 100% by 2008 and 66% by 2005
- reducing access to the drugs which cause most harm, particularly heroin and cocaine among young people (under 25) by 50% by 2008 and 25% by 2005 (Cabinet Office 25.5.99)

There is a clear focus, which will necessarily be reflected in practice through the accountability mechanisms, on the biologically damaging drugs. The inference may be that there is some element of acceptance in the use of 'soft' drugs or perhaps that reduction may best be achieved through educative processes, which under the drugs strategy, will commence at the age of 5 years (Cm 3945 p 15).

There is also the problem of measurement, notoriously difficult in the covert world of drug abuse. Simple objectives allow some manipulation by the unscrupulous and that relating to participation in drug treatment programmes, deals only with outputs and not outcomes; numbers entering programmes may or may not be related to the rate of desistance from drug use by the same subjects. There is a fruitful and important role here for disinterested and objective evaluation and monitoring.

Whatever the caveats and shortcomings, there is no doubt that the Government has embarked upon its harm reduction programme with determination. In 1997, Michael. O'Byrne, a chief constable addressing the problem of tackling drug abuse wrote:

Only one of the factors that show that the political will needed to improve the chances of success appears to be present, that is public statements. It is time that the propaganda stopped and the will to succeed was adequately reflected in the provision of resources and the funding of research into what works. (O'Byrne (1998) p 59)

The strategy has provided some of the required clarity, albeit that resources will be found from re-distribution rather than new sources.

Reassurance may be drawn from history. In the eighteenth century, alcohol was a far bigger problem than it is today. In 1735, the annual consumption of gin alone in London was equivalent to 8.5 gallons for every man, woman and child (Ascoli 1979). The problem was eventually rendered more manageable and less socially pathological by a range of factors - economic, legislative and social improvement through education and campaigning. It took a little time but it was an early example of a successful multi-agency approach.

The Structure of the Book

Young People, Drugs and Community Safety is divided into three sections. In the first, contributors address the development, theoretical and ideological assumptions of current drug policy.

In Chapter 1, *A View from Government*, Home Office Minister George Howarth MP stresses that the government is committed to a multi-agency approach to harm reduction aimed at helping young people to resist drug abuse, achieve their full potential as citizens and protect communities from drug related anti-social behaviour. Amongst these policies will be a commitment to drugs education from the age of five years, together with the involvement of parents and schools. The government also accepts that treatment intervention can be effective in reducing acquisitive crime and there will be the backing of treatment and testing orders to ensure offenders stay drug free. He stresses that there is no single solution and the principle that local partnerships can make a difference is at the heart of the new anti-drugs strategy.

Geoffrey Pearson also takes the view that multi-agency work is essential but in Chapter 2, *Drug Policy Dilemmas: Partnership, Social Exclusion and Targeting Resources*, he observes that it is not easy to accomplish. Ingrained conflicts may surface and it is important to recognise such differences. Strategies should focus on the reduction of social and economic costs but will often face resource gaps and skill deficiencies. He points to research evidence that bears powerful testimony to the cost benefits of treatment programmes and suggests there should be a shift from tackling the consequences of drug abuse towards a positive investment in preventative targeting of resources. However, programmes must link with other more difficult strategies to improve the life chances of those at risk from drug abuse.

In Chapter 3, *Between Two Stools: Children, Drugs Policy and Professional Practice*, Mike Ashton critically reviews four reports published at the end of 1997 on the issues of parents, young people and drugs. The common theme is that there should be a systematic focus on young people and the most important people in their lives. The reports, he argues, are timely, as the development of responses to an increasing problem is in its infancy. In his analysis of the reports, he draws out the themes that should form part of the construction of the developing agenda of reducing harm to young people.

Holland is often quoted as a model of tolerant policies towards drug misuse and in Chapter 4, *Dutch Drug Policy and Cannabis*, I.P.Spruit and M.W. Van Laar outline and review the principles and effects of the controlled and limited tolerance of cannabis consumption in coffee shops. They contend that this approach has achieved a separation of the markets for soft drugs within the country and those drugs that carry an unacceptable risk. The conditional acceptance of the use of cannabis may be influential in the fact that the number of hard drug addicts has stabilised and that the Netherlands has fewer drug-related deaths than other advanced countries. The authors argue that whilst cannabis is by no means risk free, its use is no more harmful than that of tobacco or alcohol.

Alex Stevens is the European Project Manager of Cranstoun Drug Services. In Chapter 5, he examines *The Development of Drug Services in European Prisons 1995–1998*. He concludes that divergence and inconsistency are the defining characteristics of policies across the continent, but in scanning educative, harm reduction and abstinence based services, there has been a rapid development over the three years. Such provision reflects service policies outside prison but with a time delay before implementation. Nevertheless, considering the high level of problematic drug use amongst prisoners, development is still inadequate.

Section 2 of the book deals with *Research and Evaluation*.

In Chapter 6, *Young People, Drugs and Community Life: the Messages from Research*, Nigel South and David Teeman look at the messages from research and from 'thinking about research'. They remind the reader that the drug scene is far from clear in its demonology. Legal and illegal substances are used and abused in 'routine ways and routine contexts' and at least in terms of acquaintance, drugs have become a normal part of life for many young people. They analyse trends by the parameters of age, social class, gender, ethnicity and types of drug. They conclude with a plea to promote a research sensitive culture amongst practitioners, as the UK is poor at seeing the value of research and evaluation. Echoing George Howarth and Geoffrey Pearson, South and Teeman stress the need for partnerships based upon a common language and understanding. To achieve this, local research, evaluation and information gathering are pre-requisites, which need not be the preserve of the professional researcher.

The enforcement of drugs legislation is distinct from most crimes as it is dependent for the construction of patterns of offending on enforcement activity itself. In Chapter 7, *Youth, Minorities, Drugs and Policing: A Study of Stop and Search*, Alan Marlow presents some empirical research that demonstrates how the exercise of stop and search powers by police officers disproportionately selected young South Asians as suspects as a result of assumptions about drug offending.

In Chapter 8, *Project Evaluation: Problems and Pitfalls*, Nick Tilley draws on his wide experience as a researcher in the fields of crime prevention and community safety strategies to point out common failings in evaluation. He distinguishes monitoring from evaluation, stating that the latter is a much more difficult discipline. Policy makers and practitioners need to develop habits of critical scrutiny, for even the best evaluations may offer only partial insights. In a timely chapter, in view of the government's targets, Professor Tilley urges the asking of sensible questions and the provision of patient answers to avoid 'a candyfloss world of appearance rather than substance'.

Section 3, *Into Practice*, brings together chapters by those engaged in or researching projects involving young people and problems of drug misuse.

In Chapter 9, *Multi-Impact Drugs Prevention in the Community*, David Teeman, Nigel South and Sheila Henderson explore the possibilities and opportunities offered by an integrated approach to drug prevention through a programme of evaluated practice. They describe a multi-impact community based initiative based on two project centres and outline the early results from a continuing evaluation. The most important factors for success involve high quality leadership from people with proper training and skills.

Geoff Wade and Trudi Barnett are professionals in the field of homelessness and in Chapter 10, *Homelessness, Drugs and Young People*, they examine links between homelessness, health problems and drug abuse amongst young people and outline a plan for co-ordinated action. Whilst the multi-agency approach is widely advocated it can often be no more than a veneer in practice and they outline a plan for co-ordinated action in the areas of need determination, service delivery, communication and information sharing.

Jenny Pearce also points to illicit drug use as just one aspect of a pathology of disadvantage. In Chapter 11, *Young Women and Community Safety; Selling Sex, Doing Drugs and Keeping Safe*, she analyses the association between the involvement of young women in prostitution and drug abuse. She concludes that young women selling sex are invariably running from violence and abuse, experiencing increasing danger on the streets and using drugs to alleviate some of the pressures on them. She concludes with a plea for a recognition of these issues in community safety strategies and suggests the principles upon which they should be based. It is easy to fail to recognise the particular vulnerability of these young women and workers and professionals should, concludes Jenny Pearce, 'shout for invisible people'.

David Barrett and Sarah Crosby would agree with Jenny Pearce's findings. They observe that drug use is a strong imperative for involvement in prostitution for many young women and the combination of the two dramatically increases their health risks. In Chapter 12, *Poverty, Drugs and Youth Prostitution: A Case Study*, they outline the principles of the Manchester Action on Street Health programme that aims to reduce these health risks through the provision of health care and advice to the vulnerable groups.

In Chapter 13, *Drugs, Young People and the Internet*, Alan Dearling points out the growing power and usefulness of the Internet as an effective communications tool in the drugs field. The breadth of information ranges from sources of illegal supply to serious research and therefore the Internet is an increasingly rich source of information for all concerned with the issue of drugs, including young people. He provides an introductory guide to accessing the Internet for drugs information.

Education is an important strand of the Government's anti-drug strategy and in Chapter 14, *Drugs and Peer Education*, Joan Bailey and Andrew Elvin provide an overview of a peer-led education project implemented in Luton high schools. The rationale for the project, its structure and administration are outlined along with the importance of independent evaluation.

In Chapter 15, *Casing the Joint: An Evaluation of Two Drugs Prevention Projects*, David Porteous of the University of Luton, discusses the method and findings of the evaluation research. Drawing from this and other research, he argues that the credibility of the peer educator is an important determinant for success. The second evaluation concerns a photography project to involve vulnerable young people in the production of posters to promote drugs awareness. The strengths and weaknesses of the approach are assessed and in particular, the extent to which young people become engaged in such projects. Tangible evaluation in educational projects is always difficult as they are based upon a 'leap of faith' in the assumption that knowledge of the harmful consequences will lead to reductions in consumption. As David Porteous concludes, 'Now there's a question'.

References

Ascoli, D. (1979). *The Queen's Peace*. London: Hamish Hamilton.

Cabinet Office (1999). Press Release CAB 111/99, 25.5.99.

Cm 3945 Government White Paper. *Tackling Drugs Together to Build a Better Britain*. London: HMSO.

Graham, J., and Bowling, B. (1995). *Young People and Crime*. Home Office Study 145. London: Home Office.

Home Office (1998). *Circular – Ministerial Priorities, Key Performance Indicators and Efficiency Planning for 1999/2000*. London: Home Office.

O'Byrne, M. (1998). Policing in an Uncertain World. In Marlow, A., and Pitts, J. (Eds.). *Planning Safer Communities*. Lyme Regis: Russell House.

Parker, H., Bury, C., and Egginton, R. (1998). *New Heroin Outbreaks Amongst Young People in England and Wales*. Crime and Detection Series – Paper 92. Police Research Group. London: Home Office.

Parker, H., Measham, F., and Aldridge, J. (1995). *Drug Futures: Changing Patterns of Drug Use Amongst English Youth*. London: Institute for the Study of Drug Dependence.

Perri 6, Jupp, B., Perry, H., and Lasky, K. (1997). Young People and *Drugs. In Findings, Social Policy Research*, 133. York: Joseph Rowntree.

Shiner, M., and Newburn, T. (1999). Taking Tea with Noel. In South, N. (Ed.). *Drugs, Cultures, Controls and Everyday Life*. London: Sage.

South, N. (1999). Debating Drugs and Everyday Life: Normalisation, Prohibition and 'Otherness'. In South, N. (Ed.). *Drugs, Cultures, Controls and Everyday Life*. London: Sage.

Section One: Drugs Policy in a New Era

Chapter 1

A View from Government

Rt.Hon. George Howarth MP

Introduction

In spring 1997 the Government launched its ten year anti-drugs strategy *Tackling Drugs Together to Build a Better Britain* and the Crime and Disorder Bill which included important measures aimed at tackling crime and improving community safety which became law in July 1998.

The Drugs Problem

Drug misuse *is* a serious problem. The 1996 British Crime Survey – which compared figures with the 1994 survey – suggested that the number of young people (in the age group 16 to 29) using drugs did not increase significantly over that period. However, it suggests that drug misuse has been rising in the North and the Midlands, but declining in London, at least, among the younger age group 16–19.

A separate survey of 27,000 schoolchildren last year showed that levels of 15–16 year-olds who had tried any illegal drugs appeared to be stable, while the figure for 14–15 year-olds declined to 26 per cent from 33 per cent, between 1996 and 1997.

On some measures, illicit drug misuse is stabilising but on others the trend remains alarming; there can never be room for complacency. But this does not mean that we are fighting a lost cause.

The New Drugs Strategy

Drug problems do not occur in isolation. They are often only a part of a range of social problems facing individuals or communities. The ACMD report published this week, suggests that deprivation can make a causal contribution to damaging kinds of drug misuse. That is why the Government's new drugs strategy will treat drug misuse together with other social and environmental factors.

The Government is also working to tackle the wider issues. For example, through the welfare to work programme and other initiatives to help prevent social exclusion, we will create a more positive environment in which the lure of drugs is less attractive.

To tackle these problems effectively we must all work together – Government Departments and agencies, police, probation and treatment services, local and health authorities, the voluntary and the private sector. Partnership and common purpose are at the heart of the new strategy.

Much has been done under the previous drugs strategy by Drug Action Teams in setting up partnerships locally. Also the Home Office Drugs Prevention Initiative is helping to show what can be done in the community to resist the threat of drugs. The new drugs strategy, which provides a long-term approach, will build on this.

The main aims of the new strategy are:

- To help young people resist drug misuse in order to achieve their full potential in society.
- To protect our communities from drug-related anti-social and criminal behaviour.

Drugs and Young People

Young People are increasingly exposed at ever earlier ages to illegal drugs, as well as to alcohol and tobacco. This does not necessarily mean that they will get involved with drugs; many will not – as the research shows. However, some *will* experiment. We want to both reduce the number that do and to reverse the trend of increasingly earlier experimentation with drugs. We know that young people are concerned about drugs; they want reliable information – information which they can trust.

To be effective, prevention has to start early, before young people begin to experiment not only with illegal drugs but all substances, including alcohol and tobacco. This is important because research shows a correlation between early use of tobacco, alcohol and illicit drugs and the development of more frequent and problematic use. Young people are often exposed to confusing and often contradictory messages about drugs. The messages they receive about drugs must be consistent and appropriate to their age and circumstances.

We propose that there is drugs education for all young people, beginning from the age of 5, to help equip them with the knowledge and necessary skills to resist drugs. Evaluation of a life-skills drugs education programme published last year by the Home Office Drugs Prevention Initiative, provides some evidence that such programmes at primary school level *do* help to prevent or delay young people's involvement with illegal drugs and tobacco.

School-based approaches are only part of the answer. What goes on in schools needs to be supported and re-enforced by approaches in the community, involving parents and others who have an influence on young people. This is especially important for those young people who may be more vulnerable to drug misuse because of other factors.

As part of the proposed programme of action under the new strategy, we will ensure that those most at risk of developing serious drug problems receive appropriate and specific interventions. Work on the ground is showing that it *is* possible to identify and reach those most at risk – for example through pupil referral units for those excluded from school, through residential care and through contact with the youth justice system. We need to build on this work.

Drugs and Community Safety

The second aim of the new strategy concerns the link between drugs and community safety.

The consequences of drug misuse affect us all to some degree and can pose very real community safety problems. Street dealing and acquisitive crime committed by drug misusers, as well as the environmental and health risks caused by drug use itself, can all contribute to fear of crime and lead to a spiral of decline in a community.

Until recently our perceptions of the extent and nature of drug-related crime were ill defined. Though we can never know precisely what proportion of crime is drug driven, Home Office research published in April sheds new light.

The research, the first of its kind outside the United States, shows two things far more clearly than ever before. First, that the levels of drug misuse on the part of offenders are remarkably high by comparison with the general population. Second, it shows that those offenders dependent on heroin and/or crack cocaine are committing far more property offences than other offenders.

Overall, 61% of arrestees proved to have taken at least one prohibited drug – and 27% tested positive for two or more. Cannabis was the commonest at 46%, heroin and other opiates were present in 18% of the sample and cocaine and crack in 10%.

Insights into the offending behaviour of these arrestees were obtained by questioning them about their illegal income both from property crime and drug dealing. The two drugs most clearly implicated here were the more costly and addictive ones – heroin and crack cocaine.

Levels of illegal income were highest among those arrestees who reported recent use of heroin or crack – roughly £10,000 to £20,000 a year.

Though this is only a first round of research, we can tentatively conclude that close to a *third* of property crime is drug driven. We are expecting to do more research in future – both to clarify the relationship between drugs and crime and to assess changes over time.

Treatment Interventions

There is a positive side to this bleak picture, however. Other recent research confirms that putting drug-related offenders in touch with treatment agencies can lead to real reductions in both levels of drug misuse and offending. The criminal justice system offers the opportunity at various stages to break the drugs-crime circle.

The point of arrest is one such opportunity. Being detained in a police cell is for many a sobering experience. At this point, at least some arrestees are ready to take advantage of offers of assistance. An evaluation of schemes in South London, Derby and Brighton showed that six to eight months after their initial contact with drug workers, one in four of those referred for help were no longer using any illegal drug. Nearly half had stopped using heroin or crack. Most of the remainder reported at least some reduction in their drug use.

Alongside this reduction in drug taking was also a reduction in property crime. The offending rate of those who were helped fell, on average, from over 130 crimes per month to less than 30. Reductions of this order go towards justifying arrest referral schemes in terms of cost effectiveness.

Treatment and Testing Order

For the worst drug-misusing offenders, we are bringing forward in the Crime and Disorder Bill a new measure to crack down on drug-related offending by getting them into treatment and ensuring that they stay there. The Drug Treatment and Testing Order will be a rigorously enforced community sentence.

It is vital to ensure that offenders stay drug free. Testing will be mandatory. Judges and magistrates will have a bigger role and will be required to follow the progress of the people that they sentence to treatment by regularly reviewing the order.

Crime and Disorder Bill

The Crime and Disorder Act places two new statutory duties on local authorities:
1. To form local multi-agency partnerships to reduce all crime and to enhance community safety.
2. To establish multi-agency youth offending teams and to ensure the provision of youth justice services.

Though the focus will lie with local authorities and the police, they will be obliged to involve a wide range of partners including voluntary groups, the business sector as well as local residents. The aim is to be as inclusive as possible, so that the wider community consequences are fully taken into account and so that all available resources are used in the most effective way. For example, health authority staff working in youth offending teams will have an important role to play in enabling the teams to access relevant local services in their work with young offenders. There will also be scope for drug workers to be included as members of youth offending teams.

Conclusion

All these proposals are based on partnership. As the ACMD report and the work of the Drug Prevention Initiative show, there is no single solution to the problems of drug misuse. But local people, working together in partnership, *can* make a difference. Partnership works and community involvement approaches can help to. make communities places where drugs and drug-dealing are much less likely to gain a foothold. Therefore partnership is at the heart of the new anti-drugs strategy.

Chapter 2

Drug Policy Dilemmas: Partnership, Social Exclusion, and Targeting Resources

Geoffrey Pearson

Introduction

British drug control policy has gone through various shifts and changes, just as the drug scene itself has changed over the years (Pearson, 1991). As the chapters in this book show, there are a multitude of difficulties to be encountered in modern Britain within the theme of 'Young People, Drugs and Community Safety', each important in its own way. Nevertheless, the major drug problem confronting Britain today is heroin misuse, in the form of the legacy of the heroin epidemic which swept through many towns and cities in the 1980s. Drug problems had not been unknown prior to that time, but in the 1980s heroin misuse began to appear in many parts of Britain where it had been previously quite unknown. The heroin problem quickly established itself in these areas, where it was to assume a characteristic form of difficulty, particularly on working class housing estates already hit by high levels of unemployment and poverty (Pearson, 1987; Pearson et al., 1985; Parker et al., 1988; Burr, 1987). Since these were the same neighbourhoods often experiencing the highest levels of crime and the 'fear of crime', as indicated by the British Crime Survey, the heroin problem thus compounded the difficulties of these already embattled communities (Hough and Mayhew, 1985).

We are still living with the legacy of the 1980s heroin epidemic which transformed the meaning of drug problems in Britain. There are also other difficulties to engage with. Local pockets of 'crack' or 'rock' cocaine misuse, for example, have had serious consequences in some parts of the country (Parker and Bottomley, 1996;Edmunds et al., 1996; Bennett, 1998). There are also indications of new heroin outbreaks among young people in several parts of England and Wales (Parker et al., 1998b), with further worrying signs of growing problems of heroin misuse among young Asian men in several of Britain's South Asian communities where youth unemployment levels are also sky high (Pearson and Patel, 1998). All this, of course, needs to be set against the fact that young people in modern Britain are much more familiar with drugs and drug cultures, although it remains true that in spite of moral panics about MDMA (Ecstasy) and other dance drugs, cannabis is by far the most commonly used drug in Britain, and that this youthful drug culture is predominantly a cannabis culture (Parker et al., 1998a; Ramsay and Spiller, 1997).

The emphasis in this chapter will not deal in detail with Britain's drug-related problems. A useful review of these can be found in a recent special issue of the *Journal of Drug Issues* (Power, 1998). Instead, we examine the dilemmas of policy and practice encountered in the drugs field, against the background of the UK government ten-year drug strategy, *Tackling Drugs Together to Build a Better Britain* (CM 3945, HMSO, 1998). The strategy lays a great deal of emphasis on collaboration and partnership between different agencies, on the targeting of resources, and on the connection between drug-related problems and social exclusion: and these will form the three central themes.

The Meaning of Partnership in The Multi-agency Maze

Drug policy is always something of a juggling act because there are inevitably a number of quite legitimate, but sometimes quite opposed, policy objectives. Primarily, the drug field is divided into three broad spheres: prevention; treatment; and law enforcement. Traditionally, prevention has been aimed at 'primary prevention' goals: that is, deterring young people who have not yet tried or encountered illicit drugs from experimentation. Treatment has been traditionally aimed at those problematic users who have become heavily dependent on drugs, and its aim has been primarily to benefit those individuals and to enable them to live drug-free lives. Law enforcement has as its primary aim to stem the flow of drugs and to make them more difficult to obtain.

Even if things were that simple, and they aren't, drug policy would still be a highly complex interplay between these different spheres of action. Further layers of complexity are introduced when we recognise that these three primary areas are themselves internally complex. 'Prevention', for example, has for many years in UK policy embraced the notion of 'harm reduction', particularly following the arrival of the HIV/AIDS epidemic and the truly path-breaking reports of the Advisory Council on the Misuse of Drugs, *AIDS and Drug Misuse* (ACMD, 1988 and 1989), which recommended the extension of needle exchange schemes and other similar initiatives.

The Advisory Council's guiding principle was clearly stated in its first report: 'HIV is a greater threat to public and individual health than drug misuse' (ACMD, 1988, p 1). Hence, 'prevention' did not mean preventing drug use, but preventing the risks and harms associated with drug use, and preventing the more harmful forms of drug use. Adjusting the route of administration of drug use thereby became a major policy objective: substituting oral methadone, for example, for injectable heroin. Or, for those who persisted in injecting drugs, making available clean injecting equipment, encouraging them not to share 'works' with other users, offering instruction in how to inject drugs properly. To many people, no doubt, this was scandalous and amounted to condoning the use of drugs, but this harm-reduction philosophy was to direct policy and practice for the next ten years, and arguably has helped to reduce the prevalence of HIV/AIDS among injecting drug users in the UK.

If 'prevention' no longer meant 'preventing drug use', for many years already 'treatment' for problem drug users had essentially meant prescribing pharmaceutically pure drugs as a substitute for street drugs. Abstinence might remain an ultimate goal, but certainly in the context of HIV risk among intravenous drug users, it was by no means regarded as paramount. Programmes such as methadone 'maintenance', which are basically another form of health-oriented harm-reduction strategy, also found a key justification as a method of crime-reduction (Parker and Kirby, 1986). It is well known by virtue of research and everyday experience that many people with expensive and compulsive drug habits, such as daily heroin users, finance these habits through property crime, drug dealing, or prostitution (Bennett, 1998). Methadone maintenance reduces the need for addicts to generate income by these illicit means, and 'treatment' thereby becomes a means of 'prevention', albeit crime prevention.

If health care and treatment strategies such as methadone maintenance thereby serve the goals of the criminal justice system and law enforcement agencies, it is equally true that one of the great paradoxes of drug policy is that through legislation such as the Misuse of Drugs Act (1971) we attempt to achieve what are essentially public health goals, reducing the availability of, and consumption of, dangerous drugs, by means of the criminal law. This paradox is the cornerstone of Mark Kleiman's book *Against Excess* (1992) which provides a sweeping cost-benefit over-view of drug policy, in terms of how to phrase a policy which maximises positive benefits while minimising the negative side-effects, always acknowledging that some drug control policies can, and do, make a bad situation worse. If criminal law in current prohibitionist drug policies is a major means by which to achieve health goals, the law is also there to punish people, and thereby also hopefully to deter drug use. But when we punish drug users by sentencing them to imprisonment, we commit them to an environment where drugs are invariably widely available, but the means of using them more safely (clean injecting equipment) are not. So that it becomes possibly more likely that drug injectors will share needles and syringes when in the custody of the State than when running free in the street. Such was the concern that prisons might become a major site for the amplification of HIV infection that the Advisory Council even went so far as to toy with the idea that needle-exchange schemes might be established in prisons (ACMD, 1988, p 65). The problem was further compounded, moreover, when, following the introduction of mandatory drug testing in prisons, worrying evidence appeared that some prisoners might be switching from the almost 'traditional' use of cannabis to the much more dangerous use of opiates in order to avoid detection, since cannabis lingers so much longer in the body-system, and is therefore more easily traced (ISDD, 1998).

We are now ten years on from the highly influential reports of the Advisory Council on *AIDS and drug misuse*, and although it is imperative that harm-reduction safeguards are maintained, and even improved, against the transmission of HIV and other blood-borne diseases, priorities have changed in terms of how the British Government frames drug policy. In its ambitious 10-year strategy which was announced in the

Spring of 1998, although prevention, treatment and law enforcement all receive mention, the emphasis has undoubtedly shifted towards crime-reduction and the reduction of other forms of anti-social nuisance associated with serious drug misuse. A primary objective is thereby to reduce the harm caused to the wider community by drug misuse, a need which could be recognised some years ago, but which had not been placed as centrally as it could have been in the past (Gilman and Pearson, 1991). A central means by which this is to be achieved is through channelling offenders with drug-related problems through the criminal justice system towards systems of treatment and support which will assist them in tackling their drug misuse.

All this, as the Minister for State George Howarth makes plain in Chapter 1, will require an emphasis on joint-working and partnership between agencies often unaccustomed to working with each other, and sometimes even suspicious of each other. What can be seen in the paragraphs above, however, concerning the complex interplay of drug policy is that 'joint working' and 'partnership' are not simply buzz words for this year's new policy spin. They are unavoidable consequences of the ways in which the field of drug policy has evolved. We are engaged in 'joint working', either working for each other, or against each other, whether we like it or not. The policies and practices adopted by one agency will inevitably do something to shape the environment of others. We need think only of the disastrous consequences of actions by the police in the Scottish city of Edinburgh in the 1980s which, before the consequences of the HIV/AIDS epidemic for the drugs field had been fully understood, adopted a policy of confiscating injecting equipment, which resulted in the increased sharing of 'works' by drug injectors, and an abnormally high HIV prevalence level in that city (Pearson, 1991, pp 205–207). A more recent research study from Australia has shown that this lesson has not always been learned, and that policing methods adopted against a network of injecting drug users in a Sydney suburb had serious consequences in public health terms, making drug users more secretive and difficult to contact by health services, and more likely to adopt risky practices such as sharing injecting equipment (Maher and Dixon, 1999).

As these examples show, joint working is not an option or a luxury; it is the shared, over-lapping and sometimes conflictual ground of drugs work. Effective multi-agency work is nevertheless not an easy thing to accomplish. Research in the mid-1980s when the multi-agency approach to crime prevention was being fashioned showed clearly that there were inevitable conflicts of interest, between the police, probation, social services, local authority housing departments, etc., and which were a consequence of the structural juxtaposition of agencies, rather than just the attitudes of agency workers (Blagg et al., 1988; Pearson et al., 1992). Some of these potential and actual sites of conflict derived from such issues as different missions and objectives, different systems of representation and internal accountability, power differentials between agencies, and varying procedures for information sharing and protecting confidentiality.

But conflicts could also arise from quite mundane issues such as the routine workloads of different agencies. Simply put, if any given problem impacted in a major way on one agency's workload, but was relatively insignificant on another agency's list of priorities, why should the second agency commit already scarce resources to a low priority target? Subsequent research has considerably advanced the understanding of how multi-agency conflicts arise and how they can be resolved, although some aspects of the underlying philosophy of the multi-agency approach remain controversial (Crawford, 1997). It remains true, moreover, at a practical level that simple exhortations to regard inter-agency co-operation as a 'good thing' will often founder against ingrained, structural oppositions between different agencies. That rather than start from a naive position that multi-agency partnership is an unquestionable virtue, a better strategy is to begin from an open and mature acknowledgement that different agencies in the State, voluntary and private sectors will not always share the same organisational objectives, professional ideologies, and personal belief systems. It is equally important that these differences of aim, mission and vision are often valuable and should not be blurred, and to plan accordingly.

Counting the Cost and Targeting Resources

One major area of contest which can be easily foreseen is that of resource allocation, involving both short-term and long-term considerations. In the short term it is hardly surprising that if government policy and legislation involves a major shift of gear, as the drugs strategy does, combined with the provisions of the Crime and Disorder Act (1998), Treatment and Testing Orders, Youth Offender Teams, etc., resource gaps are going to appear pretty quickly. Drug services were not slow to point out that, given already existing waiting lists for drug users seeking help, using the Courts to 'fast track' offenders with drug-related problems towards helping agencies could only make things worse. There are promising indications from one 'fast-track' programme already evaluated that this can be an effective means of tackling the drugs-crime connection, although waiting lists had increased significantly as a consequence of the 'fast-track' initiative, and mistrust between drug services and criminal justice agencies meant that there was also sometimes a reluctance to share information such as the outcomes of urine-tests (Barton, 1999). Another recent evaluation by Tim Newburn (1999) for the Drugs Prevention Initiative of two pilot projects which focus on youth justice, while confirming the continuing difficulties encountered in multi-agency work, suggests that skill shortages also act as a barrier to the delivery of such programmes. And yet training, significantly, goes unmentioned in the strategy document.

Where long-term planning is concerned, the emphasis must be on attempting to reduce the social and economic costs resulting from drug misuse. Reliable estimates of such things are, nevertheless, notoriously difficult to make, witness the controversy around the latest US estimates of the costs resulting from drug and alcohol misuse (Harwood et al., 1999; Reuter, 1999; Kleiman, 1999). In terms of guaranteeing effective monitoring of the UK drug strategy, it should be a matter for sober reflection that social cost estimates of drug-related harm should remain so controversial even in the USA where there is a much better developed set of drug monitoring programmes and a research capacity so much larger than our own, that the budget of the National Institute of Drug Abuse alone is said to amount to 85 per cent of total world funding on drugs research.

The UK strategy document arrives at an initial estimate of £1.4 billion drug-related public expenditure annually, and shows how this is currently deployed. Whereas 61% is spent on enforcement, only 13% goes to treatment, 12% to education and prevention, and a further 13% on international supply reduction. It is further estimated that 'the social problems generated by severely dependent drug misusers alone are in the region of £3–4 billion annually'. It goes on to say that the guiding principle of the strategy is that 'drug-related expenditure should, over time, shift away from reacting to the consequences of the drugs problem and towards positive investment in preventing and targeting it'. Furthermore, 'the bulk of targeted resources should be spent on collaborative projects which tackle high priority groups, in particular vulnerable young people, drug-related offenders and problem drug misusers'.

It is necessary to ask what this might mean in terms of future policy trends. Could 'reacting to the consequences' mean treating existing drug users, whereas 'positive investment in preventing and targeting' drug problems means enforcement measures to shut off supply? Or, conversely, in the context where already a much larger proportion of drug-related expenditure is devoted to enforcement and 'supply side' measures, 75% on the government's own reckoning, is the intention in the long term to shift the emphasis of resource investments from enforcement to health care and social support? In other words, does 'reacting to the consequences' mean picking up the social costs of drug-related crime and nuisance, whereas 'positive investment' in prevention means health care and social services?

If this crucial statement on resources means the latter, as many commentators have assumed it to mean, powerful encouragement for the government's position is to be found in a major research programme conducted by the RAND Corporation in the USA (Rydell and Everingham, 1994). This involved an economic modelling of the impact of different types of public investment and anti-drug programmes. The study focused on cocaine misuse, which has been the major social difficulty in the USA for some time, but its findings are of more general interest. Basically, the question asked was this: if an extra dollar is to be spent on drug programmes, will it yield improved benefits if it is spent on various enforcement measures or on health care? In a nutshell, health care won hands down.

Overall, an estimated $13 billion was spent each year in the USA on cocaine control, of which merely 7% was on treatment and the remainder on enforcement measures (Rydell and Everingham, 1994, p 12). Enforcement expenditure took three forms: interventions in countries which were the sources of drugs; border interdiction measures; and domestic enforcement including police, courts and prisons.

The researchers asked a series of cost-benefit questions in terms of how to obtain different goals through additional expenditure, a reduction in the number of cocaine users; a reduction in the amount of cocaine consumed; or a reduction in the social costs of crime and lost productivity. To give an illustration of how this worked, in order to obtain the same goal, namely a 1% reduction in cocaine consumption, the estimated cost for different kinds of interventions was as follows:

> *$783 million for source-country control, $336 million for interdiction, $246 million for domestic enforcement, or $34 million for treatment.* (ibid.)

If only domestic enforcement was considered against treatment, the findings were equally dramatic for a range of outcomes:

> *Domestic enforcement costs four times as much as treatment for a given amount of user reduction, seven times as much for consumption reduction, and 15 times as much for societal cost-reduction.* (Ibid., p 16)

To put the matter another way, the RAND project asked how much money would be saved, in terms of reduced social costs, by an additional dollar spent on these different forms of intervention? Here, the results were truly staggering, in that for all supply-control programmes the savings were smaller than the dollar spent on control costs, but not for treatment:

> *The savings of supply-control programs are... An estimated 15 cents on the dollar for source-country control, 32 cents on the dollar for interdiction, and 52 cents on the dollar for domestic enforcement. In contrast, the savings of treatment programmes are larger than the control costs; we estimate that the costs of crime and lost productivity are reduced by $7.46 for every dollar spent on treatment.* (Ibid.)

It is part of the New Labour stance towards the investment of public expenditure that it should be directed to areas which can reduce social costs in the long term on an evidenced basis. This is where its drugs strategy will count in the long term. The RAND Corporation study, which did not make over-ambitious assumptions about what could be expected from treatment programmes in terms of long-term abstinence, nevertheless showed the dramatic potential of investing in health care rather than enforcement measures. If this is what is meant by the somewhat ambiguous statement in the UK strategy document, 'drug-related expenditure should, over time, shift away from reacting to the consequences of the drugs problem and towards positive investment in preventing and targeting it', this would be a truly major policy innovation. It will also add a startling new dimension to what is meant by the 'multi-agency' approach, 'joint-working' and 'partnership'.

Moving Ahead: Social Exclusion and Social Integration

One final and highly significant aspect of the UK strategy document is that it is recognised throughout that the most serious drug-related problems are inter-woven with the question of social exclusion and hence broader socio-economic forces and policy considerations. Problems associated with drug misuse are certainly not the sole province of the poor, as drug casualties among fabulously wealthy film stars, rock stars and footballers testify. Moreover, on the basis of survey evidence, the recreational use of drugs such as cannabis would appear to be widely dispersed through many sections of society. Nevertheless, there is a solid body of evidence from both Britain and North America that the most serious pockets of heroin or crack-cocaine misuse (together with associated crime and the fear of crime) are reliably found in the poorest neighbourhoods and housing estates (Pearson and Gilman, 1994; Pearson, 1995a). And quite apart from questions of national strategy and resource deployment, it is here on the ground that these problems must be combated.

These connections between drugs and deprivation had been immediately obvious to those of us working and researching amidst the heroin epidemic of the 1980s, whether in Glasgow, Manchester, Merseyside, or London (Haw, 1985; Parker et al., 1988; Pearson et al., 1985; Burr, 1987). The attitude of Conservative governments and politicians in the Thatcher and Major years, however, towards the relations between deprivation, drugs, crime and disorder had been repeatedly evasive and resistant (Pearson, 1995b). It is therefore all the more important that this recognition is now grasped and placed centrally within the UK drugs strategy, together with detailed consideration of a number of related issues in the Advisory Council report *Drug Misuse and the Environment* (1998).

The practical implications are two-fold. The first is reflected in one of the strategy's four key aims: 'to protect our communities from drug-related anti-social and criminal behaviour'. Because it is the poorest neighbourhoods which experience the most serious levels of drug-related difficulty, this suggests the need to target resources on these already vulnerable communities, whether in terms of enforcement efforts directed against dealers, other forms of community safety initiative, effective housing management schemes, and a variety of social schemes intended to improve the fabric of the community. Once again, effective joint-working will need to underpin such efforts, together with the activation and participation of local people (Duke et al., 1996; Henderson, 1996).

In terms of housing management a particularly tricky balance has to be struck between providing for the housing needs of those people with drug problems, on the one hand, and safeguarding the interests of neighbours from anti-social nuisance on the other. The eviction of troublesome residents is, of course, allowed for within the provisions of the Housing Act of 1996; although the advisory council report on environmental issues suggests that this should only be used as a last resort. Models of intensive housing management can be identified which, in combination with other services, can help problem drug users to stabilise their lifestyles (ACMD, 1998, Ch. 7). The advisory council report also advised that local housing directors should be members of Drug Action Teams.

If protecting vulnerable communities is one aspect of the inter-connection between the problems associated with drug misuse and social exclusion, assisting those individuals with drug problems 'to tackle their drug problems and become better integrated into society' is how the drug strategy describes the second objective. Crucially, this is not just about 'coming off drugs'. It is also about how people re-fashion identities and lifestyles. And just as bricks are not made without straw, effective identities cannot be fashioned and sustained without the material props of jobs, housing and other meaningful life opportunities. Drugs agencies and the criminal justice system will therefore have to learn how to connect up with job creation and job training schemes, and other aspects of the wider socio-economic environment. This is probably the biggest challenge of all, since it is effectively about combating social exclusion, which just as the Advisory Council said ten years ago in the context of HIV/AIDS, is a bigger threat to communal solidarity, and a far bigger social problem, than drug misuse itself.

References

Advisory Council on the Misuse of Drugs (1988 and 1989). *AIDS and Drug Misuse*, Parts 1 and 2. London: HMSO.

Advisory Council on the Misuse Of Drugs (1998). *Drug Misuse and the Environment*. London: HMSO.

Barton, A. (1999). Breaking the Crime/Drugs Cycle: The Birth of a New Approach? *Howard Journal of Criminal Justice*, Vol. 38; No. 2: pp 144–157.

Bennett, T. (1998). *Drugs and Crime: The Results of Research on Drug Testing and Interviewing Arrestees*. Home Office Research Study 183. London: Home Office.

Blagg, H, Pearson, G, Sampson, A., Smith, D., and Stubbs, P. (1988). Inter-Agency Co-operation: Rhetoric and Reality. In Hope, T., and Shaw, M. (Eds.). *Communities and Crime Reduction*, pp 204–220. London: HMSO. .

Burr, A. (1987). Chasing the Dragon: Heroin Misuse, Delinquency and Crime in the Context of South London Culture. *British Journal of Criminology*, Vol. 27: pp 333–357.

Crawford, A. (1997). The Local Governance of Crime: Appeals to Community and Partnership. Oxford: Clarendon Press.

Duke, K., MacGregor, S., and Smith, L. (1996). Activating Local Networks: A Comparison of Two Community Development Approaches to Drug Prevention. *Drug Prevention Initiative Paper 1*. London: Home Office.

Edmunds, M., Hough, M., and Urquia, N. (1996). *Tackling Local Drug Markets*. Crime Detection and Prevention Series, Paper 80. London: Home Office.

Gilman, M., and Pearson, G. (1991). Lifestyles and Law Enforcement. In Whynes, D.K. and Bean, P.T. (Eds.). *Policing and Prescribing: The British System of Drug Control*, pp 95–124. London: Macmillan.

Harwood, H.J, Fountain, D., and Livermore, G. (1999). Economic Cost of Alcohol and Drug Abuse in the United States: A Report. *Addiction*, Vol. 94; No. 5: pp 631–635.

Haw, S. (1985). *Drug Problems in Greater Glasgow*. London: SCODA.

Henderson, P. (1996). Drug Prevention and Community Development: Principles of Good Practice. *Drug Prevention Initiative Paper 7*. London: Home Office.

ISDD (1998). Failing the Test. *Druglink*, Vol. 13; No. 5: p 7.

Kleiman, M.A.R. (1992). *Against Excess: Drug Policy for Results*. New York: Basic Books.

Kleiman, M.A.R. (1999). Economic Cost, Measurements, Damage Minimisation and Drug Abuse Control Policy. *Addiction*, Vol. 94; No. 5: pp 638–641.

Maher, L., and Dixon, D. (1999). Policing and Public Health. *British Journal of Criminology*, Vol. 39; No. 4: forthcoming.

Newburn, T. (1999). Drug Prevention and Youth Justice: Issues of Philosophy, Practice and Policy. *British Journal of Criminology*, Vol. 39; No. 4: forthcoming.

Parker, H., and Bottomley, T. (1996). *Crack-Cocaine and Drug-Crime Careers*. London: Home Office.

Parker, H., and Kirby, P. (1996). *Methadone Maintenance and Crime Reduction on Merseyside*. Crime Detection and Prevention Series, Paper 72. London: Home Office.

Parker, H., Bakx, K., and Newcombe, R. (1988). *Living With Heroin: The Impact of a Drugs 'Epidemic' on an English Community*. Milton Keynes: Open University Press.

Parker, H., Aldridge, J. and Measham, F. (1998a). *Illegal Leisure: The Normalisation of Adolescent Recreational Drug Use*. London: Routledge.

Parker, H., Bury, C., and Eggington, R. (1998b). *New Heroin Outbreaks Among Young People in England and Wales. Crime Detection and Prevention Series*, Paper 92. London: Home Office.

Pearson, G. (1987). *The New Heroin Users*. Oxford: Blackwell.

Pearson, G. (1991). Drug Control Policies in Britain. In Tonry, M. (Ed.). *Crime and Justice: A Review of Research*, Vol. 14: pp 167–227. Chicago: University of Chicago Press.

Pearson, G. (1995a). Drugs and Deprivation. In Dickerson. J.W.T., and Stimson, G.V. (Eds.). Health in the Inner City: Drugs in the City. Supplement to *The Journal of the Royal Society of Health*, pp 80–86.

Pearson, G. (1995b). City of Darkness, City of Light: Crime. Drugs, and Disorder in London and New York. In MacGregor, S., and Lipton, A. (Eds.). *The Other City: People and Politics in New York and London*, pp 85–113. New Jersey: Humanities Press.

Pearson, G., and Gilman, M. (1994). Local and Regional Variations in Drug Misuse: The British Heroin Epidemic of the 19802. In Strang, J., and Gossop, M. (Eds.). *Heroin Addiction and Drug Policy: The British System*, pp 102–120. Oxford: Oxford University Press,

Pearson, G., and Patel, K. (1998). Drugs, Deprivation and Ethnicity: Outreach Among Asian Drug Users in a Northern English City. *Journal of Drug Issues*, Vol. 28; No. 1: pp 199–224.

Pearson, G., Gilman, M., and McIver, S. (1985). *Young People and Heroin: An Examination of Heroin Use in the North of England*. London: Health Education Council.

Pearson, G., Blagg, H., Smith, D., Sampson, A. and Stubbs, P. (1992). Crime, Community and Conflict: The Multi-Agency Approach. In D. Downes (Ed.). *Unravelling Criminal Justice: Eleven British Studies*, pp 46–72. London: Macmillan.

Power, R. (Ed.) (1998). Contemporary Issues Concerning Illicit Drug Use in the British Isles. Special issue of *The Journal of Drug Issues*, Vol. 28; No. 1.

Cm. 3945 Government White Paper. (1998). *Tackling Drugs To Build a Better Britain*. London: HMSO.

Ramsey, M., and Spiller, J. (1997). Drug Misuse Declared in 1996: Latest Results from the British Crime Survey. *Home Office Research Study 172*. London: Home Office.

Reuter, P. (1999). Are Calculations of the Economic Costs of Drug Abuse Either Possible or Useful? *Addiction*, Vol. 94; No. 5: pp 635–638.

Rydell, C.P., and Everingham, S.S. (1994). *Controlling Cocaine: Supply Versus Demand Programs*. Santa Monica: RAND.

Chapter 3

Between Two Stools: Children, Drugs Policy and Professional Practice

Mike Ashton

The last half of 1997 saw publication of four important reports redefining work with drug using parents and young people who use drugs. How do they differ, what were the common themes...and what difference will they make?

Thoughts seemed to have turned to the family. Three dealt with responding to young drug users, the fourth with drug using parents.[1] This was not entirely coincidental: the Local Government Drugs Forum (LGDF) and the Standing Conference on Drug Abuse (SCODA) each had a controlling hand in two of the reports.

The only one not to bear their imprint (from the Social Services Inspectorate (SSI)) nevertheless has SCODA to thank for its data-analysis and drafting. Also, LGDF's *Children and Young People* acknowledges the roles of SCODA and of the SSI in its advisory group. The LGDF report is explicitly based on the Health Advisory Service (HAS) report of the same name, which, to varying degrees, also underlies and provides the stimulus for the other two documents on drug using children.

The reports are timely in the sense that they come when the need for a response to youth drug problems has been acknowledged, but the response is in its infancy; they have a chance to shape the agenda. What would that agenda look like, where would it converge on common themes or reflect different views and priorities – and will the policymakers reading these reports be willing and able to follow their lead?

The next section does some context-setting and explains how this review was constructed, before moving on to the main business: the prescriptions for change.

The comments and findings in the reports can be analysed under four headings: two concerned with diagnosing the problem; two with prescribing what should be done about it:

Diagnosis

- The nature, extent and consequences of youth drug problems.
- What are we doing now to prevent or ameliorate the resultant harm?

Prescription

- What sort of services are required to adequately respond to youth drug problems?
- What will it take to establish these services – money, commitment, strategies, training?

This review only briefly summarises the 'diagnosis' to make space for an extended look at the 'prescriptions'.[2] Comments not explicitly attributed to one or more of the reviewed reports are the author's or based on other documents.

Diagnosis Gloomy
Youth drug use increasing

Concern over increasing youth substance use, transmitted partly via HAS, is a driving force behind all three reports dealing with this topic. They document a 'significant increase in the use of illegal drugs' (SSI) with 'alcohol and illicit substances… increasingly accepted as part of youth culture' (*Children and Young People*) and the age of initiation dropping, but acknowledge that most youth use is experimental.

Reference to 'A greater range of drugs…being used than ever before' (SSI) over the last five to ten years suggests the dance drug phenomenon is the key break from the past. Markers of youth addiction and problem drug use are compatible with incremental rises in proportion to the overall increase.[3] It is 'recreational' use of cannabis, LSD, amphetamines, ecstasy, poppers which has grown to levels that 20 years ago would have led findings to be doubted.[4]

The severity and extent of youth drug use can be and probably has been exaggerated, but even a simple across-the-board spread is bound to draw more youngsters into contact with drug problems; there is no doubt that such a spread has occurred in recent years. For some drugs and patterns of use, notably those associated with youth dance culture, the UK seems at or near the top of the European youth drug use league.[5]

Where's the harm?

All four reports caution that any drug use entails risk, especially in relation to the young who are a) vulnerable and b) in a fluid stage of development.

As the 'impact of early substance use on the emotional and social development of…children', this theme features in the SSI report as a reason for not tolerating drug use patterns ('recreational' use) in children which in adults are 'commonly equated with non-problematic use'. LGDF and SCODA's guide on drug using parents argues that 'Any drug use has the potential to interfere with parenting ability'.

The harms associated with drug use, crime, disease, death, exploitation by adults, a disrupted education, social isolation, are not at issue. What needs to be explored is whether it is prudent to acknowledge another side, both to interventions and to drug use.

Interventions can harm

In encouraging assertive responses to 'recreational use', the SSI does not link to its own recognition (found also in the other documents) that the adult world's responses can themselves be a component of drug-related harm. Among those it itemises are school exclusion and gaining a criminal record.

This theme has particular resonance for *Drug Using Parents*, which says that drug-related harm to the young, even before birth, has arisen from past social responses. 'When local authorities saw drug use by parents as a reason in itself for putting a child on the child protection register, parents were deterred from approaching agencies or professionals for help. As a result some families did not receive the support or services they needed for their children or themselves'. Drug users are perfectly capable of creating their own harm, but awareness that this can be compounded by how we intervene seems prudent in documents intended to stimulate interventions.

Risks and benefits of negativity

The impression left by this body of documents is of a transition to adulthood which can be undesirably diverted, even derailed, by external chemical influences. The direction of the diversion is always portrayed as negative, or at best neutral in practice but negative in potential. None suggest that workers hoping to build relationships with young 'recreational' drug users (and perhaps even with more committed drug users) may have to acknowledge that, for them, enjoyment or mind-stretching gained via chemicals has its positive side, even at the same time as for some it poses problems.

Their reticence is understandable, this is not a popular point to make, and their focus is, after all, on harm rather than benefits. However, one implication of more widespread first-hand (or personal second-hand) youth experience with drugs is that, for an increasing proportion of young people, teachers and others can no longer get away with denying anything positive about the experience. Continuing in this vein will alienate young drug users and convince them that you know nothing worth knowing about drugs – the ups as well as the downs. Though risky to take on, the 'positives' issue is also a risky one to ignore. It was cogently addressed by one of the government's chief consultants for its mass media anti-drug campaigns. Emphasising the negative and denying the positive does, Arnold Cragg accepted, deter many from starting drug use, but, if his analysis holds, the balance of public health benefit between deterring the still drug-naive, and alienating the initiates, is shifting.

At special risk

The consensus of the reports is that youth drug use, and with it the potential for harm, is widespread, but also that relatively few youngsters suffer actual and significant harm, and that these are concentrated in certain groups.

Among those spotlighted are children looked after by social services, school excludees, offenders, children of drug using parents, the homeless, single pregnant girls, the mentally ill, those sexually abused or exploited through prostitution and youngsters who have suffered family disruption or abuse.

SCODA's *Drug-related Early Intervention* explains that 'In adolescence, harmful drug misuse rarely occurs without predisposing psychological or social problems', what the HAS report called risk factors such as family drug use and/or poor parenting, social isolation and psychological or physical problems including neighbourhood deprivation and disintegration.

Between stools

The other side of the diagnosis is, what are we doing now to prevent or ameliorate these harms? If good enough, or at least as good as it could be, then it's a pat on the back and a call for incremental improvements. In some sectors of drug policy this judgement may well be warranted: HIV prevention is a probable example with prescribing programmes for opiate addiction not too far behind – in both cases, when the targets are adults.

What the Health Advisory Service's report did, as recently as 1996, is to establish beyond doubt that when it comes to the young in trouble with drugs or alcohol, we are light years from an adequate response, sometimes from any response. Its conclusions (see *HAS's verdict*) seem harsh, but should be seen in the context of a society forced into awareness of drug problems in the younger teenage years only relatively recently, and which had scared itself so much about the conjunction of children and drugs that denial and buck-passing have been the automatic and natural responses.

Given the recency of HAS's findings, it is no surprise to see them reflected in this current crop of reports. Indeed, their purpose is to promote the remedies which can change this gloomy picture. All four still faced structural and demographic obstacles which pose the greatest challenge yet to co-ordination structures in the drugs field. Young people dually in need, because of their drug problems and because of what led to those problems, are still falling painfully between the stools of Britain's welfare services.

The gaps have clear historical and social origins. Drug services have developed to deal with problems overwhelmingly seen only when the constraints of school and home have been outgrown. Children's services see severe substance misuse as a risk which they are not equipped to take on. Now both are having to come to terms with an uncomfortable crossover, children with adult-sized drug problems, in numbers which can no longer be treated as isolated exceptions.

As the SSI's inspectors were told, another major gap between the stools is that young drug users especially tend to use the more accessible and cheaper alcohol or solvents instead of or as well as illegal drugs, yet service structures for legal and illegal substances are often separate. Such divides are replicated at co-ordination and policy levels, hindering a coordinated response.

Uncomfortable at the sharp end

HAS's verdict

Published in january 1996, the verdict of the Health Advisory Service's report *Children and Young People: Substance Misuse Services* was damning enough to stimulate some of the reports being reviewed here and more yet to come. This is just part of the 'gloomy picture' it found of services for young people who misuse substances.

A lack of leadership in the commissioning and provision of services.

Virtually no provision in contractual arrangements made by statutory health agencies with providers stipulating services specifically for children and adolescents who misuse substances.

Overall, an absence of individual or joint purchasing strategies for this age group.

Responses are poorly planned and poorly co-ordinated.

Lack of recognition by health services of the particular and definable needs arising from substance use and misuse by children and adolescents.

Specialised treatment for young people is extremely limited as a result of a range of factors including: lack of definition and understanding of the problem; lack of basic information about existing services; unclear and disputed funding responsibilities; and competitiveness and lack of trust between service sectors and components.

An apparant lack of clarity in most health services about the nature and extent of the problem, the roles of the services involved, and the balance to be struck between education, prevention and more direct intervention with young people who have problems.

Staff are concerned about the legal implications of working with young people. Generally, there is little proper knowledge or formal training on confidentiality and consent.

The target group at issue in these reports stretches from those facing an elevated risk of starting drug use, to young people already embarked on a serious addiction career.

Towards the bottom end, preventive responses may be inadequate but at least sit comfortably within established educational and youth welfare structures. Further up among the dabblers, and even some 'recreational' users, if a response is demanded at all, it can be handled by parents, youth workers, teachers and the police as part of 'normal' adolescent development.

The issues become sharper when prevention, education and advice, the familiar adult responses to young people, no longer measure up to the severity of the problem. The youngster has left these behind and so must their adult carers. Then we enter territory where the legal and ethical ice is thin indeed, such as prescribing dangerous drugs to children, enabling them to do very risky things such as injecting rather more safely, and taking a degree of responsibility as an adult for the life of a young person clearly at risk of losing it. Fear of failure and the instinct to cover your back may be as strong and as understandable as the urge to help.

Here, where need is greatest, experience, services and confidence are least. Commonly the response is to call for a new generation of specialist services which can shoulder the responsibility of youth drug problems. But such services face a demographic bind; as we near the sharp end of youth drug problems, so too do the numbers narrow sharply.

Preventive approaches are appropriate to the entire youth population, but addiction treatment is applicable to a few thousand,[6] raising a question mark over the viability of specialist services, particularly as local accessibility is also a priority. A youth addiction treatment clinic in every population centre is simply not on. To strain the title analogy, new child-height 'stools' may be desirable, but these reports have to be as much about spreading communication and co-operation safety nets between the existing stools, and adding a degree of height adjustment to them by retooling the staff.

Inching forward

The gloom is punctuated by a few bright spots, signs that our response to youth drug problems is inching into the decision, even into the active change, phase of Prochaska and DiClemente's famous model.[7] SCODA's *Drug-Related Early Intervention* is most upbeat: 'The needs of these vulnerable young people are gaining recognition'. Part of the proof is the Department of Health's £1 million grant allocated by SCODA itself, and projects for young people funded by the Home Office's Drugs Prevention Initiative. The 'many professionals' who told the SCI's field-workers that 'local drug agencies were developing new services for young people' may have been witnessing the fruits of these initiatives. Half the SCODA-funded projects survived and presumably totted up to 19 suitable services across the response vacuum.

SCODA has also received encouraging uptake of its current initiative to engage drug action teams in an action learning exercise to upgrade provision for young drug users.

Among the bright spots identified by *Children and Young People* are those 'few child and adolescent mental health services which take a direct interest in substance misuse and provide services ... Some operate from mobile buses; others have drop in facilities in city centres'. The SSI found that one in ten local authorities had budgets for young people's drug services and that many more may be planning specific services.

Drug Using Parents is able to list 14 residential drug services for parents and children in England and Wales, though a common experience is that it is easier to get the parent funded than their child. Legislation and official reports stress the importance of keeping the family unit intact, yet funding structures treat parent and child as unrelated individuals.

Prescription Ambitious

The services and strategies recommended in these reports flow directly from the deficiencies they record. Less clear is how they propose to create viable services in response to a need which clearly demands a specialist response, but which may not yet have reached the levels needed to sustain it.

An obvious way out of the demographic bind, the way taken up to now, is for the numbers to rise to the point where young problem drug users become a major client group. The challenge is to find the other way out, to create the services which can prevent this happening yet cater for the remaining young casualties. Meeting this challenge may be the *only way out*: given current wider policy trends, if criminally active adolescent drug users become obtrusively numerous, the response is at least as likely to be controlling and punitive as it is to be service-based.

The reports' prescriptions for change are analysed here from the 'bottom up': first the services/responses needed, then what will be required to make these happen, finally the strategic and structural arrangements demanded if these objectives are to be realised.

Child-size services

Two models developed by the Health Advisory Service form the core of the service recommendations in the three reports dealing with substance use by young people. At the deepest level are the principles which should underpin all service delivery as described in HAS's '3 Cs' (see *Key Principles of Services Provision*. The '3 Cs'). At the operational level how these principles should be expressed in services is HAS's four-tiers model (see Four-tiers model). Below are what seem the main dimensions of the desired service network implied by these models, as projected through this current crop of reports.

Broad range of provision

Such is the severity of drug problems even at young ages that the SSI argued for services to span the range from prevention to residential rehabilitation. Unpacked, this means we can no longer confine ourselves to education and advice, but must provide child-sized versions of what until now have been adult services. The SSI's call for action is uncompromising: 'there is a paucity of services for young people with substance misuse problems who require treatment. This requires *immediate* attention'. (italics added)

Children and Young People operationalises the range of services required in the form of HAS's four tiers of increasingly specialised personnel or services. The first

Key Principles of Services Provision. The '3 Cs'

The Health Advisory Service's report highlighted three guiding principles which should underpin services for young substance misusers: comprehensiveness, competency, and child-centredness (the '3Cs'). Here is how they were described by the SSI.

Comprehensiveness

- A holistic approach to the child in terms of assessment and care planning.
- Family involvement as good practice.
- Collaborationg with other children's and young people's services and substance misuse services.
- Local police procedures agreed with the relevant local area child protection committee and drug action team.
- Targeting services to groups of young people most at risk of serious substance misuse problems.

Competency

- Providing services in line with the Children Act where the welfare if the child is paramount and reflected in confidentiality and reporting procedures.
- Staff competence in working with both young people and substance misuse issues, either as an individual, in a team or through a shared care approach.
- Providing a comprehensive assessment of need, maturity, parental involvement and risk of substance-related harm.
- Utilising a care-planning approach which links to other care plans.
- Establishing comprehensive record-keeping and information-sharing systems.

Child-centredness

- Advice and treatment services separate to those from adults, appropriate and sensitive to the specific needs of children and young people.
- Services that take account of the young person's age and maturity.
- Services appealing to young people that facilitate self-referral and easy access.
- Explaining and involving the young person (and their parent or carer) in care planning and reviews.

two tiers draw on primary care workers and professionals working with young people; the next two are recognisably addiction treatment and harm reduction services, characterised by multidisciplinary team-working. As implied by its title, SCODA's *Drug-Related Early Intervention* is concerned mainly with tiers 1 and 2.

How and the degree to which the '3 Cs' principles are implemented must be seen in the light of the level at which the service operates. 'Accessibility' will often mean walk-in self-referral at tiers 1 and 2, but usually an assessment filter for the clinics in tier 4. Similarly, 'child centred' means youth-oriented workers in tiers 2 and 3 but not necessarily at tier 1. This may also be the case for some tier 4 services where child focused sub-specialisms may be too narrow a niche.

Separate from adult services

In all four reports, 'child centredness' is acknowledged as the key to meeting the needs of young people affected by substance misuse. Certainly with respect to early intervention and basic treatment (tiers 2 and 3), this is taken to mean they should be engineered to meet the needs of children and therefore separate from services for adults. Also seen as demanding separation is the call for services to appeal to the young.

This principle is spelt out by the SSI, which argues that good joint commissioning is characterised by 'dedicated budgets' supporting 'dedicated services'. *Children and Young People* explains what this might mean in practice. 'Services for children and young people should be commissioned, designed and provided to meet their particular needs', entailing provision 'separately from adults in an environment suitable to the child's age...where children and young people mix with their peers and not adults'.

Separate from young people's services?

Where the potential client base is relatively low or money tight, integration with generic youth facilities is one way out of the demographic bind. In fact, the demand for a holistic approach makes integration desirable in its own right. In *Children and Young People* we find the local authority bodies counselling 'comprehensive or 'one-stop' centres for children and young people'. SCODA's *Drug-Related Early Intervention* observes that 'Many successful projects have been set up within larger youth centres, or run alongside existing services that are well known to young people, and employ experienced staff who know their clients' needs'.

Most threatened by the demographic bind are the specialist addiction services foreseen for tiers 3 and 4, which can expect to see few but demanding (and costly) clients. Perversely, here, where most needed, the option of integration with youth services may not be available: the severity of the needs of the youngsters may preclude their being handled well in anything other than a dedicated setting. *Children and Young People*, for example, argues that 'Child and adolescent psychiatric wards may not be suitable for older adolescents who require detoxification. The development of facilities specifically for adolescents needs to be considered'.

Four-tiers Model

In a previous report on mental health services the Health Advisory Service developed a model of four increasingly specialised service tiers accepting referrals from and offering training to those below. This was adapted for their report on substance misuse services.

Tier 1 is concerned with identifying young substance users and making entry points to information, advice and referral accessible via locations and personnel such as GPs, shopfront drop-ins, voluntary workers, health visitors, the police or school health services.

Tier 2 consists of professionals with a background in working with young people in need and who have specialist interest or training in drug/alcohol problems. They remain integrated into their non-drug specialist, youth-oriented services but their knowledge equips them to assess and counsel young substance users and their parents/carers, or to refer complex cases on to tiers 3 and 4. Among them will be youth workers, educational pychologists, youth criminal justice workers, some teachers and school health workers, and staff in children's health and medical services. Access is via outreach, self-referral or tier 1 entry points.

Tier 3 consists of specialist youth-oriented addiction services working as a multi-disciplinary team, perhaps across agencies, to provide therapy, detoxification, prescribing and rehabilitation.

Tier 4 services will have the resources to address the complex and specific needs of those whose drug problem and/or personal situations are beyond the reach of tier 3 teams. Inpatient detoxification, intensive treatments, residential rehabilitation, and clinics for youngsters whose drug problems are complicated by other disorders, are among the facilities that may be needed.

Drug-Related Early Intervention supports integrated youth provision, but its service examples suggest demand is such that specialist services for young drug users are viable at tiers 1 and 2, where counselling is the top end of the services delivered and clients can be drawn from a broad range of youngsters using drugs.

Mainstreaming drug users' children

Drug Using Parents emphasises keeping children out of specialist services and in mainstream care, the reverse of the documents on drug using children.

Most mainstream are the parents: 'In developing services for children and their families, it is important...as far as possible to keep children with their parents'.

The theme is continued in relation to day care services, and we are reminded that an HIV-positive child 'is still a child' and should 'be cared for in mainstream services'; in both cases, the rider 'where possible' is added.

What of the period before the baby is born? Here again 'pregnancy and birth should be as normal as possible'. The emphasis is not on specialist services but on collaboration between mainstream maternity and drug services. Only with respect to residential rehabilitation does *Drug Using Parents* argue for specialist family-focused drug services, partly mandated by the requirement for children to have their own care plan and key worker and the desirability (may be a requirement) to meet children's home standards. The pay-off is that the family stays together and parenting skills can be developed in a drug-free environment with role models available.

Mother-to-be centred?

After the birth, *Drug Using Parents* acknowledges that 'the needs of newborn infants' come into the frame and, according to law, these must be paramount. But before birth the report says the woman should be at 'the focus of maternity care…and able to make decisions about her care, based on her needs'. The abrupt prioritising of the adult's needs is striking.

Here we enter a highly contested area where the issues are as profound as, 'When does someone become a person with their own rights?' Happily, Britain has Dr Mary Hepburn of Glasgow to defuse the debate with common sense and evidence that, appropriately advised, the mother's decisions are at worst not harmful to the foetus, so whatever she feels happiest with is likely to be best for both. If this is the case then the debate over whose needs are paramount at what stage has no practical relevance.

Age sensitive

Another dimension to child-centredness is sensitivity to the child's age and level of development. This is seen as demanding, not separate services for different ages, but that services should assess and tailor their interventions accordingly. As the SSI put it, 'it is unlikely that a service for a 17-year-old drug misuser requiring health or social care would be the same…as for a 13-year-old'.

Such maturity assessments also set important legal parameters. Generally the reports do not spell out what these mean in terms of which services should, or should not, be provided at what ages. Supplying sterile injecting equipment is the exception. *Children and Young People* says 'Needles and syringes should not be provided by outreach workers and others to young people, particularly those under 16, without appropriate and comprehensive assessment and monitoring'.

Age 16 is when children are generally regarded as competent to consent to medical treatment. Below this age, without comprehensive assessment, workers may not be able to show they had adequately determined the child's competence to consent without parental approval. In effect, we are being told that low-threshold syringe exchange and outreach-based syringe provision (such workers will practically never have the time or resources to adequately assess) are barred for the under-16s.

Children and Young People has taken its lead here from the HAS report. The issue presumably arises because providing injecting equipment is usually the only 'treatment' (as opposed to information) provided outside an office or clinic with a staff team to hand who can achieve the required level of assessment.

Easy access

The requirement for comprehensive assessment may impede another priority, ease of access to services. Doubling the irony is the fact that outreach is spotlighted as the delivery vehicle which maximises access, yet the services which can be delivered are restricted by assessment limitations.

The first dimension to ease of access is *physically* being where the child is, or at least getting there quickly, or being where children are willing and able to visit. Where this is will be influenced by the targets: a presence at school will miss truants and home visits will not reach the homeless. So we read in *Children and Young People* that services should be in 'settings that are likely to be used by young people...with opening hours convenient for them' and the SSI talks of 'services young people can get to safely at appropriate times, e.g., after school'.

Both stress outreach. *Children and Young People* recommends 'strong outreach into youth, primary health care and other settings...together with outreach into juvenile courts and residential children's homes'. The SSI calls for 'special efforts...to reach young people who are not in touch with services [including those] unaware of services, homeless or living in hostels or rural areas and young people with multiple problems'.

Many of the projects in *Drug-Related Early Intervention* target such groups and prioritise easy access. At the Early Breaks Project fronted by Ian Clements, an influential 'product champion' in this sector, 'venues for meetings are determined by the needs of the client' and referrals responded to within 24 hours. Another project provides dedicated access to counselling and harm reduction for children looked after by local authorities. Drug-related interventions integrated into the work of units for school excludees and a seafront drop-in for the young homeless are further examples. The advice and information bus is a classic easy-access tactic.

Less often seen in this light is peer education, yet few counsellors can match the accessibility of same-age contacts. For *Children and Young People*, using 'slightly older peers as educators' is one characteristic of effective prevention: 'Young people are likely to turn to their peers for advice and help'. We find an instance in *Drug-related Early Intervention* in the rare form of a service targeted at ethnic minorities.

Interestingly, the peer educators (whose shelf-life as peers of young people is clearly limited) themselves train the next generation of educators.

Peer education also scores heavily on the second dimension to ease of access – culturally being where the child is (at). The SSI and (in the following quote) *Children and Young People* both argue that 'Agencies should promote their services to young people by using language and images that are attractive to them'. For many youngsters, the last place they would want to risk being seen is a drug service, another argument for integrated youth provision.[8]

Drug Using Parents also emphasises ease of access, though with adults this is more a case of effective networking and a welcoming persona. For parents-to-be, 'Regardless of where drug-related care is based, pregnant drug users should be linked to all the services they need. Purchasing authorities should ensure that...services...encourage women to seek help without fear of discrimination'. For parents, the report links accessibility with not stigmatising them and their children by automatically invoking child care proceedings or diverting children outside mainstream provision.

The third dimension is *direct access* – not having to traverse a chain of referral intermediaries. *Substance Misuse and Young People* and *Children and Young People* call for services to 'facilitate self-referral'. Easy access and making services appealing are, of course, important ways to facilitate self-referral, and self-referral can open up access and make services seem more attractive; these dimensions are intertwined. As the HAS report clarifies, self-referral should be available to a wider range of services than for adults because young people may be reluctant to contact adult-focused referral intermediaries.

Sometimes self-referral access is neither feasible nor desirable. The more intensive treatments, if only because funding is likely to be on a case-by-case basis, require filtered access. At the other end, early intervention often means delivering remedies before the youngster thinks they have a problem. For example, one very early intervention project in SCODA's guide ('for pupils who are starting to experiment with drugs') relies on referrals from the police, teachers, parents and especially education welfare officers. Self-referral also assumes children know they are in need and how to act on it. The call in two of the reports for 'strong' or 'assertive' outreach is recognition that this is often not the case.

All this makes it crucial for adults to recognise incipient or actual need and know how to access help, tasks for which the SSI found many social workers with care responsibilities felt poorly equipped. If **they** feel this, what of the general run of, say, parents and teachers? In this perspective adult education and training becomes as important as information directed at the child.

Getting in early

To clarify the issues involved in intervening early, we need first to clarify the basis for intervening at all. All four reports imply that, with some adjustment, the

Children Act's formulation of when a child is 'in need' of local authority services fits the bill. This stipulates firstly that the child's 'health or development' is at risk and secondly that providing services can attenuate that risk. In other words, it is not enough for there simply to be risk, we have to be able to do something positive about it before intervention is required. Transposed to drugs work, this implies that if the drugtaking is at least potentially harmful, and intervening can help, then intervene we should.

If the principle is clear, its application is far less so. In the 1960s and 1970s it was feared that drug education might encourage drug use, now the consensus is that education should be universal at secondary level and perhaps also at primary. The corresponding debate is still in flux when it comes to intervention, not to prevent possible future behaviour, but to change current behaviour.

The potential for harm from say, regular injecting, is such that intervening in some way must be in the child's interests. But how far down the scale should we intervene and in what ways? There comes a point when some interventions carry more risks than the behaviour they seek to change, and we can no longer be sure they are in the child's best interests. After all, two of the most successful interventions with adults, syringe exchange and methadone prescribing, entail giving clients dangerous implements with which to do dangerous things to themselves, or addictive and potentially lethal drugs. The need to take into account all the child's circumstances is another complication and means interventions cannot be determined solely by the scale of the drug problem.

On this kind of issue HAS's lack of specificity feeds into the later reports, which call for clear guidelines but themselves give little guidance beyond 'assess fully and act in the child's best interests'. HAS was specific only about the overdose and dependence-creating risks of prescribing methadone to young people. It did caution against street syringe exchange for under-16s, but this had as much to do with whether it might backfire legally for the service as whether it might backfire for the client.

Not a problem?

A fundamental obstacle to early intervention was pointed out to the SSI's field-workers: 'Many...professionals reported that most young people saw their drug and alcohol use as 'recreational' and as not causing them problems...if a young person did not see the harmfulness of their drug use, then it was difficult to help them'. None of the reports explicitly address this conundrum. However, within them can be found a number of potential solutions.

First, perhaps the young person's self-assessment is correct and, at this level of drug use, 'help' (as opposed to information) is inappropriate. Second, some interventions do not require admitting to a drug problem, such as targeting prevention at those for whom drug use, if it starts, is most likely to become a problem. Another way is to integrate drugs into youth-oriented services. Also important is encouraging adults in contact with young people to incorporate drugs in their assessments and equipping them to deliver 'brief interventions' (anything from a heart-to-heart with mum or dad to structured input from the GP) or refer onwards. Peer education and fostering a supportive peer group can create a monitoring and care safety-net which avoids the risk of adult opprobrium.[9]

Moving up a gear, we could make the drug use a problem for the child: in this category come school exclusion, cautioning and arrest, denial of access to certain activities, and, in some circumstances, informing parents. But making these the norm might deter self-disclosure by other children.

Which brings us to a tactic not in any of the reports – fostering a climate in which children feel they have nothing to lose by admitting to drug use and everything to gain in terms of good information and advice. The fact that *once they start* trying drugs, young people turn away from authority figures and parents and towards their friends for drug information, shows we have some way to go. However, recent work from DEMOS suggests the *general* level of respect for adults may remain high, indicating that the communication channels are there if the drug-specific blockages can be overcome.

Relevant here is Arnold Cragg's thesis that anti-drug propaganda creates child-parent alienation by scaring parents about drugs and scaring children about how their parents will react if they admit trying them. The same point was made by an author of the DEMOS study: speaking of anti-drug messages, he said 'raising parents' fears creates inter-generational alienation'.[10]

When is information enough

Stepping down to less problematic users, there comes a point when information is enough and behaviour change is not explicitly on the agenda – but where?

We can gain some clues in HAS's dismissal of experimental use as not a problem in itself, and in its argument that preventive education has failed because it addressed the broad sweep of young people, including the majority who engage in 'normative behaviour in which they experiment with a cross section of activities'. Similarly, its outline of a comprehensive service network talks of making 'information and education' available to experimental and recreational users, but of helping responses to those 'engaged in dependent or harmful substance use'.

SCODA's *Drug-Related Early Intervention* similarly prescribes access to education, advice and counselling for young drug users (which could simply mean adequate information about drugs and services) but 'more intensive...support' for those engaged in harmful use.

Here we have the beginnings of a hierarchy of responses. Up to the experimental level, for the majority not at special risk, making information available (about services as well as drugs) is adequate, and perhaps more assertive responses risk making an issue of a normal phase of adolescence. For those engaged in harmful use, or whose other life problems compound the risks, then it is every adult carer's duty to intervene, whether or not the child wishes or seeks it.

Duty to intervene

The SSI makes this clearest in asking, if the interests of the child conflict with their wishes, 'Do we allow a young person to continue to engage in alcohol or substance misuse, or can and should an adult intervene to prevent them from further harm?' Its answer is found in a recent Department of Health circular (CI letter (97) 6) on children in care which could have wider applicability. This says staff in day-to-day care of a child have the 'responsibility and authority' to control the child's actions if harm is anticipated. In turn, the SSI believes, drug service staff may need to 'inform and involve' those in a position to exercise control, i.e., parents or equivalent. For the SSI this duty would extend to 'recreational use', a term which 'implies an acceptance which is quite contrary to the duties of carers and parents to safeguard and promote the welfare of children'.

So there seems consensus on whether or not to intervene with respect to experimental and dependent/harmful use, but on recreational use the debate continues.

These reports do give one concrete piece of advice over when and how to intervene: 'Treatment agencies should seek their own legal advice to satisfy themselves that they are acting within the law'. This wording is in both *Substance Misuse and Young People* and *Children and Young People*, though the latter adds: 'Records of decisions made and the reasons for them should be kept. Staff must be able to show that they believe that they are acting in the best interests of the young person'. The idea that even essentially identical services must each seek their own legal advice seems ludicrously wasteful. Thankfully, this nettle will be grasped by SCODA and the Children's Legal Centre in forthcoming guidelines.

Targeting risk groups

Targeting limited resources at groups most likely to need and benefit from them, – not just those currently in trouble but also those at greatest risk, is a common theme in these reports. While access to information should be universal, the SSI argues that 'services should target children and young people who are vulnerable and at risk'. *Drug-related Early Intervention* and *Children and Young People* concur. In its insistence that parental drug use should not in itself trigger 'at risk' procedures, *Drug Using Parents* also opts for targeting, but more from concern over deterring parental help-seeking than conserving resources.

Why is targeting *groups* central to work with young people in a way it is not for corresponding adult services? After all, if every *individual* in need was recognised or came forward, there would be no need to target the groups we suspect contain disproportionate numbers of those individuals. But children, with more to lose and perhaps little to gain, and less able to recognise they are in trouble, are thought less likely than adults to own up to drug and other problems.

The demands of targeting groups such as school excludees, truants, young offenders and the homeless to an extent dictate the shape of services, such as the importance attached to outreach and easy access. Most early intervention services in SCODA's guide rely on individuals being referred, even if from a limited risk group, but others do target risk groups as a group. Examples include the drop-in for homeless youngsters and several youth offender projects.

The Department of Health's £1 million grant targeting young people at risk of drug misuse and, given that targeting is integral to early intervention, SCODA's guide, raise the profile of targeting. There is also a demographic imperative: as experimentation with the more common drugs becomes almost the norm, so choosing priority targets gains in importance.

Holistic assessment and confidentiality

When they contact a service, HAS's '3 Cs' emphasises that the young person, and if possible their carers, should be involved in a holistic 'assessment of need, maturity, parental involvement' as well as 'risk of substance-related harm'. This wording from the SSI is echoed by *Children and Young People* and reflects not just good practice, but also what's needed to satisfy the Children Act. All four reports emphasise the need to understand what it means under that act to assess a child as 'in need' of services or 'at risk' of significant harm.

Assessing competence the other side of the table, the worker's ability to make these judgements, is the key to whether the assessment of the child is adequate. This has implications for confidentiality for, as the HAS report makes clear, adequate assessment may require 'involving other agencies and disciplines'. In arguing that thorough assessment requires 'links between social services, child and adult mental health services, child protection teams and substance misuse services', *Children and Young People* is partly making the point that drug misuse services lack staff trained in child protection issues and (as the SSI found) social workers may lack the confidence or knowledge to assess drug-related risk or need.

Joint assessment is particularly appropriate when the drug using parent is the client. *Drug Using Parents* first makes the fundamental point that 'All drug using parents should routinely be asked about their parenting and child care practices', then counsels that such assessments are best 'carried out jointly by child and adult agencies'. Next it delivers an instruction which some drug services, those for which confidentiality and distance from authority are touchstones, may find hard to swallow: 'If the drug service has concerns that children of drug using parents may be 'at risk' or 'in need'…they should contact social services'.

The qualifier 'may be' gives a potentially wide scope to this direction, particularly as the document points out that 'Where parents are heavy, dependent or chaotic users of drugs, family life **will** be affected' (emphasis added). It does however, leave the drug service with an easier judgement to make, not whether the child is 'in need' or 'at risk', but whether they **might** be: 'It is not up to the drug service to assess the need for child protection, but only to refer the child to the social services department for assessment'.

Drug Using Parents' list of factors social services should consider in their assessment of the child includes 'any relevant information [from] health care professionals'. So perhaps the drug service will be called upon not just to make the referral, but also to reveal things said to it by the client or observations pertinent to the child.

Workers reluctant to inform social services may find the pill sweetened somewhat by the Children Act's emphasis not on removing the child, but on providing support for the family to stay together. But it seems this sweetener is often illusory: *Drug Using Parents* says support services are 'frequently over-stretched and under-resourced and there may be a considerable wait'. If in practice social services intervene only when the child is a candidate for the child protection register, then warnings about how this has deterred parents from seeking help may continue to be relevant.

Collaborative care

As several documents point out, collaboration needs to continue beyond assessment into service delivery. *Children and Young People* says 'Each agency and service component should have a menu of the services, interventions, treatments and facilities that it provides and a written protocol for its contribution to packages of care for individuals when responsibility for care is shared by a number of agencies'.

HAS's assertion that it is good practice to involve the child's family in assessment and care planning is echoed in the SSI report, but *Children and Young People* recognises there is a debate: 'Some services...discourage the involvement of parents, in order to reassure young people that services are confidential'. Confirmation of this can be found in SCODA's *Drug-related Early Intervention* which illustrates a number of projects in which parental involvement is integral (such as the family-focused Early Breaks Project) and others (such as peer education) where it would be unusual. But if there is a debate over whether it is good practice to inform parents, what of whether it is legal?

Telling the parents

On the legality of not gaining parental consent before providing drug-related services, all these reports hang fire to varying degrees, with 'seek legal advice' being the concrete recommendation from the SSI and *Children and Young People*. There is also a call for guidelines on parental involvement and consent to treatment agreed through local drug action teams and area child protection committees, and *Children and Young People* recommends record keeping sufficient for staff to show 'they believe that they are acting in the best interests of the young person'.

Before coming to these conclusions, both reports use the same wording to describe the issues involved in intervening with those under 18. Services 'need to deal with any threat or impediment to the development and maintenance of a reasonable standard of health and development of the child or young person (derived from the definition of being 'in need' in the Children Act), while at the same time taking account of the relevant law...it is also necessary to consider and take into account the role of those with parental responsibility...and the age and relative understanding of the child or young person, their welfare and the rights or otherwise of those with parental responsibility under the Children Act'.

The SSI's report also approaches the issue of informing parents from a different angle, not seeking parental consent to treatment, but enabling parents to fulfil their 'duty of care' (see *Holistic assessment and confidentiality*).

The forthcoming guide from SCODA and the Children's Legal Centre should clarify these issues. Here it is worth noting that assessments of the **child's** competence to consent to treatment, including their intellectual development and emotional maturity, and of the **service's** competence to assess the child's competence, seem the key elements. The problem is that deciding what to do on these criteria, is not necessarily the same as acting in the child's best interests, the fundamental principle of the Children Act.

The crunch scenario is where a service decides the child is not competent to consent, believes they still need to intervene in order to prevent harm, but also believes that seeking parental consent will impede the provision of this service or otherwise harm the child. Do they seek parental consent because the child cannot legally consent, or do they do what they believe to be in the child's best interests and risk the wrath of the courts? And would they risk this anyhow if they withheld the intervention and as a result the child came to harm? Legally playing safe may not be the same as ensuring the young person's safety.

Making it happen

We now have a clear, and ambitious, picture of the services required to meet the needs of young drug users. Ranging from prevention to treatment, they would be separate from services for adults, sensitive to the child's level of development, easy to access, attractive to the young, and intervene before problems become severe and entrenched. Early intervention services would target risk groups, access to education and advice would be universal. What will it take to get there?

All the reports call for commissioning and training plans and collaborative structures aimed at achieving these objectives. The interest is in how they see this happening when it has not (or not anywhere near sufficiently) up to now.

Collaboration in diversity

If effective work in this area requires co-working across service sectors, then the spirit and practice of collaboration between those sectors becomes critical to service delivery. On this all four documents could hardly be more emphatic. A shared strategy provides the basis for operational collaboration, but is not in itself sufficient. The strategy may require it, contracts may insist on it, and everyone may pay lip service to it, yet collaboration may still fail to make it from paper to practice.

Which agencies need to collaborate? *Drug-Related Early Intervention* lists social workers; the youth service; teachers, governors and others involved with education; criminal justice professionals including the police, probation, court workers and youth justice teams; voluntary and statutory drug services; health workers. From its local authority perspective, *Children and Young People* adds housing departments and also prisons.

The latter gives the most explicit account of how such agencies can be encouraged to work together. First is agreeing 'definitions of 'children' and 'young people' (and) what is meant by substance use and misuse' and achieving 'a common understanding of the particular needs of children and young people'. Then telling each other what they are doing via a 'written statement which defines (each agency's) aims and objectives and identifies its role in the overall pattern of provision'. Presumably these will feed into a shared 'information base about local needs, existing services and the effectiveness of services', the latter requiring consensus on the 'clinical and social effectiveness of particular services and methods'.

Achieving such agreements will be no mean feat. For example, if local opinion is that a particular service is ineffective, it may be difficult to incorporate its managers in the consensus. Some of the debate will occur while agreeing a shared strategy. Beyond this, *Children and Young People* calls for at least health and local authorities to 'appoint lead officers to be responsible for coordinating work done across agency boundaries' – a concrete manifestation of the 'commitment of time and energy and…willingness for agencies to learn about each other' required for partnership working.

Reminding us that service differences create choice for the client, *Children and Young People* sees such commitment as making it 'possible to respect and value differences in style and approach'. Lastly, 'Frontline staff can only play their part in joint arrangements if their commitment is supported by senior management and organisational structures'.

Funding and resource-sharing

Using adult services for the young seems ruled out, and the youth services which might incorporate drug provision have reputedly withered under decades of financial stringencies. Achieving the recommended range of services would seem to demand substantial new funding.

Perhaps judging it unrealistic, none of the reports calls for this, despite the SSI's implication that dedicated budgets are the only way to ensure suitable services and the observation in *Drug-related Early Intervention* that 'A dedicated budget is generally critical to the success of new services'.

The latter attempts to square the circle through its suggestion (perhaps hope) that budgets and resources may be carved out of 'existing mainstream service resources (e.g., staff, finances, sites, facilities)'. Making a related point, it observes that 'The most effective early intervention drug projects rely heavily on existing mainstream services for children (and families). Resources can therefore be maximised by adapting these existing services to provide referrals or joint care management as an integral part of an intervention package'.

Commissioning: joint and long-term

How will the budget be allocated? In *Children and Young People* and *Drug Using Parents* we find joint commissioning between health and local authorities positioned as the core mechanism, one the SSI found already widely established, though more for adult than children's drug services.

This cooperative funding mechanism is also seen as a route to cooperation between services. *Drug Using Parents* argues that purchasing plans and contracts should encourage 'close working arrangements' between children's services and those working with drug using parents. In relation to new projects, *Drug-related Early Intervention* sharpens this up in its call for 'specific alliances' between children's services, other health and social services, police and substance misuse professionals: 'Some commissioners have found it valuable to negotiate and agree critical partnership roles and responsibilities formally before funding is awarded'.

Children and Young People argues that developing a range of services entails purchasing from a range of providers, as no single provider can meet all the needs. In reverse, to remain viable some services may need the support of a range of purchasing authorities. 'Commissioners will need to work with neighbouring authorities to plan and support' highly specialised services, presumably HAS's 'tier 4' clinics and rehabilitation units for complex cases.

Achieving separate child-centred provision is in turn seen as requiring consideration of 'separate contracts for drug and alcohol services for children and adolescents rather than including them in general mental health service or drug and alcohol service contracts'. Such an arrangement, continues *Children and Young People*, makes it 'easier to set quality standards...appropriate to children and young people', including staff vetting. Contractual specificity may also facilitate the call in *Drug-related Early Intervention* for the 'precise service specifications...essential in ensuring defined and targeted services'.

On tackling the short-termism in funding widely seen as impeding strategic development, *Drug-related Early Intervention* calls for initial three-year contracts to enable projects to establish themselves, and for a 'strategic funding commitment from commissioners', but does accept that a pilot evaluation phase may be valuable. Similarly, *Children and Young People* argues for 'three to five year agreements', pointing out that shorter funding rounds divert staff from frontline work.

Lastly, with the importance attached to staff competence, *Children and Young People* makes an important (if coded) call for purchasers to be ready to pay for this, arguing first that agency budgets should include a 'suitable level of expenditure on training' and then that 'Organisations that offer appropriate training, professional supervision, information and support services should have this recognised in their contracts'.

Retooling staff

Identification of staff training as 'essential' to adequate and lawful service provision flows directly from the deficiencies in knowledge and confidence and the incompatibility in approaches identified in all four documents. In *Substance Misuse and Young People* and *Children and Young People* it is a two-way call 'to empower those already skilled in working with children to be able to identify, assess and refer young substance misusers [and] to ensure for those working in drug services for young people, the knowledge and skills to work appropriately and effectively with young people'. In *Children and Young People* it is a broader recognition that 'All staff...in contact with children and young people need training both in substance misuse issues and working with children and young people'.

Children and Young People calls for local programmes to embrace all four levels of training recommended by HAS, roughly corresponding to the needs of staff in the four tiers of service provision. The training suggested in *Drug Using Parents* has the different but related task of meeting the 'local needs of key services in working with drug using parents and their children'.

Procedures and guidelines...

Among the SSI's 'critical success factors' was 'Policy and practice guidance for a range of professionals on a range of topics including: assessment; referral routes and procedures; confidentiality; legal issues; harm reduction services; and monitoring'. These it found distinctly lacking among the local authorities it surveyed. *Children and Young People* also calls for 'clear, written child protection procedures' approved by the area child protection committee.

The more detailed statement in SCODA's *Drug-related Early Intervention* still goes no further than listing the headings for guidelines 'agreed between the local drug action team and area child protection committee and including information sharing, parental involvement, consent to treatment, and working with children 'at risk' and 'in need'. They should dovetail with other policies (including managing drug-related incidents in schools) and address the interface between different disciplines.'

...are central to work with parents

For drug using children, generating new service provision is perhaps the priority; for *Drug Using Parents* it is getting existing services to work well together. This is why widely implemented operational guidelines lie at the heart of its recommendations in a way they do not for the other documents. The report gives two examples, one for assessing the children of drug using parents, the other for pregnant drug users.

As with drug using children, drug action teams and area child protection committees are seen as the core bodies through which such guidelines are to be agreed. Among the other participants mentioned are health and local authorities and service providers, though in part they may be involved via the coordinating bodies. Agreed policies should be disseminated 'widely to specialist and generic agencies' and to 'drug users who are pregnant or have children'. The hope is that parents will then 'understand the benefits for them and their children of contacting statutory or non-statutory agencies'. Samples are given which make it clear that 'No agency can offer you absolute confidentiality'.

For each type of policy the report seems to stipulate at least one mandatory feature: for drug using parents, it is recognition that 'drug use in itself is not a reason for considering a child to be at risk of significant harm'; and for pregnant drug users, 'All maternity services should have policies and procedures...that encourage (women) to go to antenatal services and to help the women to stabilise, reduce or stop their drug use'.

Controlling quality

Children and Young People is not alone in arguing that 'Good practice requires that the effectiveness of services is subject to review'. Here the 'clear statement of the aims, objectives and targets of the service' needed to support collaboration, can also provide a yardstick against which to measure performance and develop auditable standards.

As with training and supervision, *Children and Young People* recognises that this costs money and advises that 'Each agency should have resources allocated within its contracts to enable it to undertake systematic internal audit and evaluation of its services'.

Agreed local strategies

Collaboration across disciplines and agencies, joint commissioning, multi-agency training, agreed local guidelines, information sharing, all these and more imply the need for a base in locally agreed strategies. Among the issues are, which agencies need be involved, through which structures, what must they do, and how can it be ensured that they do it? Within this last question is the important issue of 'which body, if any, should take the lead in developing the strategy?'.

Where are the strategies?

A local strategy on children and drugs could feature in several broader plans. Ideally, they will speak with one voice, but the SSI had to call for 'Further alignment...between drug action team plans, community care plans, children's services plans and joint commissioning committees'. An obvious tactic is to reference a single strategy document on children and drugs in all these broader plans, so for the SSI one characteristic of good joint commissioning is a 'stand-alone strategy'. Without being explicit, *Children and Young People* seems to assume a core plan is desirable. *Drug-related Early Intervention* and *Drug Using Parents* also seem to opt for a stand-alone version incorporated in drug action team and children's services plans, and for parents-to-be also in health authority strategies for maternity and neonatal services. This latter aspect of planning for drug using parents argues perhaps for a strategy separate from but related to the one for children using drugs.

Children and Young People highlights another strategy need, repeating the call in the English drug strategy white paper and in the HAS report for 'adequately resourced and coordinated' local training strategies. *Drug Using Parents* also calls for such plans. Omitted from both is HAS's scepticism that 'without national leadership and coordination...it is difficult to see how the training objectives in the white paper will be achieved'. There seems sufficient overlap with the training needs identified in *Drug Using Parents* for the same plan to cater for work with children and parents using drugs.

DATs take the lead

Top of the list for potential strategy leaders are drug action teams (responsible for local drug strategies) and area child protection committees (responsible for children's services plans). In these reports the former seem favoured, though cooperating with the latter and with other bodies.

The SSI reports that 'in most areas (drug action teams were seen) as the appropriate vehicle for strategic development, planning and commissioning of services for this client group', while *Children and Young People* recommends that 'Drug action teams should bring together an overall strategy for children and young people who misuse substances'. For *Drug Using Parents*, 'Drug action teams have a crucial role in coordinating services and ensuring...arrangements for cooperation between...services...on both a strategic and operational level'.

In *Children and Young People*, drug action teams are also the 'key agencies' in developing a multi-agency training strategy.

Complexity unavoidable

The complexity of strategy formulation in this area is seen in this specification from *Children and Young People*: 'The strategy must link closely with other strategies for child protection, child and adolescent mental health services and for substance misuse services for adults. It needs to: cover educational, preventive and treatment oriented approaches; identify and prioritise children and young people in high risk groups; consider how young people can be diverted into services that provide alternatives to custody.'

Drug-related Early Intervention expands on the services the strategy should ensure: 'access to early intervention (education, advice and counselling services)' and 'more intensive and targeted support for young drug misusers (with drug and other problems)'. Matching recommendations on service contracts, SCODA argues for strategies to run for three to five years.

Drug Using Parents says plans with respect to its target group must 'separately identify the needs of:
− children
− their families
− their parents.

Informed by needs assessment

The local service mix will ideally be based on the kind of comprehensive needs assessment recommended in *Drug-Related Early Intervention*. Similarly, in developing the training strategy, 'A staff training needs analysis (specifically on working with substance misuse and working with children and families) should be considered'. SCODA says the needs assessment for service planning should:

• Assess local substance misuse trends among young people in general and among those with special needs.

• Map existing services including general health and welfare services for children and families, substance misuse services, services for young people with other problems or complex needs.

• Map existing policies and procedures for working with young drug users.

Both SCODA and the local authority bodies behind *Children and Young People* advise consultation with the young drug users who may become clients of the services provided for by the strategy, market testing to ensure they will be used and useful.

It takes commitment

Though SCODA describes needs assessments as 'essential', the SSI found them rarely carried out. It is unclear from these reports what will make comprehensive assessments the rule rather than the exception.

Perhaps again it comes down to the sort of commitment to the strategy which *Children and Young People* says must be forthcoming from 'key people at all levels, including chairs of local authority committees and chief officers of local authorities, health authorities and NHS trusts as well as drug action teams and drug and alcohol teams, managers and front line staff'.

By specifying strategy development among the action points for health and local authorities, *Children and Young People* appears to suggest this is where commitment needs to be strongest in order to place young drug users on the agendas of drug action teams and area child protection committees.

Resources

Substance Misuse and Young People: the Social Services Response. A Social Services Inspectorate study of Young People Looked After by Local Authorities. *Social Care Group of the Social Services Inspectorate*. Department of Health, 1997. Copies from: Department of Health
           PO Box 410
           Wetherby LS23 7LN

Children and Young People: Guidance for Commissioners and Providers of Substance Misuse Services. *Local Government Drugs Forum and London Drug Policy Forum*. Local Government Association, 1997. Copies £10 (including postage) from: Quote ref SS086 and send payment (payable to 'LGMB') with order. LGMB Publication Sales
           Layden House
           76–86 Turnmill Street
           London EC1M 5QU
           tel 0171 664 6600; fax 0171 296 6666.

Drug-related Early Intervention: Developing Services for Young People and Families. *Good Practice Unit of the Standing Conference on Drug Abuse (SCODA)*. SCODA, 1997. Copies £10 (£7.50 SCODA members) from:
           Standing Conference on Drug Abuse
           32–36 Loman Street
           London SE1 0EE
           tel 0171 928 9500; fax 0171 928 3343.

Drug Using Parents: Policy Guidelines for Inter-agency Working. *Local Government Drugs Forum and Standing Conference on Drug Abuse. Local Government Association, 1997.* Copies £15 (including postage) from:
           LGMB Publication Sales (address above)
Quote ref SS084 and send payment (payable to 'LGMB') with order. Reviewed report England and Wales only. Scottish edition under preparation, contact LGDF 0171 664 3256.

Notes

1. Beyond the remit of this review were two reports on the children of alcohol using parents published around the same time as the reviewed reports and raising similar issues: Brisby *et al. Under Influence: Coping with Parents who Drink Too Much* and Housten, Kork *et al. Beyond the Limit: Children who Live with Parental Alcohol Misuse*. Health Advisory Service Children and Young People: Substance Misuse Services. London: HMSO, 1996.

2. A fuller version available on request via e-mail from mike@mashton.cix.co.uk extensively analyses the 'diagnosis' as well as the 'prescription'. Send a message asking for *Between Stools: Full Report*. Specify acceptable word processing formats.

3. From 31 March 1993 to the same date in 1996 the proportion of under 20s recorded by drug misuse databases was relatively steady at 11–12%. (Department of Health. Drug Misuse Statistics). Similarly under 21-year-olds formed 24% of all opiate addiction notifications in 1986 and 20% in 1996, having dipped to 14% in 1991 (Home Office).

Statistics of Drug Addicts Notified to the Home Office, United Kingdom, 1996. However, there are very recent signs of the trend tipping upwards.

4. Among the latest evidence for more and younger drug use is a series of studies in Wales reported in Roberts and Moore *et al. Drug Use Among 15–16-year-olds in Wales.*

5. Press release relating to Plant, M. *Alcohol and Other Drug Use Amongst Students in 26 European Countries.* European Monitoring Centre for Drugs and Drug Addiction. *Annual Report on the State of the Drugs Problem in the European Union for 1997.*

6. From 1 October 1995 to 31 March 1996 doctors and drug services in England recorded 2807 new episodes of treatment of 15–19-year-olds and 180 of those under 15. (Department of Health. *Drug Misuse Statistics.*)

8. See for example the survey findings in: Gilchrist and Polley *Consultation and Local Intelligence. A New Substance Use Service for Young People in Leeds.*

9. How this might work can be seen, for example, in the responses of young people documented in Wibberley's *Young People's Feelings about Drugs.*

10. Perri 6 addressing the London Drug Services Providers Consortium, November 1997.

References

Brisby, T. et al. (1997). *Under Influence: Coping with Parents who Drink Too Much.* London: Alcohol Concern.

Cragg, A. *op cit.*

Cragg, A. (1994). The Two Sides of Fear. *Druglink*, 9(5).

Department of Health (1997). Drug Misuse Statistics. *Bulletin 1997/9*, May 1997.

European Monitoring Centre for Drugs and Drug Addiction (1997). *Annual Report on the State of the Drugs Problem in the European Union for 1997.* Lisbon: EMCDDA.

Gilchrist, H., and Polley, S. (1996). *Consultation and Local Intelligence. A New Substance Use Service for Young People in Leeds.* Leeds: RSDC.

Health Advisory Service (1996). *Children and Young People: Substance Misuse Services.* London: HMSO.

Health Advisory Service (1995). *Together We Stand: The Commissioning, Role and Management of Child and Adolescent Mental Health Service.* London: HMSO.

Hepburn, M. (1996). Drug Use in Pregnancy – Fact and Fiction. *Druglink*, 11(4): p 12–14.

Home Office (1997). *Statistics of Drug Addicts Notified to the Home Office, United Kingdom, 1996.* Government Statistical Service .

Housten, Kork, et al. *Beyond the Limit: Children Who Live with Parental Alcohol Misuse.*

Joseph Rowntree Foundation (1997). *Young People and Drugs.* Findings.

McNeill, A., and Raw, M. (1997). *Drug Use in England: Results of the 1995 National Drugs Campaign Survey.* London: Health Education Authority.

Plant, M. (1997). *Alcohol and Other Drug Use Amongst Students in 26 European Countries.* Edinburgh: Queen Margaret College.

Proceedings of SCODA Residential Services Forum.

Prochaska, J.O., and DiClemente, C. (1984). *The Transtheoretical Approach: Crossing Traditional Boundaries of Therapies.* Homewood, Illinois: Dow Jones/Irwin.

Roberts, C., and Moore, L., et al. (1995). Drug Use Among 15–16-year-olds in Wales, 1990–94. *Drugs: Education, Prevention and Policy*, 2(3): p 305–316.

Shiner, M., and Newburn, T. (1997). Definitely, Maybe Not? The Normalisation of Recreational Drug Use Amongst Young People. *Sociology*, 31(3): p 511–529.

Strang, J., and Taylor, C. (1997). Different Gender and Age Characteristics of the UK Heroin Epidemic of the 1990s Compared with the 1980s. *European Addiction Research*, 3: p 43–44.

Wibberley, C. (1997). Young People's Feelings about Drugs. *Drugs Education, Prevention and Policy*, 4(1): p 65–78.

Chapter 4

Dutch Drug Policy and Cannabis

I.P. Spruit and M.W. van Laar

The main aim of the drugs policy is to reduce the risks of drug use to the individual drug users, their immediate environment, as well as society in general. The reduction of supply and demand is also an important objective. With respect to the individual, the protection of their health is the key aim. In this context, prevention and care are core policy issues. With respect to the protection of society as a whole, measures in the field of public order and safety are important issues.

Responsibility for the drugs policy rests with both the Minister of Health, Welfare and Sports (HWS) and the Minister of Justice. The Minister of HWS bears the prime responsibility for policy on prevention and care, with the exception of administrative prevention. This is the task of the Ministry of the Interior. The Minister of Justice is responsible for the enforcement of the Opium Act. The Minister of HWS is responsible for the co-ordination of the government's drug policy.

The Opium Act is the main law in which regulations on drugs are laid down. Various other types of legislation may also be applied in investigation and prosecution. One example is the *pluk-ze* (clean them out) legislation (law on financial penalties) which makes it possible to tackle money-laundering. The Public Prosecutor's office has also issued directives for circumstances in which more severe sentences are to be used, such as selling to vulnerable groups (school children, psychiatric patients) and trade in the vicinity of schools and psychiatric hospitals. But the government policy is also based on the premise that criminal prosecution must be no more damaging to the drug users than the drug use itself.

Dutch drug policy is aimed at maintaining a separation between the market for soft drugs (cannabis products such as hashish and marijuana) and the market for drugs that carry an unacceptable risk (such as the hard drugs, heroin and cocaine). Furthermore, the policy is also aimed at preventing drug users from ending up in an illegal environment, where they are difficult to reach for prevention and intervention.

The Opium Act

The Opium Act of 1919 (amended in 1928 and 1976) regulates the production, distribution and consumption of 'psychoactive' substances. Possession, commercial distribution, production, import and export, and advertising the sale or distribution of all drugs is punishable by law. Since 1985, this has also covered activities preparatory to trafficking in hard drugs. The use of drugs is not punishable by law. Activities relating to soft drugs and hard drugs for medicinal and scientific purposes are allowed provided the Minister of HWS has granted special permission.

Since 1976, a distinction has been made between soft drugs and hard drugs. This distinction was established as a result of a 1972 report from the Working Group on Narcotic Drugs (the Baan Committee). Using a 'risk scale', based on medical, pharmacological, socio-scientific and psychological data, a distinction was made between drugs which pose an unacceptable hazard to health ('hard drugs', such as heroin, cocaine, LSD and amphetamines) and hemp products ('soft drugs' such as hashish and marijuana). Hard drugs were listed on schedule I and soft drugs were listed on schedule II (sub b) of the Opium Act. Since 2 July 1993, barbiturates and tranquillizers have been listed on schedule II (sub a) due to the fact that the Netherlands ratified the Psychotropic Substances Treaty.

Violations of the Opium Act are punished severely, but penal provisions for soft drug offences are milder than those for hard drugs. A distinction is also made between the possession of drugs and trade in drugs. This makes the possession of soft drugs and hard drugs for commercial purposes subject to harsher sentences than possession for individual consumption. The import and export of drugs has the highest priority in terms of investigation and prosecution and is subject to the stiffest sentences.

The following illustrates the penal differentiation: the maximum sentence for the sale or production of a maximum of 30 grammes of hemp is one month detention (and/or a Dfl 5,000 fine), while import or export is punishable with one year detention (and/or a Dfl 100,000 fine). The maximum penalty for the possession of hard drugs in 'consumer amounts' is one year imprisonment (and/or a Dfl 10,000 fine) and 12 years imprisonment (and/or a Dfl 100,000 fine) for the import or export of hard drugs. The maximum penalties may be increased by one third if the offence has been committed more than once.

Guidelines have been established for the investigation and prosecution of Opium Act offences (see Expediency Principle).

Coffee Shops

Over the years so-called coffee shops emerged. The sale of hard drugs at these premises is strictly forbidden, but the sale of soft drugs is not prosecuted provided certain conditions are met (see Guidelines below). The reasons for this policy is the desire to separate the markets for hard drugs and soft drugs, to avoid criminalisation and administrative clarity. The government wants to prevent (often young) soft drug users from resorting to a market where there are more drugs for them to switch to (see Stepping-Stone Hypothesis) and where they might more easily end up in criminal circles.

According to police estimates the number of coffee shops in the Netherlands was 1,200 to 1,500 in 1991. A research bureau estimated their number at 1,460 in 1995 and 1,293 in 1996, but there are both lower and higher estimates, all of which are as well founded as each other. The coffee shops are mainly small, café-like enterprises catering for a diverse public from various social backgrounds. Most offer a wide range of hashish and marijuana products from various countries and of varying quality. They have various functions. Some act solely as shops, in others people may use drugs if they buy something, while others serve mainly as meeting places where little is bought and people stay longer. These latter type may have a nuisance-reducing effect, as there is less lingering in the streets.

The majority of coffee shops adhere to national AHOJ-G criteria (see Guidelines below). The closing down of a number of coffee shops and a more rigid police control in recent years have shown that these criteria are strictly adhered to. Immediate causes for police operations are usually related to nuisance problems in the neighbourhoods or suspected hard drugs traffic. Other specific problems are coffee shops in undesirable locations (such as in residential areas or near schools), and the attraction of drug tourists, especially in the border towns.

Since 1995, the policy has been aimed at reducing the number of coffee shops, also in the context of the nuisance policy. Administrative measures are also being introduced more often at local level to prevent and fight nuisance problems in the vicinity of coffee shops. General by-laws, nuisance regulations, environmental regulations, zoning-plans and building regulations offer possibilities in this respect. Since these often result in complicated procedures which are by no means always successful, a new law is being drafted. Dubbed 'Damocles', this draft law on the executive enforcement of the Opium Act allows mayors to close coffee shops and trade locations even if there are no nuisance problems, but if, for instance, both hard drugs and soft drugs are being sold. The separation of the markets for soft drugs and hard drugs continues to be a key criterion in use of closure authority.

Data on Cannabis Use

In the Netherlands, an estimated 675,000 people use cannabis regularly or occasionally. This is about 4.6% of the population of 12 years and older. However, there are no hard figures available.

A 1994 study of drug use in Amsterdam showed that 6.4% of the population had used cannabis recently (during the month preceding the survey). In 1990 this figure was 6%. The average age of the users is 30, but most are between 20 and 24. The number of new users per year is estimated at 1%. A study among school pupils in Amsterdam in 1995 also showed a fairly small increase in use in the 1990s.

Large-scale nationwide surveys among secondary school students (aged between 12–18 years) showed that cannabis use increased more sharply before the 1990s, i.e. between 1984 and 1992. In 1984, 4.8% of pupils had ever used cannabis and 2.3% had done so recently (during the previous month). In 1988, these percentages were 8.0% and 3.1% and in 1992, 13.6% and 6.5% respectively. The difference between 'ever' and 'recent' use indicates that more than half of the cases involve experimental behaviour. Even more people stop using cannabis after leaving school. Boys score a significantly higher percentage than girls with regard to cannabis use, and the highest score in recent use is among 16 and 17 year-olds.

The increase in cannabis use among young people is often attributed to coffee shops, but this is highly unlikely. Not only are coffee shops responsible for a mere one-third of the total distribution, but the increase in use also started well before the rise in the number of coffee shops, and coffee shops are not allowed to sell to school pupils. The main argument against this connection, however, is that soft drug use among young people is on the increase in a large number of (western) countries, and in some of these more strongly than in the Netherlands, while these countries do not have coffee shops and often have a more repressive policy.

Between two and five per thousand cannabis users get into trouble. The number of registrations for problematic cannabis use in the out-patient facilities for addiction care was 2,456 in 1995, amounting to 5% of all registrations. Addiction clinics, psychiatric hospitals and general hospitals admitted a total of 237 people for cannabis addiction and 87 people for cannabis abuse without addiction in 1995. In line with increased use, there has been a rise in the number of requests for professional help over the years.

Prevention and Education

Prevention, information and education play an important role in Dutch drug policy. The project *Healthy Schools and Stimulants*, specifically aimed at secondary school pupils, was launched in 1991. The project is a cooperative effort on the part of the Trimbos Institute, the out-patient facilities for addiction care and local public health services, together with local authorities. The project provides information on tobacco, alcohol, cannabis and gambling, aimed specifically at the ages at which students generally have their first contacts with the substance in question or gambling. For cannabis this is usually around 15 years old. Besides providing information, the project is also aimed at establishing regulations (no substance use in schools), detection and guidance. By mid 1996, 30% of schools were implementing this project on a structural basis. A specific consumer public is being advised on 'sensible use' in leaflets distributed in various coffee shops. *Tips on Hash and Grass* warns against the harmful effects on concentration and the ability to react, the use of cannabis as a means of overcoming problems, eating space-cake, simultaneous use with alcohol or medication and taking hashish and grass out of the country.

Criticism and Praise

The Dutch cannabis policy has been both praised and criticised nationally and internationally. In terms of social acceptability, the current policy is regularly under discussion, particularly with regard to drugs-related nuisance. The policy has also been criticised by EU countries, which regard the Netherlands as being out of tune, particularly regarding the harmonisation of legislation on narcotics.

This has resulted in a tendency towards a more repressive approach. On the other hand, the Dutch cannabis policy has achieved the objective of a (relative) separation of the soft and hard drugs markets. The fact that cannabis is relatively easy to obtain in coffee shops has not resulted in a greater increase in use than in other countries. Furthermore, the number of hard drug addicts has stabilised and the Netherlands has few drugs-related deaths compared with other countries. In recent years, other countries have also come to realise that a certain level of decriminalisation of soft drug use is worth considering in the context of public health, the prevention of social damage to users and the limitation of aggressive small-scale trade in the street.

International Treaties

The main international drugs treaty ratified by the Netherlands is the United Nations Single Convention on Narcotic Drugs of 1961 (amended in 1972). The primary aim is to achieve worldwide cooperation in the fight against drug abuse and drug trade other than for medical and scientific purposes. In 1993, the Netherlands also ratified the 1971 UN Convention on Psychotropic Substances (pertaining to illegal drugs, as well as tranquillizers and barbiturates) and the 1988 UN Convention on Illicit Traffic in Narcotic Drugs and Psychotropic substances.

The Schengen Treaty of 1985 is an agreement between all EU member states, with the exception of Denmark, the UK and Ireland, aimed at the opening of their borders. The Treaty includes agreements on better cooperation in the fight against crime and the harmonisation of drug legislation. The implementation treaty of the Schengen Treaty dates from 26 March 1995.

Expediency Principle

The principle of expediency has been included in the Dutch Penal Code. This empowers the Public Prosecutor to refrain from prosecution of criminal offences if this is in the public interest. The guidelines for investigation and prosecution were amended on 1 October 1996. These guidelines establish the priorities in the investigation and prosecution of Opium Act offences. Punishable offences involving hard drugs other than for individual use take the highest priority, followed by punishable offences involving soft drugs other than for individual use. Investigation and prosecution of possession of hard drugs for individual consumption (generally 0.5 gramme) and soft drugs to a maximum of 5 grammes carry the lowest priority. If coffee shops comply with the guidelines (see Guidelines below), the sale of a maximum of 5 grammes of hashish and marijuana per transaction is generally not investigated. The police do confiscate all drugs discovered. Coffee shops involved in the sale of trade or consumption stocks for export are subject to priority investigation and prosecution. The same applies to soft drugs sales via other points of sale, such as cafes, shops, take-away centres, couriers or taxis, commercial telephone lines, mail order, etc.

Stepping-stone Hypothesis

The assumption that cannabis consumers run a higher risk of switching to hard drugs, especially heroin, is known as 'the stepping-stone hypothesis'. This idea was first put forward in the forties in the USA and has since greatly influenced public opinion, as well as American and international drug policies. Opinions differ as to whether or not the hypothesis is correct. As for a possible switch from cannabis to hard drugs, it is clear that the pharmacological properties of cannabis are irrelevant in this respect. There is no physically determined tendency towards switching from soft to harder substances. Social factors, however, do appear to play a role. The more users become integrated in an environment ('subculture') where, apart from cannabis, hard drugs can also be obtained, the greater the chance that they may switch to hard drugs. Separation of the drug markets is therefore essential and forms the basis of the current cannabis policy.

Guidelines

Coffee shops must adhere to the so-called **AHOJ-G** criteria: no Advertising (commercials), no Hard drugs sale, no Nuisance, no selling of soft drugs to Young persons (under 18) and no Great quantities (more than 5 grammes) per transaction. The maximum trade stock allowed is 500 grammes, but local councils may set a lower maximum. Depending on specific local problems, some local councils have added several stipulations to the AHOJ-G criteria in the form of a covenant ('no parking in front of entrance', 'closing-time at 22.30 at night', etc.). The Public Prosecution Department has proclaimed the AHOJ-G criteria to be a nationwide criminal prosecution policy in 1991.

Local policy with regard to coffee shops is a matter for the local authorities. The Public Prosecutor, the Mayor and the Chief of Police confer on these policies (the 'tripartite deliberation'). In 1996, the Public Prosecution Department laid down new guidelines which form a new basis for the tripartite deliberation. Many local councils have since been working on a coffee shop policy. The supervision of compliance with the AHOJ-G criteria has been given a more central role in this respect. It was also agreed in 1996 that alcohol and soft drugs should not be sold in the same premises.

Cannabis Confiscations

The police and the public prosecutor cooperate closely in the investigation and combat of the drug trade. International cooperation is considered of primary importance. Confiscated imported hashish (see table) was often transported via containers (from Pakistan and elsewhere) or by road (from Morocco).

Destinations included the USA, Great Britain and Sweden. Marijuana mainly came from Colombia, Jamaica, Central Africa and South East Asia.

In recent years the Dutch cannabis market has increasingly been supplied (around 50%) via the production of indigenous marijuana (Nederweed). Hemp cultivation is only permitted for agricultural and horticultural activities and for wind barriers. In the future it is possible that more measures will be developed to deal with the illegal indoor cultivation of hemp and the cultivation of illegal crops.

Nederweed

The yield and quality of Dutch-grown grass or Nederweed has improved greatly in recent years, due to more sophisticated cultivation techniques, such as climate control, crop improvement, cross-breeding and the cloning of female plants containing the highest percentage of active substance (tetra-hydro-cannabinol or THC). Various studies have shown that the percentages of THC in Nederweed can vary from 1.5% to 13% with peaks of up to 27%. Similar to many kinds of imported cannabis, some variations of Nederweed ('Skunk') may contain high concentrations of THC but this is not standard. In 1997, the Forensic Laboratory found an average THC level of 8.5% in Dutch cannabis and 6% in imported hemp.

Risks of Cannabis Use

In the Netherlands cannabis is smoked primarily in the form of hashish (resin mixed with parts of the hemp plant) or marijuana (dried tops of the hemp plant). Cannabis is also eaten ('space-cake') and smoked using a waterpipe. The main risk of smoking is the damage to the lungs. There is no conclusive scientific evidence of harmful effects on the brain, blood circulation, immune system or fertility. However, studies have established a decrease in reaction speeds and the ability to concentrate, as well as a decline in short-term memory. These may have a negative effect on school performance, job performance and participation in traffic. Frequent use of cannabis can lead to psychoses in people with a certain predisposition. Consumption of 'space-cake' sometimes leads to an overdose with passing panic attacks. Consumption of Nederweed with a high percentage of THC may occasionally cause over-reactions. Cannabis use is by no means risk free, but is certainly no more harmful than alcohol and tobacco use.

Table 1. — Confiscated hash, marijuana (kg) and Nederweed (plants)

	1993	1994	1995
Hash	28.173	43.297	57.051
Marijuana	110.049	194.961	275.035
Nederweed	194.413	558.706	549.337

Source: Dutch Criminal Investigation Information Service

Publications

The Trimbos Institute publishes a series of fact sheets each year. Those published previously are:

1. *Cannabis Policy*
2. *Hard Drugs Policy: Opiates*
3. *Hard Drugs Policy: XTC*
4. *Addiction Care and Assistance*
5. *Prevention and Education Alcohol and Drugs*
6. *Nuisance Policy*

Copies in four languages can be ordered from the Trimbos Institute, Postbus 725, 3500 AS Utrecht.Tel: +31 30297 11 00; Fax:+31 30297 11 11; E-mail: info~trimbos.nl

The fact sheets and other information can also be accessed on the Internet. Please consult the Trimbos home-page: http://www.trimbos.nl

Results

The 167 individual prisons which reported the numbers of prisoners they held contained 51,926 people (including 2,437 women) on 1st January 1998 (or nearest date for which figures were available). One hundred and thirty-five respondents reported the proportion of prisoners who were estimated to be users of illegal drugs before imprisonment. The average proportion was 46.3%.

Figure 1 shows the proportion of prisons which reported having selected drug services available in 1995 and in 1998.

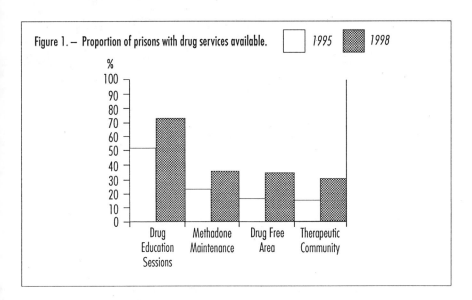

Figure 1. – Proportion of prisons with drug services available. ☐ *1995* ▨ *1998*

This graph indicates that, although there has been substantial development in the availability of prison drug services across Europe since 1995, these services – apart from drug education – are still only available in a minority of prisons. This is despite the high level of awareness that a large proportion of prisoners are at least former users of illegal drugs.

As seen in Table 1, the response rates across Europe were uneven. There follows more detailed information for those countries from where the questionnaires covered more than 10% of their prisons (excluding Luxembourg).

In the following figures, the number of prisons reporting the availability of each type of service is presented as a percentage of those that reported knowing whether that service was available at both 1st January 1995 and 1st January 1998.

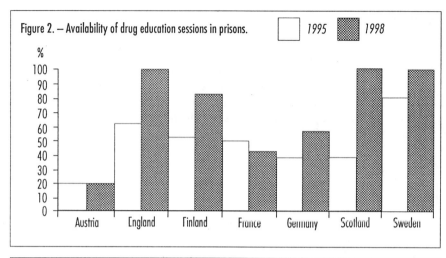

Figure 2. – Availability of drug education sessions in prisons.   ☐ *1995*   ▨ *1998*

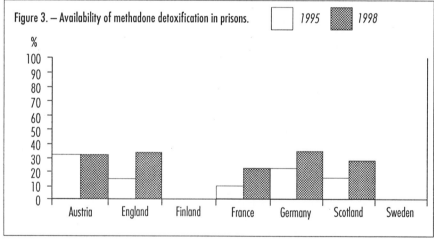

Figure 3. – Availability of methadone detoxification in prisons.   ☐ *1995*   ▨ *1998*

Drug Education

As will be seen below as a common pattern, the availability of this response to prisoners' drug use varies widely between countries. Scotland, England and Sweden have official strategies in place that require prisons to educate their inmates about drugs. This has lead to such education being provided in all the prisons which returned a questionnaire (see Figure 2). In Finland and Germany, there has also been an increase in the availability of this measure. The apparent fall in France represents the same number of prisons reporting the availability of drug education,

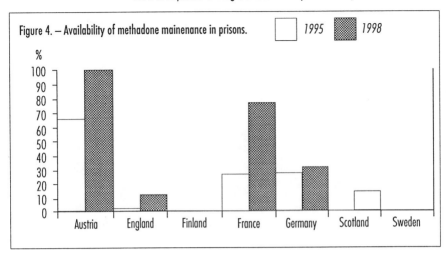

Figure 4. – Availability of methadone mainenance in prisons.   1995   1998

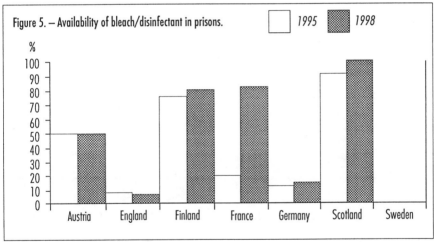

Figure 5. – Availability of bleach/disinfectant in prisons.   1995   1998

but a fall in 'don't knows' between 1995 and 1998. Drug education – both by training session and by leaflet – was the service that was reported as most commonly available across all the prisons in this survey.

Harm Reduction

The widest discrepancies between countries were reported for services that could be described as harm reduction; that is, services that focus on minimising the harm associated with drug use, rather than on eliminating the use of drugs.

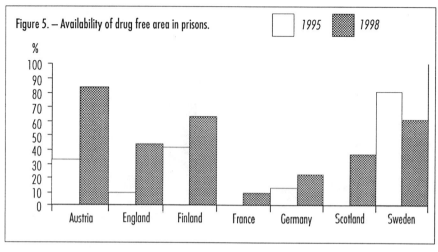

Figure 5. – Availability of drug free area in prisons.   ☐ *1995* ▦ *1998*

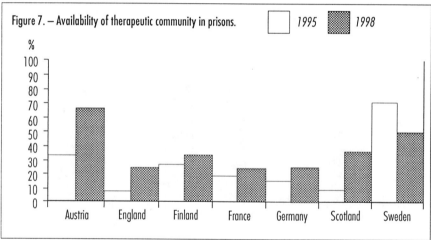

Figure 7. – Availability of therapeutic community in prisons.   ☐ *1995* ▦ *1998*

Only two prisons reported officially accepted needle exchange schemes. Both were in Lower Saxony (Germany) where the then Minister of Justice firmly supported the introduction of these schemes. One other respondent prison reported that injecting equipment was informally available from the prison health care department.

In Sweden and Finland, countries which are firmly opposed to any introduction of harm reduction strategies, no prisons reported providing any methadone treatment, whether for detoxification, or for longer term substitution. This gives a strong contrast with Austria and France, where provision of methadone

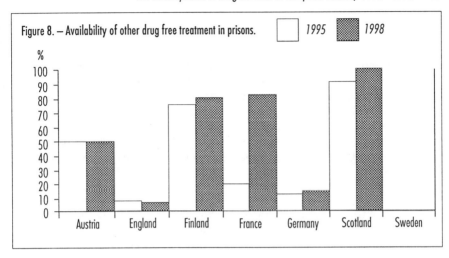

Figure 8. – Availability of other drug free treatment in prisons.   ☐ *1995*   ▨ *1998*

maintenance increased rapidly between 1995 and 1998 (to 100% and 77% of respondent prisons respectively). This echoes the growth in the provision of methadone in Spanish prisons; the number of Spanish prisoners who received methadone increased from zero in 1991 to 6,066 in 1996 (Anon, 1997). The provision of methadone substitution treatment has been shown to reduce injecting drug use in prisons, when the daily dose of methadone is over 60 mg, in both Catalonia and New South Wales (Boguña Casellas, 1997; Dolan et al., 1998).

There was an unexpected difference between the two countries who stand together against the rest of Western Europe in most arguments about harm reduction; 80% of respondent prisons in Finland reported the availability of 'bleach/disinfecting agents' in 1998, compared with none in Sweden.

There was also a revealing discrepancy between Scottish and English/Welsh prisons. An official policy review recommended the distribution of disinfectant tablets in English/Welsh prisons in 1995 (AIDS Advisory Committee, 1995), but this recommendation was quickly overturned and the tablets are yet to be made widely available south of the border, despite trouble-free distribution in all Scottish prisons.

Rapid development in the availability of disinfectants in French prisons has coincided with a low and stable availability in German prisons, as well as with uncertainty as to the effectiveness of distributing disinfectants in prison as a means of preventing viral infection transmission (see Dolan et al., 1994).

Abstinence-based Services

Given the emphasis in prison on control of behaviour that is seen as deviant, it was expected that services that require prisoners to be free from drugs would be more widespread in prisons than those that accept that some level of illicit drug use will occur.

This expectation was confirmed, in that more prisons had developed drug-free areas, therapeutic communities and other drug-free treatment programmes than had introduced methadone maintenance or needle exchange programmes.

There is an important distinction to be drawn between, on the one hand, drug free areas, in which prisoners agree to urine testing but do not necessarily receive any treatment for drug dependency, and, on the other, therapeutic communities and other drug-free treatment programmes. The two types of provision are often complementary, but the aims and target groups of each service can be very different.

Conclusions

The results of this survey give a good example of the forces and tensions involved in the process of European integration. While there are common trends across Western Europe, the directions that developments are taking often diverge within and between countries.

Within this pattern of divergence and inconsistency, we do attempt to draw three general conclusions.

The first is that prison drug services have developed rapidly in the three years from January 1995. This development can be seen across the countries involved in this survey, and across the range of types of drug service provision. The only exception to this list of countries is perhaps Sweden, which already had comparatively high provision of drug services in prison in 1995, some of which have suffered funding cuts since then (Farbring, 1998). The exception to the list of services is provided by the virtual invisibility of needle exchange in European prisons.

The second is that, in most countries, the development of drug services in prisons in each country has reflected the development of drug services outside prison, but with a time delay between the appearance of a service outside prison and its reflection inside. We suggest that the greater the degree of conflict between the type of service and the level of control that prisons seek to exercises over inmates, then the longer this time delay. A good example of prisons holding a mirror to developments outside prisons is given by the increased availability of methadone in French prisons, but not in Finnish or Swedish establishments. The time delay can be seen in the continued low level of availability of methadone in British prisons, and even more so in the provision of needle exchange, which conflicts more strongly with the repression of deviance. An exception to this rule is the Netherlands, where the emphasis in prisons is on providing drug-free areas and treatment, with little provision of harm reduction measures – in contrast to the situation outside Dutch prisons.

The third is that the availability of drug services in prisons across Western Europe, despite the rapid development of the last three years, is still inadequate when compared to the high level of problematic drug use among prisoners. In many prisons, people who are dependent on drugs will not receive the services they would get if they presented themselves to drug treatment agencies in the community. The availability of pharmacological treatment of withdrawal is limited in many countries' prisons, the full range of measures to prevent the spread of infectious disease through injecting drug use is rarely available in European prisons, and only a minority of these prisons have drug treatment programmes in place.

One could debate whether prisons are the most suitable environment to provide drug services, but the fact remains that many people with drug problems commit crimes that courts consider deserve punishment by imprisonment. If there is no dramatic shift in penal or drug policies, large numbers of problematic drug users will continue to be imprisoned. Prisons will have to provide drug services if they are to alleviate the suffering of these prisoners and to prevent future problematic drug use and crime by these prisoners.

Attempts are under way at a European level to speed the development of prison drug services. ENDHASP has provided a forum for sharing information and expertise since 1994, and is distributing recommendations on prison drug services (including harm reduction, drug-free treatment, substitution treatment, needle exchange and peer support) that were drawn up by people working in the field. These developments and recommendations will be further discussed at the 4th European Conference on Drug and HIV/AIDS Services in Prison (Vienna, 3–6 March 1999), which will provide another opportunity for all those involved in the field of prison drug services to place their own practice within the context of European developments.

Acknowledgements

This survey was funded by DGV of the European Commission, as are all the activities of ENDHASP. It would not have been possible without the assistance of the ENDHASP contacts.
Correspondence to: Alex Stevens,
Cranstoun Drug Services,
4th Floor, Broadway House,
London SW19 1RL
Tel: +44 (0)181 543 8333
Fax: +44 (0)181 543 4348
E-mail: prs@easynet.co.uk

References

AIDS Advisory Committee (1995). *The Review of HIV and AIDS in Prison.* London: HM Prison Service.

Anonymous (1997). Programas de Intervención con Drogodependientes en Centros Penitenciarios. *Boletin GID*, 13(4). Madrid: Grupo Interdisciplinar sobre Drogas.

Boguña Casellas, J. (1997). Methadone Maintenance Programmes. In O'Brien, O. (Ed.). *Report of the Third European Conference on Drug and HIV/AIDS Services in Prison.* London: Cranstoun Drug Services.

Council of Europe (1988). *Parliamentary Assembly, Recommendation 1080 on a Co-ordinated European Policy to Prevent the Spread of AIDS in Prisons.* Strasbourg: Council of Europe.

Dolan, K.A., Hall, W.D., and Wodak, A.D. (1994). *Bleach Availability and Risk Behaviours in Prison in New South Wales.* Sydney: National Drug and Alcohol Research Centre.

Dolan, K.A., Wodak, A.D., and Hall, W.D. (1998). Methadone Maintenance Treatment Reduces Heroin Injection in New South Wales Prisons. *Drug and Alcohol Review*, 17: pp 153–158.

Farbring, C.A. (1998). Prisons in Wonderland. *Connections*, 6(12). London: Cranstoun Drug Services.

Goos, C., and Kingma, S. (1997). Drugs and AIDS in Prisons in Europe: a Perspective from UNAIDS and WHO. In O'Brien, O. (Ed.). *Report of the Third European Conference on Drug and HIV/AIDS Services in Prison.* London: Cranstoun Drug Services.

Hough, M. (1996). *Drugs Misuse and the Criminal Justice System: a Review of the Literature.* London: Home Office Drugs Prevention Initiative.

O'Brien, O., and Stevens, A.W. (1997). *A Question of Equivalence: a Report on the Implementation of International Guidelines on HIV/AIDS in Prisons of the European Union.* London: Cranstoun Drug Services.

Stillwell, G. (Ed.) (1994). *Reports on the Drug Laws, Drug Treatment Systems, Prison Systems and Drug Treatment in Prisons for Countries of the European Union.* London: Cranstoun Drug Services.

Turnbull, P.J., and Webster, R. (1998). Demand Reduction Activities in the Criminal Justice System in the European Union. *Drugs; Education, Prevention and Policy*, 5(2): pp 177–184.

United Nations (1984). *Standard Minimum Rules for the Treatment of Prisoners, and Procedures for the Effective Implementation of These Rules.* New York.

World Health Organisation (1987). *Statement from the Consultation on Prevention and Control of AIDS in Prison.* Geneva: WHO Global Programme on AIDS.

World Health Organisation (1993). *World Health Organisation Guidelines on HIV Infection and AIDS in Prisons.* Geneva: WHO Global Programme on AIDS.

Section Two: Research and Evaluation

Chapter 6

Young People, Drugs and Community Life: The Messages from the Research

Nigel South and David Teeman

Introduction

This article conveys some messages from research and from thinking about research. What it obviously cannot be is a review of *all* the available research relevant to the three broad themes of this volume. For introductory purposes it may be useful to summarise the aims of the new UK drug strategy insofar as these will also inform the aims of the accompanying research agenda. These aims relate to:

- **Availability** – 'To stifle the availability of illegal drugs on our streets'.
- **Treatment** – 'To enable people with drug-problems to overcome them and live healthy and crime-free lives'.
- **Young People** – 'To help young people resist drug misuse in order to achieve their full potential in society'.
- **Communities** – 'To protect our communities from drug-related anti-social and criminal behaviour'. (Druglink, 1998: p 6–7)

Connecting to the strategy:

How does all this connect with past research questions and studies?

If this agenda does indeed shape accompanying research, then in most respects, it connects well with past research endeavours. As the new UK Anti-drugs Co-ordinator has suggested (at the conference on which this collection is based), to criticise the new strategy for absence of novelty is a reflection of short-term thinking and calls of 'so, what's new?', are perhaps symptoms of impatience, not reasonable criticism. What is needed is long term thinking, hence the acceptance by the government of a ten-year time-frame for the work of the new strategy. This argument should apply to the research agenda too, albeit with provisos. We offer our own suggestions for inclusion on this agenda below. One key point is that continuity with past research means we can build on what has already been achieved. The strategy offers some potential 'new-ish' points of departure for research although, in some areas, research intentions are unclear, and there are also some areas where research is needed but not mentioned at all so far. However, loudly and clearly, 'young people' and 'communities' are key targets within the strategy, both for practice and for research.

Three Themes

The articles in this volume engage, in varying ways, with the three themes of the title of the conference from which they originate. Let us therefore think about these three themes: 'young people', 'drugs' and 'community safety' but consider them in reverse order.[1]

'Community' rediscovered?: developments and research potential

Our view here is that the emphasis on community in the strategy and in this volume, is useful, timely and connects well with a range of other developments. By this, and more specifically in relation to research issues we mean that the theme of 'community' is at the heart of several recent and current initiatives which could contribute to multi-agency information gathering, pooling of data, inter-disciplinary research, evidence-based practice development and multi agency prevention efforts. For example:

- In the area of civic affairs, community safety is to be addressed by combined local authority and police efforts involving strategies, audits, community consultation, and, one would hope, some research. The need to share information has been urged by guidance accompanying the Crime and Disorder Act 1998. Most of this flurry of local activity has been initiated as a result of or spurred on by this Act.

- In the area of community health care and health promotion, we see the creation of Health Action Zones; the development of 'primary care groups' for the co-ordination and delivery of health services in the community; and the establishment of locally-networked primary care research consortia to promote evidence-based research and care. In the field of health promotion, there is a re-emphasis on the importance of 'community' and moves toward the 'integration' of healthy lifestyle initiatives and services, including work on alcohol and drugs. Such a goal includes maximising the use of what the Health Education Authority has called the 'social capital' residing but under-exploited within our communities (Gillies, 1997). Healthy Living Centres are also to be promoted as part of a strategy for promoting health and lifestyle change within and across communities.

- In the drugs field, the work of the Drug Prevention Initiative and the local Drug Prevention Teams, of the Drug Reference Group, and the Drug Action Teams, has done much to generate research data and research questions about drugs and community issues. These local and regional initiatives have also created or stimulated existing local fori and networks, which in turn, seem to have enjoyed a far better experience of multi-agency co-operation than earlier predecessors in the days of the Drugs Education Co-ordinators and Health Education Co-ordinators in the 1980s.

Overall, the prospects for the generation of research information within communities and localities are looking good. However, the question of what is done with such research findings remains a moot point. Not only is the UK service and development culture poor at seeing the value of, and the undertaking of evaluations and research, it is also poor at listening to findings and implementing recommended changes.

Drugs: What do we mean here?

Those who have thought about this question before will immediately recognise that this is not a straightforward question and that it does not have a straightforward answer (see e.g., Gossop, 1993; Lenson, 1995). In the 1990s, indeed since the mid-late 1980s, the UK has produced a poly-drug culture (South, 1997, 1999). Of course, this is not to say that all drug users take a wide variety of different substances, (though studies indicate that a large number do), and furthermore this is not to say that there is an overall 'national picture' of poly-drug use, the picture is patchy. For example, comparison of the 1994 and 1996 drugs-use data from the British Crime surveys shows clear regional variations in patterns of drug use. Most notably, there has **apparently** been some reduction of use in London, no change in the South and East Anglia, and significant increase in use across the Midlands and in the North. The 1997 Schools Health Survey (Balding, 1998) also provided some indicators suggesting levelling out or reduction of use among the samples surveyed. One problem of relevance to us here is that neither data set is likely to include samples of the **serious** drug users within society. Those termed the 'socially excluded', including growing numbers of young people, who have already fallen through society's safety nets, are 'hard to reach' through routine surveys, and yet are most at risk of serious drug-related harm. Hence, the information such surveys provide about trends, serious drug misuse and drug-related harm, deserves some caution in its interpretation. Furthermore, such data and other studies confirm we have to be cautious when talking about 'drugs' as a catch-all term. 'Drugs' actually refers to a lot of different substances, used in different ways, in different contexts for different reasons and with different regional trends discernible. Ramsay (1998), a Home Office researcher responsible for analysis of drug use data from the British Crime Survey, has compared this data with other studies. His findings suggest that a polydrug culture is particularly marked in the North-West where Parker et al. (1995) have conducted their research on the 'pick'n'mix' approach to drug consumption adopted by young people. Here the availability of substances is a **smorgasbord** from which selections are made; drug specific loyalties or preferences may not be as marked as they once were; but perhaps most importantly, the mix of drugs or intoxicants used contains both the legal and the illegal.

Regarding alcohol, for example, it seems clear that alcoholic drinks branded to appeal to the youth style market, e.g. white ciders and fruit flavour high alcohol content drinks, have had a 'fashionable renaissance' (Ramsay, quoted in *Druglink*,1998: 9). According to *Druglink*,

> *reports from alcohol and drug agencies around the country (suggest) that drug users in their early thirties are coming out of 'Generation E' still wanting an instant (though perhaps legal) high. This may have led to a new and worrying approach to problem drinking – going for the knock-out in the first drink.* (ibid)

As the Royal College of Psychiatrists (1986) reminded us some years ago, alcohol always has been and remains 'our favourite drug'. Drugs prevention interventions and drugs research do not faithfully respond to the real world unless we at least acknowledge the cross-over connections between drug and alcohol use and the cultures that mix or divide the two.[2]

This last point is also about 'opting into' or 'opting out of' polydrug or 'any drug' using culture and reminds us that there is a debate here, and a very important one at that. While there are some studies showing what is argued to be an increasing 'normalisation' of drug use, mixing legal and illegal substances in routine ways in routine contexts, there are also those studies which emphasise the enduring strength of barriers (peer-pressure, parental attachment, personal value systems, etc.) which keep most young people from associating with, and within, a culture in which familiarity with drugs is 'normal'.

The former position, 'normalisation', presents an argument we can summarise along the following lines. That either 'lifetime' experience of using a drug (i.e. 'ever used during your lifetime?') or at least 'acquaintance' with the availability of drugs and/or drug users, have rendered 'drugs' a 'normal' part of life for young people. Hence, it is those who have not experienced use or such acquaintance that are now the exceptions to the 'new norm' and are hence the 'new deviants' (Parker et al., 1995). The second position in this debate emphasises that the strength of drug-resistant peer group membership and identification with other values antithetical to drug use remain strong counters to involvement in drug user groups (Shiner and Newburn, 1997, 1999).

These two lines of argument can be taken to represent two emerging bodies of thought (both supported by various studies). This is a debate which we think, or at least hope, will run (albeit without acrimony) because it shows the power of good research. Both these arguments are based on studies that are exemplary in design and analysis (although they are not actually directly comparable), so the question has been 'who is right?' After all they can't both be right, can they? Of course we put the matter this way because we believe that indeed they are both right.

To put this case briefly (see South, 1999, for an expanded argument), Parker et al. present a reflection of a late 20th century culture which undeniably has seen the normalisation of our awareness of drugs issues. Simply taking them more seriously through education and prevention indicates these substances are no longer exceptional and remote, but in fact are very familiar and accessible consumption items in everyday life. On the other hand, Shiner and Newburn valuably point to the persistence of peer-group resistance and mutual support in most contexts which work against anything more than passing acquaintance or minor experimentation with drugs and their use. Addressing this debate should be a key issue for future research on 'young people, drugs and community life'.

Young people

Here our brief is to review a few key areas and research findings, albeit rather sparingly but the outline will be useful at this point.[3]

Young people, age, attitudes and risk

Use of illegal drugs is largely confined to the young. This has not always been the case and we should recall that in the 19th century, present illegal drugs were used by or administered to a wide age-range, from infancy to senility (Berridge and Edwards, 1981). Furthermore, in the late 20th century one characteristic of the drug scene is that it also embraces a wide age-range of different kinds of drug users: from those who were twenty-something in the 1960s and are now fifty-something, to those who are in their teens today. Nonetheless, with fluctuations over time and in different areas, the majority of drug users can be described as young, relatively few being over thirty five, with this being consistent regardless of class or gender. The research deficit regarding ethnic minority drug use remains a significant matter for our evidence base.

For most young people, experimentation (and little more – see the debate above) with illegal drugs involves cannabis, amphetamine and other class 'B' drugs, and from the early 1990s onward, occasional to irregular to regular use of Ecstasy and LSD (classified as Class A). Importantly, we should emphasise that, in the career of most drug users, 'escalation' to 'harder' drugs and long-term continuation of use is confined to a minority. Hence, it is a generalisation but one worth making, that most young drug users are not at significant risk of becoming casualties – their experimentation is too fleeting, their involvement too occasional. However, Gilman (1998: 17) has recently indicated that there are other young people who *are* at 'high risk of addiction and social exclusion', such risk being particularly associated with certain background factors in their lives. Gilman lists as the ten most crucial factors: mental health issues; initiation into crime; school non-attendance; unemployment as the norm; being 'looked after' (e.g. in care of local authority); homelessness (not simply sleeping rough, but not having a settled place to call 'home'); heavy use of legal drugs in early life; criminally active parent with a history of substance misuse; disruption of family unit; and use of illegal recreational drugs. Clearly there is a research agenda here!

Young people, social class, gender, ethnicity and drugs

In the 1960s the rise in the availability of opiate drugs in the West End of London gave rise to considerable concern. Although remarkably modest by comparison with what was to follow in the 1980s (Dorn and South, 1987), media and legislative attention was captured. The new trends were in part related to the emergence of a new type of user who is young and working class (Ruggiero and South, 1995). Middle class youth also used heroin but were particularly associated with images of a counter-culture: the 'hippy' life-style and drugs such as cannabis and LSD. By the 1970s, drug use was clearly an 'all-class' phenomenon although class may still be related to acquaintance with and patterns of use of drugs (Leitner et al., 1993).

Studies of women and drug use (illegal or legal) remain relatively rare. This should be addressed in further research within and without the strategy. Although research studies were once clear about a lower prevalence of problem drug use for women than for men (with the exception of tranquilliser use), the gap has lessening Giggs, 1991:166). For example, it is no longer true that drug use per se is predominantly male to the extent that it was (as far as we know) in the 1960s and the 1970s: the figures concerning the BCS 1996 cohort were, for 'ever-users' between 16-19 years of age, 48% male and 42% female. Not a very large gap at all. Nonetheless, drug **dealing** probably remains a largely male preserve and there are familiar social prejudices operating against women in the drugs economy which explain this. The drugs economy is not an equal-opportunities employer (Ruggiero and South, 1995: 138-141; Taylor, 1993; Maher, 1997). It is also important to recognise that a familiar pattern of an unequal burden of care falls upon female partners or relatives (principally mothers) of male heavy drug users (Auld et al., 1986; Dorn et al., 1992). This point draws attention to the fact that the whole area of familial and voluntary sector care remains only patchily researched in terms of its contribution, capacity, needs and lessons learned.

Drug use within ethnic minorities has received even less research attention than drug use by women. In the early part of the decade 'the Four Cities' study (Leitner et al., 1993) and data from the 1992 British Crime Survey (Mott and Mirrlees-Black, 1995) suggested that white and African-Caribbean drug use in the population (including cannabis) was of similar proportions but that whites' were more likely to have used amphetamine or hallucinogens. Asian drug use remains low generally. However suggestions from the street, as well as the BCS, are that heroin use is increasing among some Asian youth (Akhtar and South, forthcoming).

In the late 1980s and early 1990s the manufacture and sale of 'crack' was associated by the police and media with illegal Jamaican immigrants involved in 'Yardie' gangs (Tyler, 1995: 214–225). However, 'crack' does not seem to have become the dramatic problem in black or white communities predicted by earlier media and enforcement reports – providing a useful reminder (a), not to assume that US trends **always** follow here; and (b) that having data is essential before reacting or, as in this case, over-reacting. In terms of 'use' in the African-Caribbean community, cannabis is the favoured and most widely used drug.

Ruggiero and South (1995: 116–119) have pointed to both the practical research problems as well as the 'political correctness' which have inhibited further criminological and social needs research in this area in the UK. Such problems have not hampered or been detrimental to the rich history of research on drug problems and minorities in the USA (e.g. Trimble et al., 1992) – research which has been helpful for the development of community services and practice.

Young people, unemployment and Drugs

Studies on the relationship between unemployment and drug use have been contentious but surprisingly rare. Akhtar et al. (1997) reviewed the international literature and found that views contrast quite sharply between unemployment being positively associated with (i.e. 'causing or contributing to') drug use versus the view that drug use leads to unemployment. Whatever the 'causal' direction (if there actually is one), both kinds of account contend that 'outcomes resulting' can be any of the following: job mobility; job separations (i.e. loss of job); the economic status of unemployment; the social condition of unemployability; and addiction.[4] According to Kandell and Yamaguchi (1987: 837): 'The dynamic relationships between drug use and employment history have yet to be established. Few relevant findings based on longitudinal data have been reported.' Over ten years on from this study, the evidence remains inconclusive.

Concerning the effects of unemployment on use of drugs, Hammarstrom (1994: 699) notes from the literature reviewed that there is evidence to suggest that unemployment is a 'risk indicator', affecting several concerns. Amongst these are increments in the use of illicit drugs.

Overall, we suggest that it is unlikely that unemployment, independent of other factors, leads to 'addiction' and hence related problems for the individual and community. However, as Simmons and Gold (1973:15) contend, unemployment may nevertheless substantially influence patterns of recidivism amongst ex-addicts post-treatment, who are unable to locate a job and participate in employment and social life. These authors therefore view the role of employment in the rehabilitation process as being of 'peculiar significance'. We think this is of clear importance as an issue for communities and community strategies seeking to re-incorporate serious drug-misusers and a key issue for research within the new ten-year strategy.

Young people, drugs and crime

There is, of course, a huge literature on this area. To summarise, there are links between drugs and youthful offending and they are varied but there is no clearly demonstrable causality. In brief, 'hanging around' with youths who do risky things like offending may bring contact with drugs; alternatively 'getting into drugs' and hanging around with drug users may ease, encourage or require the passage into various forms of crime, usually acquisitive, to generate funds for purchasing drugs. The Audit Commission's report on *Misspent Youth* 'noted that of the 600 (young) people studied, 15% were classed as having a drug or alcohol problem and of the persistent offenders the figure rose to 37%.' (cited in Arnull, 1998:21). Furthermore,

We also know that there are some differences between adult and youth offending, one difference being that young people's offending might be less about feeding a habit, but

more about 'lifestyle', about a young person's general way of life and behaviour at that time. Drugs and crime might be two of those factors. Thus in the words of Hough (1996) such offending may be more 'drug related' than 'drug driven'. (Arnull, 1998:21)

Future research: bringing the community into the research process?

We have suggested earlier that the late 1990's are seeing something of a proliferation of initiatives emphasising and related to community development. In part this reflects a new agenda from central Government but also other influences, whether these are US inspired as with the idea of 'integrated programmes' of health promotion and drugs prevention, or home-grown, as with the Health Education Authority's identification of the 'social capital' available in our communities and ready to be brought to bear in community health work (Gillies, 1997). Emphases on community and the integration of agencies and resources are certainly a part of the spirit of the new responses to drugs problems in the UK. With this in mind, thought should be given to the role that the 'community' itself, or at least some of its 'ordinary' representatives, could play in 'community research'. In this sense, our position is that future research about drugs, young people and community life and safety should not just 'parachute in', as has traditionally been the case, but could and should also learn from other areas of enquiry which aim to be *empowering* of communities in the research process.

For example, we might look at the kind of 'participatory research' that has been carried out in other disciplinary areas concerned with the quality of life in the community. Of particular value here is work to be found within the area of environmental studies. Here then, briefly noted, are eight models of community participation in research methodologies which empower participants rather than treating them and their communities simply as subjects or objects![5]

1. **Community appraisals:** local people develop and self-administer questionnaires; gather responses, produce and circulate a report identifying key issues and priorities. People participate on several levels.

2. **Participatory appraisal:** development of action plans and formation of community groups.

3. **Future search:** 'vision building events' involving 64 representatives of the community split into 8 stakeholder groups of equal size – reviewing the past and present of an area and asking where do we want to go, how can we address our problems (e.g. drugs/youth crime) and put them in perspective (e.g. drugs/youth crime are actually not as big or bad a problem as we thought…however, xyz are more worrying than we thought…).

4. **Community audits:** to motivate local people while retaining distinctiveness of localities (e.g. rural areas), produce action plan presented as public exhibition, produces feedback and revised five year plan.

5. **Parish maps:** what do we value about our community? Bring in as many points of view as possible – young and old (etc.) who say what is good and

how it may be enhanced rather than what is bad and how it must be eradicated!

6. **Action planning:** multi-disciplinary teams of specialists work with local people in five day, intensive process to produce a package of information about making the most of community resources, design of the community and its infrastructure etc.

7. **'Planning for Real':** a consultative technique used in community development programmes and to get local views on key policies or local issues.

8. **Citizen's Juries:** small groups of 12 to 25 people brought together for three to five days to consider an issue of public policy and/or local concern. Jury represents cross-section of society/the community, and hears experts present different sides of the argument. (see Pretty, 1998)

Welcoming the evidence base

The recognition in the new strategy that we need to build a more adequate evidence base is an excellent development. However, ideally, and following on from the spirit of the previous section, we suggest that this does not just mean more research studies undertaken by 'professional researchers'. What we have here is the opportunity to also seriously consider how to promote a research-sensitive culture among *practitioners* within the drugs field: getting them involved in local research, evaluation and information-gathering exercises. Taking this opportunity would help to increase the research capacity in the drugs field. It could also help ensure that new initiatives are cost-effectively monitored, evaluated and findings disseminated. Probably everyone in the drugs practice field knows of examples of good practice and real innovation that have not been evaluated or reported on, and have then read or heard an account of something very similar developed quite independently elsewhere.

An evidence-based culture must therefore pay attention to dissemination and ways of ensuring material is accessible. In the UK the origin of the idea of evidence-based practice, care or research, lies in the NHS and the impact of the Culyer Report 1994.7 The aim is to promote a culture of research **and development** – the latter is very important to note. If we are seeking an improvement in services and measurable outcomes as required in the new drugs strategy then research alone, no matter how informative it may be, is less useful than research which contributes to development of practice, services, community initiatives, treatment and rehabilitation. Practitioners themselves need to feel confident about working with and using the findings of research. In this respect, as for the NHS and its varied professionals, some training in using and doing research is vital. In this vision, we see research as being important for drug users, their services and their communities but also for the various practitioners involved in the drugs field. We should not forget that those working with serious drug users in the community are entrusted by society and government with a great deal of responsibility in their professional dealings with some of the most difficult problems and individuals in society. Their status, contribution and potential should be recognised and 'continuing professional development' which involves research training could have significant pay-offs all round.

However, a caution. While EBC/ EBR (etc.) are ideas that are certainly buzzing in the NHS, the actual development and emergence of a broad evidence-based culture is slow. There is also some scepticism about whether the identification of the need for an 'evidence base' will really widen the research agenda and projects funded in ways that are needed, or whether it will simply mean the reproduction of more of the same kinds of research on topics already well covered, conducted by the same familiar names, and missing the opportunity to add new energy and new research staff to the field. As Eldridge and South (1998) found in relation to the development of evidence-based research and practice in the NHS, this is a 'slow acting' initiative. Furthermore, to return to an earlier point, the really big question is whether anyone with control over resources will actually listen to and 'act upon' research findings?

Conclusion

A recent report from the Public Health Alliance was concerned with the links between crime, fear of crime and public health. It is both obvious and of great significance, that drugs represent an empirical link between crime, fear of crime and health problems, and also that use of drugs in the community can be a very potent symbol. In this latter respect, a 'community drug problem' may represent the suggestion or indication that a community is in decline, is facing increasing crime, with attendant increase in anxiety among residents, deteriorating quality and enjoyment of life in the community, and so on. One of the joint authors of the PHA report, Angus McCabe of Birmingham University, recently made several remarks which seem fitting concluding thoughts here. Partnerships, he says, are needed to tackle the kinds of linkages at issue: 'But they depend on a common language and common understanding.' What is required he suggests, is 'closer co-operation between the Department of Health, the Home Office and other ministries to develop integrated crime prevention and health promotion strategies, and the development of shared policy agendas on crime and public health' (Millar, 1998: 13). This should sound a familiar message. The drugs field is now enviably poised at the kind of point that is aspired to here. The accumulation of recent developments (through the DPI and other sources and initiatives mentioned), accompanied by the push and agenda of the new Strategy, mean that, perhaps, for the first time since the early 1920s and the turf war between the Ministry of Health and the Home Office over who would be 'in charge', the drugs field is promised the possibility of a future in which it is not a 'political football' or a 'Cinderella', but an area of services and research which is genuinely valued and which will genuinely be helped in working among and with communities. We shall see.

Notes

1. We are also addressing broader issues than just community safety and hence refer to community life.
2. The smoking of tobacco has not seen a reduction of use among young peole, particularly young women, that health promotion professionals had at one time expected, and is another 'across the divide'.
3. The following sections are based on South, 1998.
4. The literature in this field obstinately refers to 'addiction' rather than misuse or dependence.
5. The following are adapted from a discussion paper prepared for other purposes by our colleague at Essex, Dr Jules Pretty, Director of the Centre for Environment and Society. We are most grateful to Jules for sharing these ideas with us. See also Pretty, 1998.
6. And relatedly the establishment of the Cochrane Centre for literature reviews and dissemination of meta-reviews etc.

References

Akhtar, S., Nightingale, R., and South, N. (1997). *Drugs, Unemployment and Unemployability: Possibilities for Rehabilitation and Training?* Research Report. HSSI, University of Essex.

Akhtar, S., and South, N. (1999). *Dealing, Entrepreneurialism and Heroin Distribution in the Asian Community.* In preparation.

Arnull, E. (1998). Crime, Drugs and Young People. *Criminal Justice Matters*, 31, Spring: pp 21–22.

Audit Commission, (1996). *Misspent Youth*. London: Audit Commission.

Auld, J., Dorn, N., and South, N. (1986). Irregular Work, Irregular Pleasures: Heroin in the 1980s. In Matthews, R., and Young, J. (Eds.). *Confronting Crime*. London: Sage.

Balding, J. (1998). *Young People and Illegal Drugs in 1998*. University of Exeter.

Berridge, V., and Edwards, G. (1981). *Opium and the People: Opiate Use in Nineteenth Century England* (2nd edition). New Haven, CT: Yale University Press.

Dorn, N., and South, N. (Eds.) (1987). *A Land Fit for Heroin? Drug Policies, Prevention and Practice*. London: Macmillan.

Dorn, N., Henderson, S., and South, N. (Eds.) (1992). *AIDS: Women, Drugs and Social Care*. London: Falmer Press.

Druglink (1998). Building a Better Strategy. *Druglink*, 13(3): p 4–7.

Druglink (1998). Drug Use in Freefall. *Druglink*, 13(3): p 9.

Eldridge, K., and South, N. (1998). Evidence Based Practice: Slow Acting Remedy. *Health Service Journal*, 21st May: p 24–25.

Giggs, J. (1991). The Epidemiology of Contemporary Drug Abuse. In Whynes, D., and Bean, P. (Eds.). *Policing and Prescribing: The British System of Drug Control*. London: Macmillan.

Gillies, P. (1997). Social Capital: Recognising the Value of Society. *Healthlines*, 45, September: p 15–17.

Gilman, M. (1998). Onion Rings to Go: Social Exclusion and Addiction. *Druglink*, 13(3): p 15–18.

Gossop, M. (1993). *Living with Drugs*, (3rd edition). Aldershot: Ashgate.

Hammarstrom, A. (1994). Health Consequences of Youth Unemployment – Review from the Gender Perspective. *Social Science and Medicine*, 38(5): p 699–709.

Hough, M. (1996). *Drug Misuse and the Criminal Justice System: A Review of the Literature*. London: CDPU, Home Office.

Kandell, D.B., and Yamaguchi, K. (1987). Job Mobility and Drug Use: An Event History Analysis. *American Journal of Sociology*, 92(4): p 836–878.

Leitner, M., Shapland, J., and Wiles, P. (1993). *Drug Usage and Drugs Prevention*, London: Home Office.

Lenson, D. (1995). *On Drugs*. Minneapolis: University of Minnesota Press.

Miller, B. (1998). Prevention is the Cure. *Health Service Journal*, 5th February: p12.

Mott, J., and Mirrlees-Black, C. (1995). *Self-reported Drug Misuse in England and Wales: Findings from the 1992 British Crime Survey*. London: Home Office.

Maher, L. (1997). *Sexed Work*. Oxford: Clarendon Press.

Parker, H., and Measham, F. (1994). Pick 'n' Mix: Changing Patterns of Illicit Drug Use Among 1990s Adolescents. *Drugs: Education, Prevention and Policy*, 1(1): p 5–13.

Parker, H., Measham F., and Aldridge, J. (1995). *Drugs Futures: Changing Patterns of Drug Use amongst English Youth*. London: Institute for the Study of Drug Dependence.

Parker, H., Measham, F., and Aldridge, J. (1998). *Illegal Leisure: The Normalization of Adolescent Recreational Drug Use*. London: Routledge.

Pretty, J. (1998). *The Living Land*. London: Earthscan.

Ramsay, M. (1998). Tracking Drug Misuse: News from the British Crime Survey. *Focus on Police Research and Development*. London: Police Research Group, Home Office.

Royal College of Psychiatrists (1986). *Alcohol: Our Favourite Drug*. London: Tavistock.

Ruggiero, V., and South, N. (1995). *EuroDrugs: Drug Use, Markets and Trafficking in Europe*. London: UCL Press.

Shiner, M., and Newburn, T. (1997). Definitely, Maybe Not?: The Normalisation of Recreational Drug Use Amongst Young People. *Sociology*, 31(3): p 511–529.

Shiner, M., and Newburn, T. (1999). Taking Tea with Noel: The Place and Meaning of Drug Use in Everyday Life. In South, N. (Ed.). *Drugs: Cultures, Controls and Everyday Life*. London: Sage.

Simmons, L.R.S., and Gold, M.B. (1973). Notes Towards a General Theory of Addict Rehabilitation. In Simmons, L.R.S., and Gold, M.B. (Eds.). *Discrimination and the Addict*. Beverly Hills, CA: Sage.

South, N. (1997). Drugs: Use, Crime and Control. In Maguire, M., Morgan R., and Reiner, R. (Eds.). *The Oxford Handbook of Criminology* (2nd edition). Oxford: Oxford University Press.

South, N. (1999). Debating Drugs and Everyday Life: Normalisation, Prohibition and 'Otherness'. In South, N. (Ed.). *Drugs: Cultures, Controls and Everyday Life*. London: Sage.

Taylor, A. (1993). *Women Drug Users*. Oxford: Clarendon Press.

Trimble, J., Bolek, C., and Niemcryk, S. (1992). *Ethnic and Multicultural Drug Abuse*. New York: Howarth.

Teeman, D., South, N., and Henderson, S. (1999). *Multi-impact Drugs Prevention Programmes in the Community*, this volume.

Tyler, A. (1995). *Street Drugs*. Hodder and Staughton.

Chapter 7

Youth, Minorities, Drugs and Policing: A Study of Stop and Search

Alan Marlow

Introduction

This chapter, which describes the findings of research into the use of stop and search in one police area, is a cautionary tale about a relationship assumed by patrolling police officers, linking young male members of an ethnic minority group and drug offences. The consequence of this assumption was that ethnic minority young people became an unwarranted focus of stop and search interventions by the police. In this chapter, the situational logic through which this occurred will be described. In doing so, it will be suggested that if pursued without a careful consideration of issues of equality in policing practice, government performance indicators could lead to an increase in this form of discriminatory practice.

Constructing 'pictures' of the drug scene

In his objectives for 1999/2000, the Home Secretary indicated that it will be a priority:

> To target and reduce drug-related crime in partnership with other local agencies, via Drug Action teams, in line with the Government's strategy Tackling Drugs to Build a Better Britain. (Home Office Circular. Ministerial Priorities for 1999/2000)

Performance will be measured by two indicators:

1. The number of arrests for supply, and possession with intent to supply, controlled drugs per 10,000 population and, of those, how many related to heroin.

2. The number of offenders referred to and entering treatment programmes as a result of arrest referral schemes.

Crimes such as burglary are relatively easy to quantify as information is the product of reports from victims. The peculiarity of drug offences is that they are predominantly consensual crimes and therefore information on patterns of misuse, abusers and suppliers is dependent to a significant extent upon enforcement activity. As Hough notes, although inter-agency approaches are advocated, more problem drug users pass through the hands of the police and the courts than any other agency (Hough 1996). Thus, enforcement is an important selection mechanism for the construction of information about drug users and that mechanism may be influenced by the assumptions police officers make about drug users. Nevertheless, research does support intuition based upon experience. Graham and Bowlings valuable work on 'Young People and Crime' concluded that the use of drugs is widespread amongst young people (Graham and Bowling 1995). The pattern of drug use and abuse amongst young people is also extremely volatile, with new trends and fashions emerging and evaporating rapidly. For example, the increased availability and cheapness of heroin has resulted in changed patterns of abuse amongst young people:

> *Most of the new young users taking up heroin can be described as 'socially excluded', coming from the poorest parts of affected towns and cities. However, there is a spectrum of susceptibility and clear signs of a broader penetration with heroin in use being found amongst those youths 'bonded' in education/work from more affluent families.*
> (Parker et al. 1998)

It is not surprising, therefore, that young people should receive disproportionate attention by those concerned with enforcement. Young (1994) points out that it is rational for patrol officers to focus on those sections of the population which their experience suggests are most likely to be involved in crime – i.e. young working class males. Given that ethnic minorities are young populations and tend to be concentrated in the lower socio-economic groups, some over-representation is to be expected. Although police performance will be judged by the arrest of suppliers of controlled drugs, in the absence of information as to their identity, traditional street enforcement activity can be perceived as an effective way of 'working from the user up' to generate information on suppliers and networks. One of the practices most frequently employed to do this at street level is the power to stop and search individuals under Section 1 of the Police and Criminal Evidence Act 1984.

The law and practice of stop and search

The powers contained in Section 1 of the Police and Criminal Evidence Act 1984 make uniform provision for the exercise of stop and search throughout the country. For the first time, police officers, wherever they may work, had recourse to a codified general power. Hitherto, there had been some limited statutory provisions and local powers in some large cities (including London). The local powers did not exist in most other parts of the country (Zander, 1995).

The Codes of Practice (Home Office 1995) made under PACE stress the desirability of obtaining the co-operation of the subject, but it seems that in law, where a search takes place with the co-operation of the subject, the various safeguards of the Act do not apply (Zander, 1995 p 22)

The stopping and searching of persons has always been viewed as a core street policing skill contributing to the overall construction of intelligence. The influence of the Audit Commission report *Helping with Enquiries: Tackling Crime Effectively* (1993) which proposed intelligence-led offence detection, as well as the Home Office's key performance indicators, gave added impetus to the exercise of stop and search powers. Research indicates an annual increase in the frequency of use (Brown, 1997).

Practice has varied widely between Forces. For example, the distinction between a PACE search and a voluntary search is an extremely uncertain area for interpretation. In difficult or contentious encounters, particularly where ethnic minority subjects are concerned and officers perceive the possibility of an allegation of racism, an interaction may be formalised by recording, whereas in other cases a 'voluntary' definition will be applied and no record ensues. This practice will have the effect of over-representing minorities in the published records.

Previous research findings

Brown (1997) in Home Office Study 155, a review of the research on PACE 'ten years on' , concluded that adherence to the Act is much stronger in procedures that take place inside the police station than outside. Stop and search is a street procedure. His conclusions were that their use varies widely between police areas, with the Metropolitan Police being the most frequent users. Currently around one in eight searches are 'successful', in that an arrest results. It is doubtful whether the police always carry out stops on the basis of reasonable suspicion (Brown, 1997).

In 1983 (pre PACE) in a study based on police records, Willis found rates of police stops were higher for black people than for the population as a whole and in the predominantly white area of Kensington the rate was three times higher for black men aged between 16 and 24 (Willis, 1983).

In 1986, the Policy Studies Institute produced survey evidence (independent of police records) to show that black people were stopped more frequently than white people, who were stopped more frequently than Asians and that the average stops per year (5.06) for black youth was much higher that than for whites (1.94) (Smith, D. 1986).

Jefferson et al. (1992) found that in areas of low ethnic minority concentration, the stop rate is higher for black than for white or South Asian people, whereas in areas of high ethnic minority population the stop rate is lower for black than for white or South Asian people (Jefferson et al., 1992).

Skogan conducted an analysis using data from the 1988 British Crime Survey. He concluded that, taking all factors into consideration, there is a disproportionate stopping of blacks by the police which is unattributable to any other factor but their ethnicity (Skogan, 1990).

It may be concluded from the research that the desired clarity of accountability based on explicit conditions and documented procedures has tended not to emerge since PACE codified stop and search. Explanations of the statistics will probably be confused and certainly conditional. Stop and search activity will always reflect local custom, practice, procedure and population structure. Records will significantly under-represent all stops of members of the public.

Ethnic differences in participation in offending

Accurate data on differences in participation in offending is extremely difficult to obtain. All criminal justice data is mediated by the agencies that produce it and is therefore never free from selectivity or bias. Graham and Bowling's research was based upon self-report data on offending by young people aged between 14 and 25. Although self-report studies have limitations, at least the information they generate is not filtered through criminal justice agencies.

The study indicated that male offending increases to the age of 18 and remains at more or less the same level until the early twenties. Female offending peaks at 16 but by the early twenties the rate is five times lower than male offending. The survey analysis revealed similar rates of offending among Afro-Caribbeans and whites and substantially lower offending amongst Asians. In this study, Bangladeshis appeared to have the lowest offending rates. With regard to drugs, minority groups, including those of Afro-Caribbean origin, were less likely than white respondents to have used drugs (Graham and Bowling 1995). The British Crime Survey, however, found little difference between whites and Afro-Caribbeans, although three times as many of both groups admitted using drugs as Asians.

Graham and Bowling's work provides a broad national snapshot of offending by young people and establishes a bench mark against which data produced by criminal justice agencies can be assessed. Nevertheless, as an overview of differential offending rates, there are caveats that should be entered. The self-report method is reliable at predicting absolute offending but it reveals little as to how offences become reported, how particular patterns of criminal activity become priorities for enforcement or which forms of behaviour become more 'visible' either to the public or criminal justice agencies.

It can be concluded from the foregoing that stop and search is arbitrary in its application and highly discretionary. It is an unreliable technique for the construction of information on patterns of offending and particularly drug offences where other data, such as reports from victims, is largely absent. The following case study illustrates how a distorted picture could have critical implications for police-community relations.

The research

The research was based upon the scrutiny of the records of stop/searches for a three month period in 1996 for the Borough of Barchester. Records were analysed to establish the ethnicity of the subjects, reasons for the search, arrest rates and other patterns of activity that were reflected in the data. This investigation was not supported by formal interviews but some comments by officers were used to suggest reasons for their operational practice.

The setting

Since the Second World War, Barchester, initially through a high demand for unskilled and semi-skilled workers in light engineering, has been an area for immigrant settlement. Immigration from the Indian Sub-continent and Caribbean peaked in the 1950s and 1960s and whilst terms such as 'minorities' are used, many minority ethnic residents are well established in the Borough with long periods of citizenship.

Barchester has a high proportion of visible minorities at 19.7%, of which 4.8% are of Afro-Caribbean and 13.1% of South Asian origin. The South Asian population tends to be younger than other groups. The proportion of South Asian males in the 15–24 group is 19.8%.

Minorities tend to be concentrated in two electoral wards – Austin and Melrose. These are the most socially deprived, with youth employment twice the borough average.

The practice of stop and search in Barchester

Frequency and trends

The proportion of minorities who were subjects of the formal stop and search for the period was 51%. Whilst the formal records demonstrated that in excess of 50% of the stop searches involved minority individuals, that proportion reduces to 42.2% if the recorded individuals are grouped in terms of single 'incidents' where the power is exercised (e.g. four individuals in a vehicle become four records but amount to one 'incident' where the power is exercised). However the data is viewed, there is a significant over-representation of minority groups.

Reasons for the exercise of stop and search powers

PACE empowers officers to search for stolen goods or prohibited articles, which will include items such as offensive weapons, implements with which to commit crime, and drugs. The records are often ambiguous as to the precise reason to justify the exercise of the power. Nevertheless, a broad analysis of reasons to search can be attempted.

Figure 1 – Recorded Reasons for Stop and Searches by Racial Group in Barchester				
	White	**Asian**	**Afro-Carib**	**Total**
Theft/Prohibited Items	159	83	42	284
Drugs	31	57	9	97
Other	25	14	4	33
Total	215	154	55	414

The table shows that in the cases of Asian subjects, more than one third of the searches were for dangerous drugs. The proportions of drug searches are much lower for other groups.

Arrests

Of the 436 occasions stop and search powers were exercised under PACE in the three month period, 73 arrests resulted. At 17%, this is a high figure, being 4.5% above the national average. The following table shows the numbers arrested, by ethnic groups:

Figure 2 – Arrests Resulting from Stop Searches

	White	Asian	Afro-Carib	Total
Total Stops	214	141	59	384
Arrests	32	12	29	73
Charge	17	6	13	36
Caution	4	0	0	4
Released*	9	6	12	27
Untraced	2	0	4	6
% Arrested	15%	8.5%	49%	19%

*Records often unclear so there may be errors in this category

The findings indicate that the arrest rate for Afro-Caribbeans was an astonishing 49% although less than 25% resulted in charges- conversely, the arrest rate for Asian subjects was precisely half the overall rate with only 50% of those arrested resulting in charges.

As far as can be ascertained from the records, 55% of those arrested were charged or cautioned. This may be an under-estimate. According to research, the national figure is 67%.

The geography of stop and search in Barchester

The minority population in Austin ward comprises 60% of the total and in Melrose ward 53%. Both areas are crime prone with much higher than average levels of victimisation in terms of property crime. One hypothesis for the over representation of minorities in particular is that police activities that lead to the exercise of powers are concentrated in these areas due to the high victimisation rates. A ward analysis compared the number of minority stop/searches for each ward with the minority population resident within it.

Ward	Number of searches	% Minorities searched	% Minority population	Variation
Melrose	34	51.5	52.8	-1.3
Austin	41	72.5	60.4	12.1
Gurney	119	62.1	11.3	50.8
New Town	50	30.6	15	15.6
Meadow	27	55.6	15.7	39.9
Renfrew	35	42.9	12.1	30.8
Starling	8	63.5	14.8	48.7
Ashton Park	8	12.5	13.4	-0.9
Western	6	100	12.8	87.2
Peabody	16	73.3	25.1	48.2
Roundtree	9	56.4	11.6	44.8
Greenacres	20	35	6.8	28.2
St Francis	9	55.6	47.7	7.9
Northills	26	23.1	7.7	15.4
Comerfield	16	100	11.4	88.6
High Wells	11	18.2	5.2	13
Borough	435	50.6	19.76	30.84

Fig 3 – Searches Involving Minorities Compared by Ward and Population

The variation between the percentage of minorities searched and percentage of minorities in the population of the ward indicates whether or not the minorities searched balances with the population – zero would indicate a perfect balance and a positive value an excess of minorities searched compared with the level expected in the population.

What emerges from the analysis, even by excluding those wards with low search levels, is that the disproportionate searching of minorities occurs not in the areas of greatest minority settlement but in the predominantly white areas. This observation seems to support the research by Jefferson (1992) that the stop rate for minorities is higher in areas of low minority residence. It may be that there are issues of 'visibility' of minority suspects 'out of geographical context' that prompt the attention of patrolling officers.

Conclusions

The study suggests the following conclusions:

- When compared to the ethnic minority population of young men between 15–25, the probability of an individual member of a minority group being stopped was very high.

- Minorities are significantly over-represented amongst the individuals subject of PACE stop and search powers.

- In Barchester, South Asians are stopped and searched on suspicion of possessing controlled drugs more frequently than other groups.

- South Asians who were subject of stop and search were less likely to be arrested than other groups.

- In areas of high minority settlement, stop and search subjects are broadly proportional to the population mix. A disproportionate stopping of minorities and Asians in particular tends to occur in predominantly white areas.

In order to make sense of these findings, observations and comments were sought from operational police officers about ways in which working practices produce an over-representation of minorities in the stop and search statistics. In respect of this case study, these conclusions relate only to the South Asian subjects.

Officers in Barchester had associated young South Asians with the use and supply of hard drugs such as heroin. There is a basis for the assumption that heroin is freely available in some areas in South Asia and the belief was that young South Asians were acting as conduits for its supply locally. The evidence from the volume of arrests and seizures did not support this linkage. This reasoning focused suspicion upon young South Asian males and this accounts for the disproportionate number of stop/searches in respect of drugs for this group.

As long ago as 1970, Lambert pointed to the importance of 'stereotypes' as an essential working tool of the police officer (Lambert 1970). Reiner, drawing on Banton's work, pointed out that stereotyping is an inevitable tool of suspiciousness endemic to police work.

The crucial issue is not its existence, but the degree to which it is reality -based and helpful, as opposed to categorically discriminatory in a prejudiced way – and thus not merely unjust but counter-productive for the police force's own purposes.
(Reiner, 1992: p 115)

Police suspicions are heightened when South Asian subjects are observed 'out of geographical context', i.e. in white residential areas of the Borough. It may be assumed that the question 'What are they doing here?' is often asked in such circumstances. The fact that subjects are members of a minority means that the interaction is more likely to be formalised and recorded as a PACE stop and search, as officers seem more likely to be aware of the consequences for accountability when dealing with minority subjects. The search is also likely to only be half as successful as the average.

Race as a factor in the construction of stereotypes may be simultaneously in-discriminate, in the sense that all members of a minority may be so labelled, and intensely discriminatory in that it singles out people for the focus of suspicion purely on the grounds of their visibility as a minority. The construction of stereotypes for white people are likely to be much more discriminating in terms of social class, attitude, or style of dress. Racial appearance has no selective qualities whatsoever.

Stop and search powers are a valuable tool for police officers and it may be the case that this type of discrimination is unconsidered and unconsciously formulated. It is the product of unexamined racist stereotypes rather than a deliberate attempt to draw a particular minority population into the justice system. Where the statistics reveal such over-representation, forces should carefully analyse the working practices, beliefs and assumptions that lead to them .

As the Stephen Lawrence Inquiry has tragically demonstrated, it is imperative that the police develop habits of critical reflection and evaluation in their dealings with minorities. Whilst Home Office guidance stresses that 'the guiding principles should be fair treatment for everyone' (Home Office 1998), the pressure to perform can, as has been demonstrated here, lead to the construction of 'pictures of the drug scene' which are at best unfairly stigmatising. Information on drug misuse is always likely to be patchy and partial. It is important, therefore that a wide range of sources and methods are used for its construction.

This research revealed that for males in the 15 to 25 age group in Barchester, the chances of being the subject of stop and search in an average year was 1 in 36 for white males, 1 in 10 for black males and 1 in 8 for South Asian males. Left unaddressed, the consequences of such discriminatory policing could be catastrophic for community relations, producing the seething resentment that triggered the disturbances in Brixton in 1981.

References

Brown, D. (1997). *PACE Ten Years On: A Review of Research.* Home Office Study 155. London: Home Office.

Graham, J., and Bowling, B. (1995). *Young People and Crime.* Home Office Study 145. London: Home Office.

Home Office (1998). *Ministerial Priorities, Key Performance Indicators and Efficiency Planning for 1999/2000.* Circular to Chief Officers of Police and Chairs of Police Authorities – Nov 1998.

Hough, M. (1996). Drug Misuse and the Criminal Justice System: A Review of the Literature. In *Criminal Justice Matters*, No. 24. London: ISTD.

Jefferson, T. (1992). Ethnic Minorities in the Criminal Justice System. *Criminal Law Review*, p 83–95.

Lambert, J. (1970). *Crime, Police and Race Relations.* Oxford: OUP.

Parker, H. et al. (1998).*New Heroin Outbreaks Amongst Young People in England and Wales.* Police Research Group Paper 92. London: Home Office.

Reiner, R. (1992). *The Politics of the Police.* London: Harvester Wheatsheaf .

Skogan, W. (1990). *The Police and Public in England and Wales.* Home Office Research Study No. 117. London: HMSO.

Smith, D. (1994). Race, Crime and Criminal Justice. In Maguire, M., Morgan, R., and Reiner, R. *The Oxford Handbook of Criminology.* Oxford: OUP.

Willis, C. (1983). *The Use, Effectiveness and Impact of Police Stop and Search Powers.* Research and Planning Unit Paper 15. London: Home Office.

Young, J. (1994). *Policing the Streets: Stops and Search in North London.* Middlesex University.

Zander, M. (1995). *The Police and Criminal Evidence Act 1984.* London: Sweet and Maxwell.

Chapter 8

Project Evaluation: Problems and Pitfalls

Nick Tilley

Introduction

Where public expenditure is at stake, requirements to make provision for evaluation of programmes, projects, policies and practices have become ubiquitous over the past decade. The rhetoric of efficiency, effectiveness and economy (originally efficiency, effectiveness and equity), of evidence-driven policy and practice, of cost-benefit analysis, of best value, of value for money, of performance indicators, of league tables, and of performance review have all contributed to an evaluation culture. My focus here is on ways of making the best of evaluation, not with questioning the very idea of it.

My particular concern springs in large part from a period attached to the Home Office when I was asked to receive evaluation reports for each of the 3,500 separate schemes funded through Phase 1 of Safer Cities, and to elicit transferable lessons from suites of related ones. It was a sobering experience. With a few exceptions, the quality of the work was low: mostly shoe-string efforts (where there were any at all) by hardworking staff attempting to keep stakeholders happy with good news.[1] This paper has four aims:

1. to distinguish monitoring and evaluation, and suggest when each is appropriate
2. to clarify the purpose of evaluation
3. to highlight potential dangers of misconceived evaluations
4. to consider problems and pitfalls in commissioning, conducting and using evaluations. My main target is evaluation which has external, public purposes, rather than routine self-evaluation, a potentially valuable habit which may have a significant role in improving practitioner performance.

Monitoring and evaluation: what and when?

A bewildering array of terms has come to be used to talk about evaluation (for attempted clarification, see Hough and Tilley 1998). The main distinction to be made here, however, is that between monitoring and evaluation.

Monitoring itself refers to two different types of exercise, both of which are important. First, it is used to refer to efforts to track what a project is doing: what is being put into it, its inputs; what issues are coming to it, its problems; what is going on within it, its processes; and what it is delivering, its outputs. 'Monitoring' is used also to refer to tracking the level and nature of the problem or problems that a project aims to address.

Good management practice will require that all project work is monitored in both senses. Proper oversight of what the project is doing, allowing for the introduction of remedial action when required, is routinely needed to keep projects on track. Especially where innovative work is planned, systematic monitoring is likely to be crucial in identifying, diagnosing and responding to teething troubles. Monitoring in the second sense is also usefully undertaken routinely. Thus, for example, if reductions in drug-taking are the aim, then using indicators to try to track drug taking is desirable to see whether the problem is changing, on the basis of which adjustments to the project may be needed.

'Evaluation' is rather different, and requires other skills. It is concerned with causal attribution, normally in quite complex settings. Finding out what changes relevant to the project have taken place, whether they are attributable to the project, how the project has brought them about, and what conditions would be needed for a like project to produce similar effects in the future are technically and conceptually difficult. The appropriate methods have been hotly debated in the evaluation literature (see Chelimsky and Shadish 1997; Pawson and Tilley 1997). Relatively robust answers, however, using any of the more sophisticated methodologies, will be costly and answers will not emerge quickly. In many (probably most) cases the amount of investment in the project, potential uses of findings in the future, and current areas of uncertainty will not warrant the heavy expenditure required for high quality independent evaluation.

The monitoring of problems being addressed by projects can be and often is mistaken for evaluation. Performance indicators sometimes track levels of problems, with the assumption that measurements signifying change reflect project impact. There is a host of problems with performance indicators and their use, which are beyond the scope of this paper (see Tilley 1995). Most importantly for the purposes of this discussion, problem levels can and do change for many reasons, other than because the project has had an impact. Detailed review alongside (well-designed) performance indicators, may enable some informed guessing about project contributions. It will often be tempting to attribute changes in levels of problems to a local project where the change is in the intended direction. Monitoring changes in problem levels is, however, a different order of activity from project evaluation. There are no direct efforts to work through the difficulties in attributing causation to the project and its measures.

Evaluation: what is it for?

Two main reasons are typically given for conducting evaluations: to learn useful lessons for future actions and to make past actions accountable. It will, however, rarely be worth the high costs of commissioning and conducting a formal evaluation in criminal justice simply for accounting purposes as provision for systematic monitoring and review should normally be sufficient. Thus, unless an evaluation contributes to decisions about future policy, practice or resource allocation, it is probably a waste of effort and money.

It is important that evaluations be capable of surviving critical scrutiny by peers if they are to be used as the basis for significant decisions. Even though political conditions sometimes prevent results from being heeded at particular points in time, what is important is that work has the capacity to inform rational decision making when and where that becomes possible.

Evaluation: how can it mislead?

The consequences of a misconceived or misconstrued evaluation may be more deleterious than those from no evaluation at all. Here are seven risks.

1. **Deception.** Where those conducting an evaluation have an interest in the work being evaluated, or are seriously dependent on those with such an interest, there are risks that findings will be (consciously or otherwise) massaged to fit those interests.[2] There were clear cases in Safer Cities where data had been massaged to produce the appearance of success. Independent rigorous evaluations produce positive findings far more rarely than less rigorous ones by project workers (Weatheritt 1986).

2. **Failing to find an impact where there is one (often termed Type 2 errors).** Evaluation studies require judgement, often using statistical data. In statistical tests there are conventions about ways of construing significance levels. Normally, where there is a more than a one in twenty probability that results could have occurred by chance, findings are treated as non-significant. There is a risk though that real effects will have been missed. Here the 'null hypothesis' (that there is no effect) is accepted when it is false.[3]

3. **Finding an impact where there is none (often termed Type 1 errors).** Lowering required significant levels risks concluding that there has been a real impact where there has been none. Here the null hypothesis is rejected, when it is true.

4. **Erroneous conclusions about external validity from findings of success.** Even where rigorous evaluations provide strong evidence that intended changes are linked to the intervention, achieving 'internal validity', this is a far cry from showing that it would always produce the same changes. I was told at one meeting that if a scheme worked in Eastbourne it would work anywhere on the planet: think about Chicago, Jerusalem, Mexico, and Kigali. The settings and subjects are crucial. Undiagnosed success risks invalid inferences about implications for the future.

5. **Erroneous conclusions about external validity from findings of failure.** Even where there is strong evidence that a particular project has not had its intended effect, it can be difficult to decide whether the lack of impact was

due to implementation failure (the intended measure not introduced or not introduced properly), to the introduction of the measure in an inappropriate setting (context failure), or to mistaken hypotheses about the potential of the measure to bring about the change[4]. Undiagnosed failure risks invalid are inferences about implications for the future.

6. **Boom-bust cycles.** There is a familiar cycle. First, a well-thought out, carefully implemented demonstration project, installed in conditions in which its prospects look good, is found to yield benefits. Capitalising on its apparent promise many others rush to emulate the project. The projects are less well thought out and implemented, and are installed in less promising conditions. Evaluations of many of them do not find the expected benefits. Confidence dwindles. New projects dry up. Old ones close. Unless evaluations are very clear about how and why they produce their benefits (or lack of them) in the conditions in which they are introduced, they risk unintentionally feeding into this unhelpful boom-bust cycle.

7. **Changing social world.** The modern social world continuously throws up intrinsically unpredictable new conditions, especially in local settings (see Popper 1957). Given that the effectiveness of interventions is contingent on conditions in which they can generate their impacts, this openness of social settings undermines any confidence we can have that we have found a panacea and any aspiration to find one. Evaluations can, at best, help test and refine abstract theories about what works for whom in what circumstances, recognising that the real-life expression of these may be quite fluid.

The production and use of evaluation goes through several stages, from the commissioning of a study, to the conduct of it, to the composition and publication of a report, and finally to its readership and the application of findings. There are problems and pitfalls at each.

Commissioning evaluations

The need for selectivity in targeting evaluation resources has already been mentioned: a thin veneer of inadequate evaluation across a large number (or all) projects will predictably lead to little that is sufficiently robust to produce a sound basis for decisions. Where there is agreement to commission an evaluation, it is important to make sure the right question is asked. Asking whether a given project produced its intended effects is insufficient. Though technically difficult and complex if done well, it will produce a more or less internally valid simple, 'Yes it did', or 'No it didn't' answer. Given the rationale for evaluation (to inform policy, practice, or resource allocation), unless there is explicit attention to the ways in which the effect was brought about and the conditions needed to generate these effects, or, where there was no effect, why the project failed, the evaluation will not be fit. for its purpose. Those commissioning evaluations must frame the evaluation question in a way that will elicit useful answers. They often fail to do so.

The evaluation question posed has implications for the relationship between the commissioner of the evaluation and the evaluator. If the 'wrong' question is asked, such as did it produce the intended effects?, all the evaluator needs to know is what the intended changes are, and what the project is delivering. The evaluator can then go away and make appropriate before and after measurements and come to his or her conclusions. If the 'right' questions are asked, say, what effects were brought about in the conditions in which this project was introduced, what was it about the project, its implementation, or the context that explains the lack of effect?', the evaluator needs to be privy to the thinking behind the project. A theory is being tested and refined, and the evaluator cannot test that theory without being informed of it. This does not mean, of course, that the evaluator relies exclusively on the commissioner of the evaluation for theory. As policy-makers agreeing to the project, however, they will normally be one key source (on eliciting and using theory see Pawson and Tilley 1997).

Where projects lack aims and, at least embryonic, theories about how what is being planned is expected to have its impact, it is unlikely that any form of evaluation is going to be worthwhile. Similarly, if monitoring arrangements are not in place to assure, track and adjust the implementation of the intervention in the planned way, it is unlikely that any meaningful evaluation will be possible.

Policy-makers, under pressure from the Treasury, are apt to demand premature answers about costs and benefits. It is difficult enough to trace the effects of projects and how they are produced in context. The expectation that the costs and benefits can be calculated and that alternative means to a given end can be costed and the benefits assessed will often be premature. I was asked once to work out the costs and benefits of forensic science in crime investigation. It was a well-intentioned and common-sensical question. It just happens to be barmy. It is not forensic science per se but its appropriate use in context, alongside other investigative methods that does or does not bear fruits, and this varies very widely (Tilley and Ford 1996). There is, and can be, no definitive answer.

Conducting evaluations

This is not the place to discuss technical difficulties in the conduct of evaluation studies. There is, though, a host of tricky issues to be considered: about research design, sample selection, sample sizes, data recording, questionnaire design and implementation, response rates, selection of comparison groups, choice and interpretation of statistical tests, use of qualitative and/or quantitative data and their synthesis and so on and so on. Only trained and experienced social scientists are likely to have the knowledge and skill to carry through an evaluation study with dependable results. Others are apt to come unstuck, and not always to realise when they do so.

Assuming, though, that the work is in the hands of a technically proficient social scientist, there are still problems and pitfalls in the conduct of work. Three important ones relate to independence, thoroughness and timing.

Independence. There are significant risks that evaluators will become too associated with a project, and will no longer be able to examine its impact dispassionately. Yet, failure to engage with the project and the thinking of those not only sanctioning it but also delivering it, risks ignorance of the ideas being put to work within the project. This understanding is important in providing a basis for selecting targets for measurement where effects can be expected. Moreover, not unreasonably, those commissioning evaluations often ask for interim reports, on the basis of which they will make adjustments to the project. At this point the evaluator risks riding in the project bus he or she is supposed to be observing from the outside, independently!

Thoroughness. The American evaluator, Lee Cronbach (1982), coined the phrase, 'self-defeating thoroughness'. Lay folk are apt to refer loosely to 'proofs' that a programme works or does not do so, especially where they are strongly committed to it or against it. Science can not, and does not, 'prove' (Popper 1959). It can only falsify (and even then decisions are taken on the basis of judgements about evidence). Evaluators can go on collecting and analysing evidence indefinitely. There is a risk of trying to say everything indiscriminately about a project to do it justice. What the user needs is an account that abstracts relevant transferable lessons, as soon as these can reasonably be elicited, and notwithstanding the fact that no single piece of work can be the last word.

Timing. One of the issues related to timing is connected to that of thoroughness. If the findings of an evaluation arrive too late for key decisions they cannot inform them. Of course, strong evaluations developing and refining accounts of how projects produce effects in context will have enduring value. Nevertheless, self-defeating thoroughness can unduly delay the provision of usable results. A second issue to do with timing relates to the point at which an evaluation is worth undertaking. The desirability of evaluating novel projects is often stressed. Yet, projects can take time to bed down so that they are sufficiently coherent and well formed to comprise something with enough facticity for evaluation. Too early and the evaluation will be 'will o' the wisp'. Moreover, projects can easily have Hawthorne or showcase effects in the early stages. That something is being done may produce an impact rather than the content of what is being delivered. If the evaluation is to examine the causal efficacy of what is being implemented rather than the fact that something is being done (often with the impetus of bags of initial publicity, see Laycock 1997), then the potential early honeymoon effects need to be avoided. A third issue to do with timing relates to impact itself. Differing projects bite at different points following their introduction. Informed decisions, based on the project theory, are needed to determine when potential effect measurements can sensibly be introduced. In the case of projects aiming at long-term impacts, such as those addressing future criminality, where much other than any individual project is liable to impinge on behaviour, it is clearly going to be especially difficult to draw causal inferences. There may be significant benefits in examining intermediate expected benefits.

Composing evaluation reports

I have argued that the rationale for evaluations is to inform policy, practice and resource allocation. Reports need, thus, to be tailored to the relevant readerships. Brevity and clarity are crucial. Few busy decision-makers will have the time or inclination to read long tomes, written in the peculiar argot of academic social science. They will also not find useful innumerable tables of data showing everything that the evaluator has counted, measured or cross-tabulated. Sadly, academic evaluators are apt to write for colleagues and to follow up issues that are of interest only to other academics. They are also often apt to be prolix. The academic may be proud of his or her all-encompassing 400 page report. It is unlikely, however, to be of any significant value in relation to its purpose, because it is unlikely to be read. The Police Research Group sets a maximum word limit of 14,000 words for its reports. Those contracted to do work (and internal researchers also) find the limits irksome. The word-limit is, however, well-attuned to the needs of users. George Bernard Shaw ended a long letter once with an apology, 'I'm sorry. I didn't have time to make this shorter.' Brevity does indeed take more time. It also requires skill and effort.

Using evaluations

Evaluations are there to be used, but can easily be misused. Policy-makers and practitioners may be tempted to jump to conclusions when reading evaluation reports. They need to be read critically, and in order to avoid falling into the boom-bust trap, must be examined for what they can tell us about what projects have achieved in relation to which types of person, and in what circumstances. It will be rare for a single project evaluation to be adequate for major decisions about changes in practice or policy. It is more likely that series of evaluations, withstanding critical scrutiny, can be read for findings about what sorts of measures work in what ways in what circumstances. It is for the policy-maker and practitioner then, intelligently, to use this increased understanding to make decisions about where and when similar interventions make sense. Series of evaluations can and have been instructive. See, for example, Pease, 1998 on repeat victimisation, Painter, 1995 on street lighting, and Sherman, 1992 on mandatory arrest for domestic spousal abuse. In each case a sustained series of studies produced much that was new and relevant to policy and practice.

Conclusion

In interview research, respondents keen to please will answer almost any question you ask of them (Schuman and Presser 1981). In evaluation, where you offer to pay someone to give you an answer, they will contrive even harder to answer almost any question. Indeed, they will often work hard to give you the answer you want, or they think you want. If you ask people to evaluate their own work or put the evaluation into the hands of their friends or dependants, you will not be surprised that good news findings typically follow. If evaluation is to avoid becoming a bit of post-modern frippery, part of the style and rhetoric of a ludenic catch-as-catch-can candyfloss world of appearance rather than substance, sensible questions have to be asked and to be answered patiently. Whilst the traditional modernist grand narratives of scientifically grounded panaceas may be past us, with that should not go the systematic search for suites of answers about what produces what outcomes in what circumstances. Getting there, however, is not easy.

Notes

Presented at the Conference on Young People, Drugs and Community Safety, University of Luton, June 4-5 1998.

1. The evaluation of *Safer Cities* overall, however, was very sophisticated (Ekblom et al. 1996). See Tilley and Webb (1994) for an overview of some of the better evaluations within *Safer Cities*.

2. Samual George Morton was noted by Oliver Wendell Holmes for the 'severe and cautious character' of his works, which 'from their very nature are permanent data for all future students...' Stephen Jay Gould (1981) shows in devastating detail the unconscious finagling that went into Morton's craniometry. It is a sobering lesson for all who believe trying hard is enough for objectivity, especially where interest and ideology are at stake.

3. David Weisburd (1998) has recently produced a clear and reliable guide to statistical analysis in criminal justice.

4. On implementation problems, see Hope and Murphy 1983, Laycock and Tilley 1995.

References

Chelimsky, E., and Shadish, W. (1997). *Evaluation for the 21st Century: A Handbook.* Sage

Cronbach, L. (1982). *Designing Evaluations of Educational and Social Programs.* Jossey-Bass.

Ekblom, P., Law, H., and Sutton, M. (1996). *Safer Cities and Domestic Burglary.* Home Office Research Study 164.

Gould, S.J. (1981). *The Mismeasure of Man.* Norton.

Hough, M., and Tilley, N. (1998). *Auditing Crime and Disorder: Guidance for Local Partnerships.* Crime Detection and Prevention Series Paper 91. Home Office.

Laycock, G. (1997). Operation Identification, or the Power of Publicity? In Clarke, R. (Ed.). *Situational Crime Prevention: Successful Case Studies*, pp 230–239. Harrow and Heston.

Laycock, G., and Tilley, N. (1995). Implementing Crime Prevention. In Tonry, M., and Farrington, D. (Eds.). *Building a Safer Society. Crime and Justice: A Review of Research*, Volume 19: pp 535–584. University of Chicago Press.

Painter, K. (1995). *An Evaluation of the Impact of Street Lighting on Crime, Fear of Crime and Quality of Life*. Unpublished Ph.D. thesis. University of Cambridge.

Pawson, R., and Tilley, N. (1997). *Realistic Evaluation*. Sage.

Pease, K. (1998). *Repeat Victimisation: Taking Stock*. Crime Detection and Prevention Series Paper 90. Home Office.

Popper, K. (1957). *The Poverty of Historicism*. Routledge.

Popper, K. (1959). *The Logic of Scientific Discovery*. Hutchinson.

Schuman, H., and Presser, S. (1981). *Questions and Answers in Attitude Surveys*. Academic Press

Sherman, L. (1992). *Policing Domestic Violence*. Free Press.

Tilley, N. (1995). *Thinking about Crime Prevention Performance Indicators*. Crime Prevention and Detection Series Paper 57. Home Office.

Tilley, N., and Ford, A. (1996). *Forensic Science and Crime Investigation*. Crime Prevention and Detection Series Paper 73. Home Office.

Tilley, N., and Webb, J. (1994). *Burglary Reduction: Findings from Safer Cities Schemes*. Crime Prevention Unit Paper 51. Home Office.

Weatheritt, M. (1986). *Innovations in Policing*. Croom Helm.

Weisburd, D. (1998). *Statistics in Criminal Justice*. West.

Section Three: Into Practice

Chapter 9

Multi-impact Drugs Prevention in the Community

David Teeman, Nigel South and Sheila Henderson

Introduction

This chapter will describe an attempt by the Home Office (HO) Central Drugs Prevention Unit (CDPU), to explore the possibilities and opportunities that are offered by using an integrated approach to drug prevention. The chapter will first look at what kind of influences contributed to the CDPU's decision to fund integrated projects and will go on to explore the CDPU's initial intentions and methods, before describing the nature of the ongoing interventions. Finally, the chapter will reflect on a number of the key learning outcomes that are presenting themselves at this early stage of research.

The geographical areas that serve as the sites of the programmes discussed are anonymous here at the request of the funders (the Home Office).

Background

At the end of the first phase of the Drug Prevention Initiative (DPI). (1990–1995) the CDPU found that it had accumulated significant learning and experience on different aspects of drug prevention. The CDPU decided that in the DPI's second phase (1995-1999), it would attempt to put this learning into a programme of evaluated practice. The first phase learning produced information and guidance on the co-operative or community development approach to drug prevention (Henderson, 1995). This was hardly surprising as the then Conservative Government's White Paper, *Tackling Drugs Together* (1995) had sought to develop such an approach, intending that the DPI would facilitate local co-ordination in response to drug use in local communities.

Learning in this area came from a variety of different sources. In the UK, the DPI's Drug Prevention Teams (DPTs) had, during their first phase, been associated with different kinds of semi-integrated drug prevention approaches. These included programmes that sought to develop joint working, usually in defined geographical or service specific areas, amongst a group of like-minded or interrelated service providers. Independent research did not accompany any example of this approach in the UK until the second phase of the DPI, hence there was little learning available to inform future integrated programmes. As a result, in the context of a newly developing policy culture that encouraged integration across areas of service provision, CDPU began to look elsewhere for tested integrated intervention models. Senior members of the CDPU were aware of models of integration in substance misuse intervention that had developed in the USA and Canada. Initially designed to promote prevention of heart disease, community wide interventions had also been developed to impact on substance use (Caswell and Gilmoore, 1989; Penz et al., 1989). This development was largely the direct result of a wide breadth of learning, suggesting that single issue/impact projects had little or no effect on their respective target audiences (Anderson Johnson, 1985; Dorn and Murji,1992; Goodstadt, 1987; Salz, 1988). Therefore, the development of integrated, multi-impact community interventions was preferred, enabling the targeting of a range of risk factors, while offering the opportunity of enhancing protective factors.

These programmes varied in ambition, methods and outcome, but crucially they were accompanied by independent research. In fact this approach had been developed as one that was research-led. This resulted in a series of accountable and significant research-led developments such as the model of community intervention known as 'Communities That Care' (Peterson et al., 1992). By the early 1990s the USA had over 10 years experience of developing such approaches. Included here were detailed evaluations of specific projects and associated issues (e.g. identification of risk factors associated with problematic adolescent substance use) and developing valid learning on 'protective factors'. The CDPU took this approach as the intellectual and practical foundations for its own planned initiative.

Original Intentions

The CDPU determined that whatever was to be implemented had to be accompanied by a research programme so that available learning about 'process' and 'impact' could then be used to construct a model of intervention for wider use in the UK. The CDPU began to develop its own ideas for funded community interventions but also drew heavily on the model developed by 'Communities That Care'. This model provided a template for a community-wide, 'all-substance' programme, with the specific aims of reducing 'risk factors' and enhancing 'protective factors'. Importantly, the CDPU sought to utilise the longstanding research model used in the USA, one which itself was integrated. There would be preliminary site research, once suitable sites had been selected. This would be qualitative and quantitative in nature to build a picture of the lives of young people and adults and issues of concern to them, enabling it was hoped, the accurate identification of need. Preliminary research included a parents survey, longitudinal in nature, to be carried out before the project started and again when in its final year. Impact surveys, largely quantitative and longitudinal, would be carried out in all secondary schools in the areas involved. This survey element would follow certain 'year-groups' during programme implementation, mapping change and helping to identify what, if any, impact the programme had had. Finally, qualitative 'process research' would help develop a picture of project implementation, change and levels of success, and be responsible for constructing a template of implementation principles on which future programmes could be based.

While recognising the inherent weaknesses of using comparisons, especially in community research (Pawson and Tilley, 1996), the decision was made to choose pairs of sites which could offer some comparison. The DPTs interested in applying for the available funding chose these and a random selection between each pair then determined which became the 'action' site and which the 'comparison' site. For the purpose of monitoring and evaluation, this meant that both the impact and process research would be carried out in both sites. This was considered important so that any change that the impact surveys picked up in the comparison sites could be accounted for by the process research.

The CDPU consulted within the extensive network of local DPTs regarding the areas that might be suitable for the development of what became known as the Integrated Programme Project (IPP). As part of a rolling consultative process with the short-listed DPTs, the criteria for site-pairing were agreed, as well as aims, objectives, methods, costing and duration for the implementation of the two subsequent IPPs.

As has been noted the CDPU wanted to develop clear learning on best practice for the implementation of such integrated approaches, however it, in consultation with the DPTs, also identified other key aims and requirements for the IPPs. The operational aim was to impact positively on minimising risk factors while enhancing protective factors for the young people in the two action-sites thereby reducing initial experimentation as well as raising levels of awareness and knowledge. All of this would be achieved by accessing young people in schools and out in the wider community, usually via community organisations. The IPPs were also targeted at reaching those in the community who have influence with young people. Included here are parents, service professionals, voluntary sector providers and any others that the IPPs could identify. Crucially, the programmes aimed to work with local service providers and their communities in ways that would draw participants into integrated and complementary arrangements. Hence all local efforts aimed at drug prevention would be strengthened in their planning and delivery by the power of co-operation and combination which integration would bring.

The CDPU decided that the projects would be funded for a two-year period. Research would pre-date and follow their establishment. The particular DPT Team Leader (TL) would have overall responsibility for the management of 'their' IPPs, while a dedicated integrated programme Development Officer (DO) would be employed to facilitate implementation. The CDPU also foresaw the need for the DOs to make use of existing learning about good practice and projects already underway, as the implementation schedule left little time for trailing new initiatives.

The DO's role would be that of facilitating the integrated approach among those involved in the 'action sites', achieving common purpose, continuity of aims, message and methods, motivating involvement, drawing-in and identifying relevant participants, and helping to engender a responsive, needs-based IPP provision amongst those concerned. The CDPU were especially keen that the IPPs were reflective of the needs of young people in their respective Action-sites, while more generally developing a sense of ownership of the IPP amongst the wider 'action site' community and the service providers involved.

IPP implementation

The two DPTs concerned undertook site selection, based on certain demographic variables considered desirable as a result of the consultation process, e.g. choosing communities with a similar size of population, ideally, including a higher than average proportion of younger families. It was considered preferable to pair communities with similar socio-economic environments, as well as communities that reflected regional ethnic compositions. The TLs sought to find two alternative pairings and employed the help of their Local Authorities in researching the demographic variables that were most relevant to them. In consultation with CDPU, team leaders selected one pair of sites. They then developed their contact base in the areas concerned, concentrating on approaching the schools who would be surveyed as well as managers of service agencies who were likely to be interested in IPP participation once implementation began. It was considered important to get the schools to commit to the 'action' and 'control' survey work before the random selection of Action-site was made and therefore before one of the paired areas found they had not been selected as a recipient of the available extra funding for new initiatives. There were concerns about the ethics of this approach and the TLs ensured that the schools understood that there would be random selection between the two areas before implementation could begin.

The implementation of the IPPs began properly with the recruitment of the DOs. In the two IPPs the DOs initially used different implementation models to develop their respective programmes. However, the process research has shown that they have both sought to engage and impact on similar groups and services in their respective areas. Key project partners have been: the schools, youth service, parents, health professionals, and more generally, local community groups.

Both DOs relied on existing DPT contacts in the action areas to help initiate the consultation process. Each DO chose to form a group of participants that have, in both cases, provided a forum for information sharing, consultation and integration. The pressure of time clearly influenced the choice of early projects in both IPPs although with the support of other DPT staff and TLs, the DOs were able to choose from a wide range of popular and already evaluated projects. Sub-task groups were established to address key issues such as the needs of young people and parents. However, neither the main steering/working groups, nor their associated sub-groups, have developed significant decision-making powers.

Both DOs have had to contend with the difficulty of facilitating integrated, community-owned projects in areas where local community networks already concerned with relevant issues were rare. In one case nothing similar had ever been tried before – although there are various ways in which this has proved to be an advantage. Facilitation strategies have therefore had to invest significant time in developing intelligence about key service providers and individuals and their various historical inter-relationships. The DOs have also developed similar and different methods of accessing the wider community, especially parents. In one IPP, dedicated community-outreach initiatives and mailings of leaflets and booklets have brought access to local parent networks based on small family/ friendship groups, who have self-referred for drugs-awareness training. In the other IPP, extensive use of the local media and leafleting has resulted in the formation of a parents support group, extensive awareness courses for parents and a generally heightened awareness of drugs prevention issues among those reached.

A significant problem for implementation in each IPP has been the lack of well-informed potential participants, given the time and commitment which working in the IPP demands. This has forced both DOs, certainly during the initial period of implementation, to shoulder much of the responsibility for decision-making. Subsequently, the IPPs have sought to raise levels of expertise and knowledge among participants via their working groups and through funded training. Interviews in both IPP areas have shown marked change among participants in their attitudes towards joint working, substance use, the role of others and their knowledge of good prevention practice.

Both integrated programmes have attempted to impact on young people within and outside of schools. 'Life skills' projects in primary schools include the teacher-friendly and recently evaluated Project Charlie (Hurry and Lloyd, 1997). Regular and school-specific meetings among teachers from all the schools concerned have helped develop a consultative process that has enabled schools to take ownership of their part of the IPP while also allowing them to share learning and develop comparative knowledge. In one IPP, there has been a concerted effort to build an integrated approach to the issue of substance-use among all the schools in the area, attempting to ensure, among other things, that there will be continuity between the approach of primary and secondary schools. The IPPs have helped and encouraged all the schools to develop policies for dealing with substance-related issues and incidents.

The most popular projects used in schools, based on responses from the young people themselves, have been Theatre In Education (TIE) and Drama In Education (DIE). These have involved either presented theatre followed by workshops and exercises for teachers, or participatory drama during which young people develop their own ideas on a prescribed theme, again with further class-room backup. Training for teaching staff has been extensive and varied e.g. all primary school teachers in both IPPs have received training for the use of Project Charlie. PSRE teachers, year-heads and other staff in both Ipps, have received substance-familiarisation training enabling them to better formulate school policy and funding-bids for teacher replacement for the training time needed. It should be recognised that the Ipps have been implemented during a period of a great deal of change in schools and, often, during periods where schools were preparing for inspection.

Projects aimed at impacting on young people in the community have largely used young peoples groups and community education/youth service resources. Support for existing youth service provision to include drug prevention activities has been provided. In both Ipps the DOs have sought to develop community youth projects that are closely reflective of the local needs of young people. This has been done via extensive outreach work using youth groups, individual workers and in one IPP, an 'action van' that has now toured the area for two summers. The van attracts and engages young people in drug prevention activities and provides information and advice on where to get further and more specific help. In the other IPP, a youth forum has developed into a self-reflective, responsive and motivating force for young people in the area. Other events and activities for young people have been supported by the IPPs, often including multi-agency efforts such as a 'health-fair' in one IPP.

Adults, as interested professionals, parents or members of the general public, have been accessed in both IPPs. This is seen as vital to successfully reaching young people in a multi-impact way. Training for professionals such as health visitors and youth workers has been provided, always attempting to meet self-assessed needs. Awareness training for parents and others who express a need is continuing in both IPPs. Accessing these groups has been a significant achievement given the lack of established networks in each community and has been helped by the way both IPPs have marketed themselves. Interestingly, one IPP has made extensive use of local media, while the other has not, preferring instead to develop their identity using distributed information, dedicated outreach work and leafleting. Both methods have proved successful in their own right.

Intermediate learning: what we can say about the process so far...

Site selection

Site selection was undertaken within time and funding constraints. Subsequent research and interviews suggest that in both IPP locations the differences between 'action' and 'comparison' sites may preclude significant and reliable comparison.

Time

Time as a factor has impacted both positively and negatively throughout preparation for, and implementation of, both IPPs. The short duration of funding (two years) has focused participants on the efforts needed. However, the lack of time before implementation meant that the USA ideal of formative research mapping of community need and current provision could not be undertaken adequately. Therefore the DOs have had to address that task as well as the task of building interest and participation in the IPP. There has been little time to train participants, to ensure basic standards of substance-misuse knowledge and understanding. This would have been particularly useful for those serving on the IPP consultative bodies. Lack of specialist knowledge has probably affected the development of these bodies and possibly hindered their potential as decision-making forums.

The DOs

The use of DOs, crucially seen by all participants as neutral, has proved a major factor in the success that both IPPs have enjoyed. All participants agreed that having a facilitator without historical attachment to any local service provider has been of significant importance in developing the IPPs and widespread confidence and trust so widely, so quickly. The appointment of a suitable person as DO is vital. Characteristics have included: being non-prescriptive in consultation and showing sensitivity to the needs of participants, their opinions and historically grounded insecurities; as well as an ability to manage sometimes difficult, sensitive and potentially damaging situations and individuals.

Importance of people

Our research reinforces existing learning regarding community service provision, that **people** are a key ingredient in their own right. Both DOs have been fortunate to have found, or been referred to, a small pool of participants whose expertise, influence, experience and commitment have been invaluable. The loss of such individuals has a disproportionate impact on the activities of the IPPs and procedures to limit these effects are currently being developed and tested.

Individuals who provide projects have a similar significance. Often it is as much the individual, in the particular circumstances, delivering to a certain group of recipients that accounts for the level of success of a project. Dynamic, experienced and committed people are especially significant in community youth provision and often projects can be highly reliant on a single person. Again both IPPs are working at managing the disruption caused by individuals moving on. On the other hand, some influential individuals can have significantly disproportionate negative effects on the IPP, for various reasons. Limiting the impact they have has depended on the personal management skills of the DOs and, if necessary, both have 'managed out' negative impacts by some individuals.

Need for training.

Given more time a formal programme of training would have been preferable. The DOs would have benefited from training regarding the research-based learning available from evaluations of community interventions in the USA. Furthermore, as has been mentioned, standard training for participants, especially those on IPP forum bodies, could have helped these forums develop their roles more fully and with greater confidence, thereby enabling the 'ownership' envisaged by the CDPU to have been more easily achieved.

Integration

Defining and developing an idea of 'how?', and 'to what extent?' the IPP has achieved its development aims, is a key task of the research team. However, at the end of the day, it is necessary to acknowledge that the assessment of 'integration' must be measured within the local context of a particular IPP intervention. This means that identifying 'what went before and how the IPP has changed the environment' is of crucial importance. Only then is it appropriate to proceed to describe the nature and extent of integration achieved in both sites,

What we can say is that relatively comprehensive integration marks the process of IPP development, although this has been individually and comparatively different in the two Action-sites. There has been integration between participants at different levels, such as strategic integration at project forum level, provider integration at project level, and integration at recipient level, thanks to the multi-impact nature of the IPPs. Integration may take the form of formal co-operation and input between participant-providers, as well as informal co-operation on other issues enabled by the development of relationships. Vertical integration between the various levels of the IPPs, the projects and service providers and into the community is very apparent, achieving a key aim of the CDPU. Additionally, integration of approach, methods and message is largely being achieved. This has been done within the constraints, mainly in time and resource, placed on the IPPs.

Funding

As has been mentioned, the IPP forums have not really been decision-making bodies. Rather the funding decisions have been made, albeit after consultation with participants, by the DOs. Sometimes this has been in response to funding applications and in consultation with their TLs. Participants have not registered any opposition to this process, believing they lack the expertise to make such management decisions. However this does mean that 'ownership', in the sense of deciding what is provided, has not been in the hands of 'the community'. Ideally, a body that is widely representative of the community should make funding decisions, perhaps with the guidance of a facilitator.

Project content

Young people have made clear their frustration with didactic, exclusively substance-focussed prevention approaches. Instead they prefer methods of information delivery, either in school or the community, that reflect what they want to see and do. The use of DIE and TIE in schools and diversionary activities in the community, have proved most popular with young people. Effective and affective drug prevention can only be carried out if audiences are attracted in the first place and engaged once attracted. There is therefore no point to using 'single-issue' methods that fail to achieve this goal.

In this study, young people have repeatedly voiced frustration with various projects some elements of which they have nonetheless enjoyed. The basis for such frustration seems to be that they are nearly always told, 'We are not going to tell you what to do, just give you the facts and provide you with information, so you can choose for yourself.' When in fact what follows is the usual and familiar itemising of 'bad things about drugs'. This approach has been criticised as patronising, dishonest and insulting and it therefore fails to properly benefit from the parts of the project the young people have enjoyed.

Exit strategies

Virtually all respondents in the IPP areas have expressed concern about 'what will happen after the central funding for the IPPs ends?' Most respondents have expressed hope and / or determination that the positive outcomes and learning achieved through the IPP will not simply evaporate with withdrawal of CDPU funding. In both IPPs, formal and informal consultation and planning is underway to try to ensure that the positive aspects and outcomes of the IPPs can be carried forward after funding ends. Respondents agree that it is vital not to generate expectations and action in the IPPs and then simply 'pull the plug'. Many of the community participants have already suffered from the effects and disappointments resulting from earlier initiatives in which funding has been 'parachuted in', but only for a short time.

Conclusion

This chapter complements Chapter 6, by South and Teeman, by providing specific examples of integrated, multi-impact community-based initiatives aiming to prevent, educate about, and minimise risk associated with drug misuse. The IPPs are a valuable experiment in the design and pursuit of a new approach to community-based drugs-prevention work. They provide examples of good practice and imaginative thinking that should be taken up elsewhere within the context of the new ten-year strategy.

References

Anderson Johnson, C. (1985). Comprehensive Community Programs for Drug Prevention. In Glynn, T.J., Leukfield, C.G., and Luford, J.P. (Eds.). *Preventing Adolescent Drug Abuse: Intervention Strategies.* NIDA Research Monograph No. 47, pp 76–113. Rockville, MD: National Institute on Drug Abuse.

Caswell, S., and Gilmore, L. (1989). An Evaluated Community Action Project on Alcohol. *Journal of Studies on Alcohol*, 50: pp 339–346.

Dorn, N., and Murji, K. (1992). *Drug Prevention: A Review of the English Language Literature.* Research Monograph, 6. London: ISDD.

Goodstadt, M. (1987). Prevention Strategies for Drug Abuse. *Issues in Science and Technology*, pp 28–35.

Henderson, P. (1995). *Drugs, Prevention and Community Development: Principles of Good Practice.* DPI paper 7. London: Central Drugs Prevention Unit, Home Office.

HM Government (1995). *Tackling Drugs Together: A Strategy for England 1995–1998.* London: HMSO.

Hurry, J., and Lloyd, C. (1997). *A Follow-up Evaluation of Project Charlie: A Life Skills Drug Education Programme for Primary Schools.* DPI paper 16. London: Central Drugs Prevention Unit, Home Office.

Pawson, R., and Tilley, N. (1996). How (and How Not) to Design Research to Inform Policy-making. In Samson, C., and South, N. (Eds.). *The Social Construction of Social Policy.* London: Macmillan.

Pentz, M.A. Dwyer, J.H., Mackinnon, D.P., Flay, B.R., Hansen, W.B., Wang, E.Y.L., and Anderson Johnson, C. (1989). A Multi-community Trial for Primary Prevention of Drug Abuse. *Journal of American Medical Association*, 261: pp 3259–3266.

Peterson, P.L., Hawkins, D.J., and Cataneo, R.F. (1992). Evaluating Comprehensive Community Drug Risk-reduction Interventions: Design Challenges and Recommendations. *Evaluation Review*, 16(6): pp 579–602.

Saltz, R.F. (1988). Research in Environmental and Community Strategies for the Prevention of Alcohol Problems. *Contemporary Drug Problems*, 15: pp 67–81.

Chapter 10

Homelessness, Drugs and Young People

Geoffrey Wade and Trudi Barnett

Introduction

Homelessness is a shameful national problem and is arguably the most visible symbol of division in our society today. It is estimated that around two million people are homeless in Britain, 2,500 of whom live on the streets as rough sleepers, surviving a harsh and violent life.

This chapter sets out the nature of the homeless problem, the consequences and implications of homelessness and provides a historical perspective of past approaches to overcoming the problem. It considers who is involved in the processes to ease homelessness and associated problems and assesses how our failure as professionals costs, both socially and financially, when trying to get the appropriate services for these vulnerable people

An alternative approach is outlined which learns from past practice. Based on multi-agency partnerships and community involvement, it addresses the causes of homelessness and drug and alcohol abuse, reducing the symptoms of low self esteem, poor health and high crime which result and helping people feel valued.

The Nature of the Problem

The definition of homelessness according to the 1977 and the 1985 Housing Acts is:

...someone is homeless if there is no accommodation which that person can occupy...

(Department of Environment 1991)

Homelessness is symptomatic of the sort of society that Britain has become and is all around us. People are regarded as 'homeless' if they:

- Live on the streets (roofless homeless – rough sleepers).
- Are resident in temporary shelter.
- Sleep on friends floors (hidden homeless).

Statistics show that 1 in 20 of the homeless population sleep rough by choice, 1 in 3 has been through the care system and half are ex-offenders.

Homeless people are vulnerable and include:

- people with learning difficulties
- people with mental health problems
- people who are disabled
- people who are escaping violence and abuse

- people with life threatening diseases
- ex-offenders
- young people at risk
- people with drug or alcohol dependencies

It is widely documented that high proportions of single homeless characterise their health status as poor. Research literature consistently demonstrates high levels of physical and mental illness among homeless people. Many have medical problems that limit their activities of daily living and have potential long-term consequences. The causes of poor health and housing are closely linked and are both symptoms of poverty. As a result the average life expectancy of a homeless person, particularly the rough sleeper, is 42 years, compared to 73 years for a person of the general population (Grenier 1996)

The best information in respect of rough sleepers relates to London where numbers sleeping rough have fallen significantly from 2000 per night in the early 90s to 400 following efforts by the voluntary sector and government action through the Rough Sleepers Initiative (RSI).

The single most common reason given for the first episode of sleeping rough is relationship breakdown, either parents or partner. Many problems in later life stem from family problems, poor parenting and lack of support.

Older homeless people identify family crises as a key reason for their situation, the main factors being widowhood, marital breakdown, eviction, redundancy and mental illness. Elderly homeless questioned in surveys have experienced broken or disturbed homes in their childhood. Of those with children over half had had no contact with them for more than five years.

Outside London the largest concentrations of rough sleepers reported are in Birmingham, Brighton, Cambridge, Manchester, Oxford and Bristol.

Behind the statistics are people who have lost hope and are trapped in fatalism.

Implications and Consequences of Homelessness

Not only does Britain have the highest number of homeless people in Europe, but it also has the highest number of consumers of illegal drugs.

Some homeless groups have a high dependence on drugs, including alcohol, so before considering the statistics it is important to develop some understanding of how drugs can affect the lives of homeless people, or how the homelessness can affect the use of drugs.

When a person becomes homeless they face enormous and often drastic changes in their life. They have no home, no income and no support networks. Decisions about where to live are no longer dictated by choice, only by circumstances. For many homeless people this lifestyle is comfortless. No-one to turn to and no-one to talk to. Legal, illegal and prescription drugs become tempting. They provide an escape from the harsh realities of life, suddenly there are no problems. Britain's homeless drug users are victims of circumstances.

Around 70% of homeless people are believed to be drug dependent although statistics vary. The Office of Population Census and Surveys (1996) suggests that:

- 6% of hostel users are drug dependent
- 18% of hostel type residents with a neurotic disorder are heavy drinkers or drug users
- 22% of night shelter residents are drug dependant
- 13% of rough sleepers are drug dependent

A homeless person with a drug dependency is three times more susceptible to other health problems and three times more likely to have or develop a mental health problem. The University of York suggests that:

- 33% who sleep rough are mentally ill
- 20% of temporary accommodation residents are mentally ill

The National Homeless Alliance report *Beyond Help* aimed to improve service provision for street homeless people with mental health or drug/alcohol dependency problems. It highlights just how suffering from a combination of mental health and drug/alcohol problems (also known as dual diagnosis) is likely to lead to a pattern of losing accommodation, behavioural problems and an unwillingness to access services. The report indicated that drug or alcohol dependency is also most common amongst those sleeping rough and those using hostel accommodation, highlighting that it is inevitably the task of social services, the police, health service and voluntary sector to cope with these difficulties when they appear,

Drugs have a harmful effect on peoples' behaviour and feelings. They affect the mental and physical health of the person using, they affect the user's social networks and housing situation. Drugs can mean social exclusion, particularly after penalties have been imposed.

Revolving Doors Agency (1996) found that housing (or lack of) and social problems are very closely linked to offending. Thus, the painful reality is that being homeless, unemployed and suffering from dual-diagnosis is more likely to cause offending behaviour.

Drugs and crime

For many years there has been speculation that a high proportion of crime committed in this country is drug related – crime to fund the habit. Until recently the statistics to put this problem into perspective have been lacking. However, recently published research by the Home Office Research Directorate outlines the scale of the problem. *Drugs and Crime in the UK – Findings of a five City Survey* the Home Office Research and Statisitics Directorate, 1998

61% of arrestees had taken at least one illegal drug.

Cannabis was most prevalent – detected in 46% of arrestees.

High proportions tested positive for the costly drugs heroin/opiates (18%)

and cocaine/crack (10%) – it is often thought that these are funded by acquisitive crime.

Nearly half confirmed their offending was connected to their drug use emphasising they need money to buy drugs.

Some reported illegal incomes two or three times higher than other arrestees. Those arrestees who had taken heroin within three days of arrest reported incomes of £10,000 to £20,000 a year compared with the average arrestee income of £4,000. 32% of illegal income was spent on buying heroin or crack.

Illegal income mainly resulted from acquisitive crime against property. Arrestees had a high level of drug dependency, 1 in 10 on heroin and more on cannabis.

1 in 5 expressed an interest in treatment.

A study based on the US Drugs Use Forecasting Programme, now known as the Arrestee Drug Abuse Monitoring Programme provides quarterly information from surveys of arrestees in police bookings facilities and their use of drugs. A wider knowledge of the nature of drug use in the UK would inform and assist treatment and enforcement agencies to strike a balance when planning remedial action.

Acting to Solve the Problem
Historical perspective

All too often in the past action has been based on slicing up problems into separate packages. People's needs cannot be so neatly compartmentalised and there should be greater flexibility .

There have been, and continue to be, many dozens of agencies and professions working in parallel, often doing good things but often operating at cross purposes with far too little co-ordination and co-operation. This has led to poor inter–agency communication, poor policy and wasted resources.

Large sums have been spent on the same people through different programmes without improving their capacity to participate in the economy or society and too much has been spent on easing the effects of being excluded from society without action to prevent social exclusion. There remains a risk of short termism and not devoting sufficient attention to preventing problems that will arise in the future.

At national level no government department has overall responsibility for the total impact of government policy on rough sleepers and so no-one has the remit to prevent the causes of rough sleeping.

Central government has 5 programmes helping rough sleepers:

- Rough Sleepers Initiative (RSI)
- Homeless Mentally Ill Initiative
- Off the Streets and Into Work
- Drug and Alcohol Specific Grant
- DSS Resettlement Grant

These are run by three different departments through three different routes and current management arrangements do not sensibly match up on the ground. Government programmes are widely regarded as parallel programmes – they never meet. At local level the temptation for housing associations and hostels to avoid assisting difficult people is an acute problem. Borough/district councils are deciding territorially on who to help and are reluctant to develop services that attract the homeless into their area. Much of the progress made in recent years has been due to valuable work and dedication of the voluntary sector and yet this contribution is not fully acknowledged or adequately funded locally.

Inter-agency working has become a cliché in recent years and yet the degree of openness and honesty between partners varies from, 'will you be my partner so that we can get a grant from Government', whilst maintaining the long established divisions between agencies, to a situation where information is passed between organisations, minimising duplication of action and resourcing and assisting more informed decision making. The latter is still sadly lacking in many districts.

Action is needed against the push factors, the sources of homeless individuals – those from broken homes, leaving care, the armed forces or prison. Early intervention must be the pre-requisite for reducing rough sleeping. Social exclusion is not only a result of homelessness but also a cause of it. Promoting solutions by encouraging wider co-operation is fundamental if further progress to reducing homelessness is to be achieved.

Government is now taking decisive action to deal with the problems and has set some ambitious targets to reduce to as near zero as possible the numbers sleeping rough in streets.

An alternative approach

A Social Exclusion Unit, part of the Economic Domestic Affairs Secretariat in the Cabinet Office, has been set up to improve the understanding of key characteristics of division in society. At the heart of the work is the aim to rebuild Britain as one nation in which each citizen is valued and has a stake, no-one is excluded from opportunity and has the chance to develop their potential. It is about more than income, it is also about prospects, networks and life chances, building self esteem in a society where individuals prosper in a strong and active community of citizens.

The social exclusion unit is a step towards putting ideas into practice, helping government to work in a more coherent integrated way across departmental and external agencies, be they public, private or voluntary. The unit is there to solve problems and to achieve results. But what makes these commitments any different from those of previous governments? There are many questioned to be answered.

Attitudes towards drugs have become much more sophisticated as they are more common and easier to get hold of. In March 1996 a 'Drugs Tsar' was appointed as part of a 10 year programme to reduce the number of under 25 year olds using illicit drugs. This is a positive step forward to prevent misuse but as there are many homeless people over the age of 25 who are using drugs, how does the Government propose to help them?

There is growing emphasis on drugs education but as time is spent on 'Education' what is being done to stop suppliers? Recent reports have revealed that, despite the appointment of the Drugs Tsar, there have been significant increases in illegal drugs being available on the streets, which, when coupled with a significant decrease in drug prices, make it all the more tempting for homeless people to spend the little money they have on illegal drugs.

March 1999 will see the appointment of a 'Streets Tsar'with a £145 million budget to cut homelessness in London and get people off the streets but are the root problems of homelessness to be tackled? How can we get homeless people off the streets and into accommodation when Britain does not have the supply of good quality move-on housing to give homeless people independence? How can a Streets Tsar cut homelessness without overcoming the acute problems that are associated with being homeless, the drug dependency, the mental illness and the lack of services to meet the needs? How can two people build a better Britain by clearing up the drugs trade and eradicating homelessness?

Past programmes have been full of good intent but have failed. 'Care in the Community' is an example that has not met expectations. Grants were made to the voluntary sector so that services could be set up to meet the needs, but the scale of needs exceeded available funding. The whole system of service delivery and homelessness legislation needs to be reviewed and the findings of the Drugs Tsar translated into practical changes to service delivery. Action is needed in a systematic and determined way to ensure people are found the right route off the street and there is good reason for optimism.

In the past there has been a tendency to institutionalise poverty rather than solving it, but there are encouraging signs that Government is adopting a holistic view of community development, generally shifting resource distribution from cure to prevention.

The policies of Whitehall departments are to be 'joined up' and their efforts closely co-ordinated, working to consistent objectives to prevent the flow of individuals into rough sleeping. Attention is to be focussed on returning people to training, employment and independent living.

- Responsibilities of the Department of Environment and Transport for the Regions (DETR) are to be expanded to cover the co-ordination of the overall strategy for England on rough sleepers, including housing, health, training, employment and benefits.

- A Ministerial Committee is to supervise the prevention of rough sleeping, focusing on steps to improve the preparation for independent living amongst those leaving care, the armed forces and the prisons.

- The Department of Health will announce changes to improve local authority support of those over the age of 16 leaving care.

- Through the Home Office, the Prison and Probation Service will have a new focus on preventing homelessness.
- The Ministry of Defence will introduce improved education to aid the transition of service personnel into civilian life.
- The Dept of Education and Employment will issue guidance to Local Education authorities to give young people a clear idea of what homelessness means, that is, targeting action at high-risk groups in high-risk areas.
- The DETR will issue guidance to housing authorities to clarify those regarded as vulnerable, provide central points of contact for other agencies and encourage the development of integrated strategies for preventing single homelessness which is good practice in tenancy support.
- The DETR has launched the Youth Homelessness Action Partnership to bring together central and local government and the voluntary sector to prevent youth homelessness, evaluate good practice and monitor the impact of action.

Government has set itself the task to reconnect the workless class to bring jobs, skills and opportunities and ambition to all those who have been left behind, concentrating on helping individuals who can escape their situation. A climate for action is being created with a commitment to release capital receipts held by councils from the sale of council houses to begin building and renovating homes to attack chronic homelessness.

Opportunities for the future   _+ drug problems_

Government cannot solve the problems of the homeless on its own but, building on the work of the last administration, it is creating a climate for action. The homeless are beset by a range of difficulties requiring the intervention of many support agencies and needs genuine partnership to be effective.

More importantly, solving homelessness and many other social issues facing society today is not simply a matter of process, the challenge is one of capturing the hearts and minds of the private and voluntary sectors, and in particular the general public.

The public knows from experience the dangers of a society that is falling apart in terms of worsening inequality, hopelessness, crime and poverty, and yet working to overcome difficulties is someone else's problem.

There is a real possibility of an alliance between the haves and have nots. To overcome the underclass of people cut off from the mainstream of society without any sense of shared purpose. There is a need to bring this workless class back into society and into useful work and bring back the will to win along with self-reliance, but this cannot be done without a radical shift in values and attitudes. Without better integration at policy planning and service delivery levels there is little that can be done to reduce the numbers of people sleeping rough. Everyone, all sectors and the public, needs to be involved in helping to solve the homeless problem.

What makes a successful partnership? Are they talking shops or action based? Are they responsive or bureaucratic? Who are the key participants? Who is involved? What are the priorities for action?

These topics were considered by a workshop of delegates from the public, private and voluntary sectors at the Young People, Drugs and Community Safety Symposium at Luton University in June. Delegates concluded that there are a growing number of innovative and committed multi-agency teams emerging around the country, but many are still inhibited by historical practice, lack of genuine openness, professional jealousy and vested interests, with limited community access to decision-makers. As a consequence, decisions have been made without a full knowledge of the problems being addressed, the choice of solutions available and the scope for joint resourcing. Duplication of action is still widespread and there is an urgent need to take down the inter-departmental and inter–agency barriers, which obstruct open partnership.

Delegates outlined an action plan they believed could deliver more focussed and effective action to address the causes and reduce long term homelessness.

A Plan for Action

Assessment of needs

Develop a detailed knowledge of street homelessness, putting the needs of the homeless into perspective against a wider community profile. Homelessness can then be prioritised with other social local problems requiring action.

Improving the sharing of information

To assist decision makers improve effectiveness and plug service gaps for rough sleepers whilst monitoring:

- where rough sleepers come from
- why they have come
- what has drawn them to an area
- tracking where rough sleepers go and how fast

In this way problems in the system can be identified and action taken to overcome them.

Service delivery and project leadership

Where there is a clear problem in an area there should be a clear leader to co-ordinate action as part of a single strategy and local authorities are well placed to fulfil this role, particularly Social Services or Housing.

Target experience, prioritise and assess availability of skills. Don't re-invent the wheel – local action groups have been formed in many areas – integrate, consolidate and strengthen what already exists in all sectors of the community:

- Services must be responsive and flexible.
- Community action – through volunteering/mentoring.
- Business action – providing jobs and daytime activities.

Budgets and funding

At a time when public spending is being squeezed and public services agencies are expected to deliver more for less, partnerships must be innovative and make optimum use of available resources.

Annual Spending Reviews – redistributing revenue budgets to service areas of greatest need as putting extra money into already fragmented channels won't solve the problem. Allocating annual revenue funding on based historical patterns should also be questioned because community needs change.

Re-align service strategies – identify areas of duplication and rationalise service delivery according to who is best placed to deliver services, pooling resources and joint funding where necessary. Government has introduced the concept of 'Best Value' to replace the practice of competitive tendering/privatisation of public services. This is not simply a political expedient but a matter of common sense, ensuring that all resources being directed at a problem are closely monitored

Develop funding mechanisms for clearly focussed contracts – with the voluntary and private sectors to reduce rough sleeping to as near to zero as possible, awarding contracts for defined geographical areas, measuring outcomes and success rates.

Community led funding bids – for public, private and voluntary sector for regeneration and rehabilitation projects.

Communication

More communication with community and service consumers. The 1996 Housing Act already requires housing authorities to ensure there is an advice service in their area to cover homelessness and how to prevent it, so local authorities should build on this to define a contact for rough sleeping:

- Communication should be in plain language – jargon free, honest and accurate.
- Information provided should be of value and timely – it is crucial to avoid an information overload.
- Support agencies must listen more to the homeless.

The Big Issue is a ready made publicity network and government is willing to provide start up funding for pilot proposals from the voluntary sector to improve communication.

Conclusion

People have developed low expectations and a crushing belief that things cannot get better. If the homeless are to be given back the will to win there must be a visible demonstration by the community that support is available to those who want to help themselves.

Services, facilities and distribution of resources must be related to the scale of problem to be overcome, striking a balance to reduce the symptoms of homelessness in the short term with a long term social development programme to overcome the causes of homelessness and reduce the homeless problems in the future.

Chapter 11

Selling Sex, Doing Drugs and Keeping Safe

Jenny J. Pearce

Introduction

In this chapter I argue that community safety initiatives should reach out to include safety issues facing young women who are running away from home or Local Authority Care and/or selling sex on the street. I link the intricate ways that many young women's previous and current experiences of violence and abuse, drug use and misuse inter-relate. I argue that multi-agency approaches coordinated by Local Authorities should openly recognise and work with these interconnections.

I develop these themes below firstly by clarifying why I concentrate on community safety issues for young women selling sex. Secondly I argue that in so doing care must be taken not to isolate young women themselves as a problem for the community. I then identify points from existing research which looks at routes into selling sex for young women, illustrating the range of problems facing them. Fourthly, I look to an example where police have played a positive role in trying to support young women who sell sex, playing an active role in enhancing community safety within specific neighbourhoods. Finally, I briefly draw on innovative work developing in Tower Hamlets which aims to provide support for young women who may be selling sex, using drugs and/or experiencing violence.

I shall draw on data from Centrepoint, a charity aiming to house young people at risk, and on my own research work with a team of women in Sheffield funded through two multi agency groups: The Sheffield Domestic Violence Forum and the Prostitution Forum. In this research forty six women who live and work as prostitutes in Sheffield were interviewed about their experience of drug use and violence and the types of support they would like to be offered. The women were provided with a list of support agencies that they could contact and were put in touch with a mobile van which provides an outreach service offering free advice, condoms and coffee during the evenings

Young Women and Community Safety

So, why young women? It is important to clarify that although I concentrate on issues facing young women as opposed to young men who sell sex on the street, I acknowledge that young men face similar difficulties and exploitation in their work. I concentrate on young women to add weight to the argument for Local Authority Community Safety strategies to accommodate issues of domestic and personal violence against women. Many debates within community safety focus on creating a feeling of safety through the control of an outside 'other': usually a male predator, criminal or vandal within the public sphere. Both The Morgan Report (1991), published from The Home Office Standing Conference on Crime Prevention, and The Audit Commission report (1996) 'Misspent Youth', place emphasis on the importance of Local Authorities taking the lead in creating multiagency crime prevention strategies which focus on the circumstances and environments, as well as the behaviour, of young people in trouble. Both reports rightly emphasise on 'community safety', a term which acknowledges the role of the community in crime prevention and which encourages participation from different sections of the community. That such an emphasis is correct has been widely supported by research within the field (Marlow and Pitts 1997). It is essential, however, that this ethos extends to all sections of the community. It must not fail to recognise the 'private violence' against women taking place within 'private concerns' (Mooney 1998). Emphasis has rightly been placed on the importance of addressing the economic circumstances of high crime neighbourhoods and the employment prospects of 'marginalised, disaffected and disadvantaged young men' (Edwards 1997:12). Such a focus is important but must not take place to the exclusion of addressing the impact of the economic circumstances in high crime neighbourhoods on young women. Young women running away from home and so living in poverty, using drugs and selling sex are invariably running from one high crime, economically deprived neighbourhood to another. Various publications demonstrate how young and adult women selling sex on the street are seen as a threat to a stable community, a threat which has resulted in different policing and traffic control strategies aiming to displace prostitution from one neighbourhood to another (Benson and Matthews 1996) However, other research shows that many local youth work projects and residents on some estates are keen to accommodate the needs of young and adult women who are working as prostitutes, failing to see the advantages of 'moving on' policies (Campbell et al. 1996). If local authority community safety strategies fail to accommodate the needs of all young people, they fail to see the way that young women experience violence in their homes and on the street. Equally, they fail to analyse how women can contribute to creating a feeling of safety or danger for themselves and/or their neighbourhood. While I concentrate on young women for these reasons, it is important to note that many of the issues raised are also relevant to young men who may be selling sex, using drugs and coping with violence in their everyday lives.

Avoiding Pinpointing Young Women as the Problem

I refer throughout to the need for multi-agency strategies to accommodate the fact that many young women are struggling with poverty, previous experience of abuse, inadequate social, legal and emotional support, poor health, homelessness and drug misuse. However, I do not assume that all those who sell sex do so as a result of deprivation or depravity. Such assumptions only reinforce the myth that all prostitutes are poor, sick, unlike 'us' and beyond 'normal' life. As McKeganey and Barnard have argued, prostitution, like sex, is surrounded by myths, the main one being that the prostitute is always 'someone else'; the woman who sells sex is never our mother, our daughter, or our sister, but some anonymous other who is infinitely more desperate than those we love' (McKeganey and Barnard 1996:1)

To separate the prostitute, and consequently the punters who buy sex, out as alien others provides the rationale for 'moving on and away' strategies, which do nothing but displace the sex-workers and punters into often isolated, poorly resourced, badly lit industrial areas where there are often additional health and safety problems to be faced (Campbell et al. 1996). Although I insist that the social, financial and emotional problems facing young women must be acknowledged, I argue that this should not be done in a way that adds to existing stigma and abuse. Neither should interventions exaggerate the idea of a young woman as a 'victim' of her circumstances. Although many young women do sell sex because there are few better choices available to them, there are many devices and strategies that they develop to exert some control over their day to day routine (Pearce and Roache 1997, Mckeganey and Barnard 1996). The 'victim' label takes away any credibility that young women hold for organising their lives effectively against great odds and hardships.

Routes into Selling Sex: Poverty, Drug Use and Violence

The last decade, and particularly the last few years, have seen an upsurge of concern about the safety of young people who are living on the street as a result of intimidation and fear and who are selling sex in exchange for money, drugs or temporary accommodation (Barrett 1997). Research has shown that many women began their work in the sex industry as children, often at times when they were vulnerable, marginalised and excluded from the forms of support usually available to young people (Green, Mulroy and O'Neill 1997, Lee and O'Brien 1995, Green 1992, Jesson 1993, Rees 1993, Stein et al. 1994). Our research in Sheffield shows that 75% of the 43 working women interviewed started work when they were under 21 years old, with 27% starting when between 13 and 16 years old, predominantly as a result of poverty and previous experiences of violence and abuse (Pearce and Roache 1997:28).

Although it is not exclusively young people from 'socially excluded' families and neighbourhoods who experience family conflict and violence, it is more likely to be these young people who find themselves isolated on the street living in poverty. Shaw et al. (1996) and Patel (1994) show that family breakup, emotional and financial pressures which can lead to children running away from home befall families across class, race and income divides.

However, it is invariably young people who are fleeing from 'unstable' neighbourhoods where overcrowding, poor job prospects and recent demographic change are common place, who find little support in coping with the problems they face (Pitts 1997).

Compelling evidence exists to demonstrate how many young people who run from abuse and violence and who have no access to other support structures within their immediate family and community, end up living in poverty on the street or in temporary accommodation. Centrepoint statistics show that the majority of children running and staying away from home come from regions characterised by economic stagnation, high unemployment and family poverty (Pitts 1997:142). Of young people using Centrepoint resources 39% of those who were provided with temporary housing in the refuge for under 16 year olds had no money or income, with 48% having up to £39 to their name (Centrepoint 1997:6). Overall, 40% of young people surviving on the streets have no income to their name. (Centrepoint 1997:12)

As noted above, it is not all young people who run away that end up living in poverty on the streets. Neither is it the case that all homeless young people sell sex to earn money. Indeed, much of Centrepoint's work proves the contrary, with 80% of those using their services from 1996–97 having never been in trouble with the police. They estimate that although between 200,000 and 300,000 young people experience homelessness each year a large proportion will return home. A survey of 43,000 children between 14 and 16 years old who left home to escape violence and abuse shows that two thirds were estimated to return home within 24 hours (Abrahams and Mungall 1992 in Barter 1996:8). However, Barter notes that as the running away career develops, so does the risk of poverty, isolation and exposure to additional abuse and violence. She studied young people aged 15 and under who used the Centrepoint refuge between 1993 and 1995 and notes that young people who run away and return home within 24 hours, may subsequently run away again for a longer period further afield. (Barter 1996:47)

As they move further away from familiar locations, the more vulnerable young women can become. The numbers of young women on the streets with little or no money are not insignificant. Although there is increasing evidence that young men are sexually abused at home, Barter (1996) argues that young women rather than young men are more likely to run from family conflict, noting that 57% of those using the refuge between 1993 and 1995 were female, and 70% of the 300 applicants for refuge support in 1997 were female (Centrepoint 1998:3). A range of different young women approached the service: black and minority ethnic young people being over represented in the refuge, despite the fact that they had more qualifications than their white counterparts (Barter 1996:17). 24% of those using 12 Centrepoint projects had been in Local Authority care at some point in their lives. (Centrepoint 1987:25)

This provides a clear argument for local authority led initiatives to make services accessible to a range of young women at the early stages of running from home as well as at the crisis point of no return. Such approaches would have to be supported by temporary respite housing provision, acknowledging that it may not be possible for all young women to return home.

Those who do leave home for good soon find that refuge provision across the country is sparse and inadequate to meet their needs. For these young people, the street can be the only option left available to them (Barter 1996:8). Once away from home or from Local Authority Care, it has been estimated that within six weeks most young people will resort to crime, drugs and/or prostitution as a survival strategy or as a way to make existence feel more tolerable (Kirby 1995). These observations are supported by Green, Mulroy and O'Neill (1997) and Green (1992). Of the women interviewed in our research in Sheffield, 39% said that they started to sell sex due to a need for ready cash, and 43 per cent started specifically to pay for drugs. Once they had worked for a while, their drug use increased and 56% said they continued working in order to pay for drugs. Once on the street, young women will develop relationships with others, finding peers to be the most accessible contact point (Barter 1997). But while peer group support can provide a life line to many young people, it is important not to romanticise an image of self-help at the expense of acknowledging rivalry and violence between young people themselves. Despite 22% of the women interviewed in the Sheffield research saying that their main source of support was other working women, 68% noted that they had themselves been violent, usually towards other working women in fights over territory and payments. This, with the high number of young women being forced into work by peers such as boyfriends and partners, raises questions about the strength of the support available from other young people.

Many young women start work selling sex not only to fund their own drug habit but also that of their partner. In the Sheffield research, 39% of the women started work to buy drugs for their partner (Pearce and Roache 1997:39). A total of 70% stated that they were working against their will, being forced to by their boyfriend or partner. Only one of them said that she was forced into work by her pimp, evidence which questions the existence of a powerful, entrepreneurial pimp running young women's lives, and raises concerns about violence and force from partners and boyfriends. All respondents aged 17 and under worked on the street in preference to saunas and private homes, although 53% recognised the street to be the most dangerous place to work, with 21% saying they experienced violence on a daily basis, a further 35 per cent on a weekly basis and 29% on a monthly basis. (Pearce and Roache 1997). The connection between drug use and violence within personal and professional relationships appeared to be clear to the women interviewed, who noted that it was more difficult to secure safe sex when drugs had been used, either by themselves, their partner or a punter. 35% of the women had been forced into unsafe sex, 63% having been raped by punters or partners. The usual self defence strategies: working in pairs, negotiating the arrangements before entering a car, maintaining a time limit and keeping a step ahead of the business was easier to maintain if either party were not under the influence of drugs.

The vicious circle, in which young women use drugs to help them cope with the pressures of the work but then need to sell sex in order to pay for their drugs, is evident to them. As time progresses the health hazard for young women increases (McKeganey and Barnard 1996, The Marigold Project 1997). Community safety strategies to support young women must be firmly linked into health care provision. This is not only a concern in this country. A growing body of work in the United States concerns the risk posed to the welfare of working women and their clients by crack cocaine. A study of 789 ante-natal patients in the United States showed 5.3% of the women using crack cocaine with 26% of them being HIV positive, compared to 2% of the non-crack using women (Schoenfisch et al. 1993). Henderson (1997) notes an increase in the numbers of types of drugs being used by young women in Britain and, in particular, raises concern for the increase in sexual risk taking amongst young women while under the influence of certain drugs such as crack and Ecstasy.

A number of projects have been developed by Local Health Authorities in response to concerns about the spread of HIV/AIDs. EUROPAP (1994), referred to 81 projects working with prostitutes in the UK, around fifty of which were funded by local Health Authorities. However, these projects tended to be targeted at older working women who may well have been familiar with sexual health clinics and harm reduction programmes. Faugier and Sargeant (1997) argue that work on children selling sex fails to connect with work on female drug use which itself tends to focus on harm mininimisation and the prevention of infectious diseases. Conversely, work on child prostitution has focused on family alienation and child abuse. Like Faugier and Sargeant, Green (1992) argues that while evidence of the fact that young people selling sex are also using drugs exists, there has been a dearth of work in co-ordinating the services which aim to provide support.

Community Safety and Community Policing

While there has been an increasing recognition of the fact that young women who are selling sex are invariably running from violence and abuse, experiencing increasing danger on the street and using drugs to try to alleviate some of the pressures placed upon them, there is little overt recognition of these interconnections by the key statutory players in community safety partnerships. The foregoing arguments pose real questions about the extent to which young women who are using drugs and selling sex are able to practice self determination (Campbell et al. 1996, Lee and O'Brien 1995). Yet young women are seen to bear full responsibility for their work and are penalised accordingly. Until the recent DoH pronouncements which represented a de facto decriminalisation of child prostitution, instead of helping young women develop survival strategies on the street and build, under supervision, on the peer group self help support that they find useful, we, in the main, penalise and punish young women pushing them further into the criminal justice system and into poverty. Home Office figures show a significant number of cautions and convictions relating to children under 18 involved in prostitution. Between 1989 and 1995 a total of 2,380 cautions were issued and 1,730 convictions were secured against those under 18 in England and Wales (Aitchinson and O'Brien 1997). This is taking place despite the fact that girls under the age of 16 cannot, in law, consent to sexual intercourse.

The Local Authority Role in Multi-disciplinary Work

We can see from the outset that many young women selling sex on the street are aware of the interconnections between the basic commodity they have, that is their bodies, which can be sold for sex, with the commodities they want, such as a roof over their head, some money and some pain-reducing substances such as drugs and alcohol. Young people's stories demonstrate the range of ways that they work independently and in groups to survive under extreme circumstances, a strength that work such as 'Safe in the City' described by Hayes and Trafford (1997) aims to build upon. While voluntary agencies are in an ideal situation to initiate multi-agency work, the 1998 Crime and Disorder Act requires local authorities to play the key role in multi-agency Community Safety Partnerships. Each Local Authority should, under the umbrella of Community Safety, be pulling together all services targeted at supporting young people who are either at risk of homelessness or who are living in temporary accommodation or on the street, drawing upon and spreading out Central Government support through initiatives such as Single Regeneration Budgets and Health Action Zones.

The London Borough of Tower Hamlets has supported initiatives to co-ordinate services between the voluntary and statutory sectors. The local branch of the NSPCC has prioritised one and a half posts for the development of outreach work with young women selling sex within the local vicinity. They have allocated a building for the workers and young women to use. At a series of meetings with the Youth Service and representatives of the Education Department it was decided to place trained peer educators with the NSPCC project. It is proposed that the peer educators would help with the outreach work with young women on the street, ensuring that regular user involvement develops in the day to day running of the work, encouraging a feeling of all young women being active citizens within their community (Pitts 1997a). The project will build training materials about working with conflict at home or while in care, looking to equip young people with basic knowledge regrading their legal rights and responsibilities, sexual health and safety, harm minimisation and harm reduction regarding drug use and misuse. The main focus of the work will be to encourage a holistic approach to the information, looking at how conflict and violence at home relates to spending time on the street which relates to sexual politics and safety on the street. It is also hoped that plans developing within the local health authority could lead to the provision of outreach sexual health work with young women who are selling sex, young women who have traditionally found it difficult to access sexual health clinics. (Pearce and Roache 1997)

Tower Hamlets, with the NSPCC, has played a key role in initiating this work, and acted as a focal point for its development. The long term aim is to provide both preventative work and crisis intervention, linking closely with the police, other local voluntary projects, legal services, community safety programmes, drug action teams, health services, youth justice, social services area child protection committee and housing. A steering group will be meeting to oversee the development of the work.

The challenge facing workers to liaise and collaborate is a small task compared to some of the struggles experienced on a daily basis by young women coping to survive their work on the street. I want to finish with examples from some of the Sheffield women's responses to the question 'how do you protect yourself?' which gives some insight into the immediate threat of danger experienced by young and adult women in their work:

- pretend that someone is working with you
- act hard
- take registration numbers
- look out for one another
- carry scissors and hope
- act confident
- never carry money
- do a self defence course
- never go on the street alone
- never get in car with more than one man
- hit them first

The aim of our work with young women should be to ensure that the 'shout for invisible people' made by one young woman is heard and produces a service.

References

Aitchinson, P., O'Brien, R (1997). Redressing the Balance: The Legal Context of Child Prostitution. In Barrett, D. (1997). *Child Prostitution in Britain*, pp 32–59. London: The Children's Society.

Abrahams, C. Mungall, R. (1992). *Runaways: Exploding the Myths*. London: National Children's Homes.

Audit Commission (1996). *Misspent Youth*. London: The Audit Commission.

Barrett, D. (Ed.) (1997). *Child Prostitution in Britain: Dilemmas and Practical Responses*. London: The Children's Society.

Barter, C.(1996). *Nowhere to Hide: Giving Young Runaways a Voice*. London: Centrepoint.

Benson, C., Matthews, R. (1996). *Report of The Parliamentary Group on Prostitution*. London: Middlesex University.

Burroughs, L., Barrett, D. (1997). Youth Prostitution and Planning for Safer Communities. In Marlow, A., and Pitts. *Planning Safer Communities*, 158–168. Lyme Regis: Russell House Publishing.

Campbell, R., et al. (1996). *Street Prostitution in Inner City Liverpool*. Liverpool: Liverpool Hope University.

Centrepoint (1995). *Statistics: April 1994–1995*. London: Centrepoint.

Centrepoint Statistics 1996–1997. *Twelve Projects Excluding the Refuge*. London: Centrepoint.

Centrepoint (1997). *Centrepoint Annual Report 1996–1997: Getting Young People Out of Boxes*. London: Centrepoint.

Centrepoint (1998). Refuge Update. In *Centrepoint Supporters Newsletter*, Issue no 7: p 3.

Edwards, H. (1997). Planning Safer Communities. In Marlow, A., and Pitts, J. *Planning Safer Communities*. Lyme Regis: Russell House Publishing.

EUROPAP (1994). *Final Report Department of Public Health*. Ghent, Belgium.

Faugier, J., Sargeant, M. (1996). Positive Awareness: Health Professionals. Response to Child Prostitution. In Barrett, D. (Ed.) (1997). *Child Prostitution in Britain: Dilemmas and Practical Responses*, 106–122. London: The Children's Society.

Green, J. (1992). *It's No Game*. Leicester: National Youth Agency.

Green, J., Mulroy, S., O'Neill, M. (1997). Young People and Prostitution from a Youth Service Perspective. In Barrett, D. (Ed.). *Child Prostitution in Britain: Dilemmas and Practical Responses*. London: The Children's Society.

Hayes, C., Trafford, I. (1997). Issues for Voluntary Sector Detached Work Agencies. In Barrett, D.(Ed.). *Child Prostitution in Britain: Dilemmas and Practical Responses*. London: The Children's Society.

Henderson, S. (1996). E Types and Dance Divas. In Rhodes, T., Hartnoll, R. (1996). *AIDs, Drugs and Prevention*. London: Routledge.

Kirby, P. (1995). *A Word From the Street; Young People who Leave Care and Become Homeless*. London: Centrepoint/Community Care/Reed Business publishing.

Jesson, J. (1993). Understanding Adolescent Female Prostitution: A Literature Review. In *British Journal of Social Work*, 23: 517–530.

Lee, M., O'Brien, R. (1995). *The Game's Up: Redefining Child Prostitution*. London: The Children's Society.

Marigold Project Report (1997). *A Report of Female Commercial Sex Workers in Tower Hamlets*. London: The Maze Project.

Marlow, A., and Pitts, J. (Eds.) (1997). *Planning Safer Communities*. Lyme Regis: Russell House Publishing.

McKeganey, N., and Barnard, M. (1996). *Sex Work on the Streets*. Buckingham, PA: Open University Press.

Mills, H. (1998). Lifeline Given to Teenagers Forced into Prostitution. In *The Observer*, April 1998.

Mooney, J. (1998). *Gender, Violence and the Social Order*. London: Macmillan.

Morgan Report (1991). *Safer Communities: the Local Delivery of Crime Prevention Through the Partnership Approach*. London: The Home Office.

Patel, G. (1994). *The Porth Project: A Study of Homelessness and Running Away Amongst Vulnerable Black People in Newport, Gwent*. London: The Children's Society.

Pearce, J., and Roache, P. (1997). *The Links Between Prostitution, Drugs and Violence*. Sheffield: S.O.V.A.

Pitts, J. (1997). Causes of Youth Prostitution, New Forms of Practice and Political Responses. In Barrett, D. (ED.). *Child Prostitution in Britain: Dilemmas and Practical Responses*, 139–158. London: The Children's Society.

Pitts, J. (1997a). Young People, Crime and Citizenship. In Marlow, A., and Pitts, J. (Eds.). *Planning Safer Communities*, 84–98. Lyme Regis: Russell House Publishing.

Rees, G. (1993). *Hidden Truths: Young People's Experiences of Running Away*. London: The Children's Society.

Rhodes, T., and Hartnoll, R. (1996). *AIDS, Drugs and Prevention*. London: Routledge.

Schoenfisch, S., Ellenbrock, T., Harrington, P., Bush, T. et al. (1993). *Risk of HIV Infection and Behavioural Changes Associated with Crack Cocaine in Pre-natal Patients*. PO-C15-2920 International Conference on AIDS, Berlin.

Shaw, I., Butler, I., Crowley, A., Patel, G. (1996). *Playing the Price: Young People and Prostitution in South Glamorgan*. School of Social and Administrative Studies, University of Wales, College of Cardiff.

Stein, M., Rees, G., Frost, N. (1994). *Running the Risk: Young People on the Streets of Britain Today*. London: The Children's Society.

Chapter 12

Poverty, Drugs and Youth Prostitution: A Case Study

Sarah Crosby and David Barrett

Introduction

In recent years there has been considerable concern expressed about the problem of youth prostitution, particularly the problems existing abroad. Furthermore, recent research (Barrett, 1995) has confirmed that young people's involvement in street prostitution is becoming a significant problem in Britain. More generally, concern has been expressed about the increasing involvement of young people in drug use (Parker et al. 1995; Home Office Police Research Group, 1998). This is the context in which we now intend to examine some of the established links between poverty, drugs and the involvement of young people in prostitution. We will do this by using a service provider as a case study (Manchester Action on Street Health – MASH) to further consider relationships between these factors. MASH is a non-statutory agency providing a service for drug using street prostitutes in Manchester. It works primarily with young female prostitutes and, to a lesser extent, some males.

Prostitution and Drug Use

Whilst the reasons for women's involvement in prostitution are varied and complex, there is a wealth of research evidence to support the notion of an inextricable link between prostitution and poverty. Research continues to point to economic need as the underlying factor which motivates women to sell sex (Edwards and Armstrong, 1988; Faugier et al. 1992; O'Neill, 1991; Townsend, 1979) and numerous studies have highlighted that most women turn to prostitution against a backdrop of unemployment and social deprivation (Edwards, 1991; English Collective of Prostitutes, 1992; Faugier et al. 1992; Green, 1992; Maher, 1995).

In addition to poverty, young people's involvement in prostitution cannot be disentangled from factors such as family conflict, homelessness and sexual or physical abuse (Barrett and Beckett, 1996). In particular, the relationship between the residential care system, young care leavers and prostitution has been identified by a number of authors, with care leavers being disproportionately represented amongst young runaways who may adopt 'sex for money' as a survival strategy (Barrett, 1997; Green, 1992; Lee and O'Brien, 1995; O'Neill 1991). Alternatively, it is not uncommon for young women who have been in local authority care to 'drift' into prostitution, as the following comment highlights:

I run away from the home...and the Social wouldn't give me any money or anything...and they told me to go back to London...so I ended up meeting a couple of girls who I started knocking about with and one of them was actually a working girl and she told me what she did and that and what the money was like and I didn't get forced into it, I just at the time thought it was a good idea, it was an easy way of making money, and at the time I just didn't see any other way out and I didn't have much choice, so I just started then.
(All quotations are from personal interviews cited from Crosby, 1997)

Whilst the prevalence of young people's involvement in prostitution is difficult to establish, it is estimated that nationally there are up to 5,000 juveniles under the age of 18 who are working as prostitutes (Thompson, 1995). Recent research highlights that 40% of a sample of 50 prostitutes in Manchester started working before the age of 18 and 82% started work under the age of 26 (Crosby, 1997). Whilst some young people may be coerced into prostitution, in the majority of cases, it appears to be a combination of factors which result in an individual's involvement in prostitution. The following comment is not untypical:

The people that we knew all used to hang around Piccadilly Gardens, they all knew about the red light area, we started off coming down here, robbing the punters, saying we'd do business with them, taking the money and running, but you can't do that all the time, can you?

Whilst the reasons for young people's entry into prostitution are complex, an involvement in street prostitution cannot generally be examined without reference to drug use. The link between prostitution and drug use has been well documented in the research literature, with levels of injecting drug use among female prostitutes found to be 25% in Birmingham (Kinnell 1989); 71% in Manchester (Faugier et al. 1992); 75% in Glasgow (McKeganey and Barnard, 1996) and 84% in Liverpool (Bellis et al. 1996). Recent research at MASH revealed that 82% of female prostitutes in contact with the service are current drug users and, furthermore, 74% of the women indicated that drug use was the main reason for their prostitution (Crosby, 1997).

The variance in these findings reflects both differential injecting rates in various regions of the country, and is also a result of distinct sampling techniques used by different researchers. However, it is generally accepted that women who work from the streets are more likely to use drugs than those in off-street locations (McKeganey and Barnard, 1992; Philpot, Harcourt and Edwards, 1989; Scambler and Scambler, 1995). Furthermore, street-working women prostitutes who use drugs in Manchester can typically be described as poly drug users. Heroin is usually the primary drug of use, but there are increasingly high levels of crack cocaine use. It is also apparent that a woman's involvement in prostitution can often lead to a rapid escalation in drug use which then necessitates them working longer hours and more frequently in order to make enough money to fund their habit. (Crosby, 1997; Taylor, 1993; Wolfson and Murray, 1986)

Rationale for Service Provision

The link between prostitution and drug use, particularly injecting drug use, and associated concerns around the transmission of HIV in the late 1980s, led to the establishment of a range of new services across the UK targeted at street prostitutes. However, the original focus on HIV prevention and other sexually transmitted diseases, implicit in many of these services, often neglected the wide ranging health care, social and economic problems affecting drug using prostitutes. For many young people involved in prostitution, sexual and general health matters are often a low priority. Issues relating to violence associated with their work, child care difficulties, social isolation, and financial problems, are of far more pressing and immediate concern (Cameron et al. 1993; Hartnoll and Power, 1989; Jacquet, 1992; Synn-Stern, 1992).

This situation is exacerbated by the reluctance of many prostitute women, particularly young women with children, to use mainstream services for reasons which include: the fear of admitting to illicit drug use and losing custody of their children; the chaotic lifestyles often associated with drug use and prostitution; and the perception of a hostile and dismissive attitude from health staff. (Casey et al. 1995; Faugier and Cranfield, 1993)

Overview of the MASH Service

MASH was originally established in 1991 at a time when similar services were emerging in other major cities under the auspices of HIV prevention. As a non statutory service, MASH came into being with a non-recurrent grant of £5,000 and the donation of a transit van from the Local Authority. From its inception the service has operated at night (between 8:30pm–1:00am) from a mobile unit located in the city's main 'red-light' area. From a harm reduction perspective, MASH provides advice and information around safer sex and safer drug use, a needle-exchange service and a wide selection of condoms.

In light of the factors discussed earlier, MASH has increasingly attempted to provide a broader range of health services which are more attractive and accessible to this client group. Over the years the service has expanded to adopt a more holistic model of health care without giving up its low threshold street based approach. One of the key developments came with the purchase of a purpose-built trailer in 1995, comprising a needle-exchange, a medical / consultation room and a general area where clients can sit down and have a cup of tea and a chat. In addition to the original advice and information, needle exchange and condom services, this enabled the improvement and expansion of facilities to include the following:

Primary health care, including genito-urinary medicine (GUM) service. The primary health care sessions were developed in response to a recognised need for a broader health care facility which is easily accessible on a no-appointment basis. The weekly service is run by a female GP, and incorporates a sexual health service providing STD testing and treatment, cervical smears, a range of contraception, and hepatitis B testing and vaccination, as well as being able to address some of the more general health care concerns of prostitute women which may include respiratory infections, asthma and skin infections.

Sexual health service for male prostitutes and male partners of female prostitutes. The male sexual health service is a more recent development aimed at responding to the sexual and wider health needs of both prostitute men and the male partners of prostitute women. Reference should be made to the 'red-light' area in Manchester, a distinctive feature of which is that both women and men prostitutes work in the same vicinity. Also, a significant proportion of the male partners of prostitute women are also injecting drug users. In a recent survey, of those working women who had a regular sexual partner, 69% of those partners were also drug users, and 45% of them were injecting drug users (Crosby, 1997). Many of these men regularly use the needle-exchange service at MASH. In this context there was a recognition that as well as responding to the sexual health needs of prostitute women it was also imperative that we began to address the needs of their sexual partners.

Nursing and specialist input. In recognition of the practical and other limitations which may prevent women from using statutory services, MASH negotiated with the relevant health authorities to have mainstream clinical staff seconded onto its street-based service. This currently includes:

- Nurses whose role includes wound dressing, injury treatment, first aid and safer injecting advice.
- Staff from statutory drug services who can offer on-site assessments for drug treatment, including fast-track access to methadone prescriptions.
- A specialist Drug Liaison Midwife who can provide pregnancy testing, basic ante-natal check-ups, referrals for terminations and ongoing follow-up and support for pregnant women. This midwife also offers a range of other forms of contraception in addition to condoms, including emergency contraception. This has particular relevance in the light of research findings which highlight substantial condom failure in relation to prostitute women's commercial activities, coupled with low levels of condom use in private sexual relationships. (McCullagh, 1996; Faugier, 1996)

Other interventions:

- Referrals to appropriate agencies and organisations.
- Advocacy and support with longer term interventions to help support those young people seeking to exit prostitution.

Reflections on the Service Provided by MASH

Whilst there are no ready-made formulae for success in terms of establishing and running an effective health-care service for young people involved in prostitution, we hope to have outlined some of the key issues in relation to practical responses. In terms of young people engaged in sex work, street-based services are often best placed to address health care and other needs simply because they are often the first and only point of contact with these young people. It is essential that any such services are available in the vicinity where prostitutes work and operate opening hours that suit their working patterns (i.e. late at night). In contrast to some of the more traditional models of health and social work, such services need to function on an easy-access, 'user-friendly' basis that is less likely to alienate this often marginalised and distrustful group of young people.

Conclusion

Recognising that, like drug use, prostitution does not exist in a vacuum, future services need to address some of the broader problems associated with young people engaged in prostitution. This may involve tackling issues such as isolation, lack of self esteem, poverty, violence and sexual abuse.

Accordingly, it may be necessary for service providers to attempt to respond to some of these wider social issues through the provision of education, training and employment opportunities; financial, welfare and legal advice; housing and child-care support all in conjunction with support and help with drug problems. There may also be a need to help women work through, and deal with, the not uncommon experiences of sexual abuse, recurrent violence and low levels of self esteem. Agencies should ideally offer a range of service options such as one-to-one counselling, personal safety training and , perhaps more pertinently, advice and information on relevant 'tricks of the trade' that includes tips to promote healthier and safer working practises.

In conclusion, it is clear that a more holistic model of service provision is necessary in order to address the range of issues relevant to the lifestyle of young people involved in prostitution. However, in the context of ever dwindling resources, such a holistic approach may require the development of collaborative ways of working, involving a number of agencies, both statutory and non-statutory.

A range of relevant agencies attended a workshop on young people, drug use and prostitution at the Conference and debated some of the key issues outlined in this chapter. Many of the suggestions and proposals which emerged during the workshop were not uncommon to those already working in the field – financial and staffing resources, multi-agency responses, raising the profile and prestige of street-level work, establishing a dialogue with local communities, training of specialist workers, ensuring the personal safety of staff, responding to child protection issues etc. Whilst responses to poverty, drugs and prostitution remain problematic, one key outcome of the workshop was that it further strengthened the resolve of the participants to promote a more collaborative approach in this area of work. Finally, at a localised and practical level, participants also agreed that MASH provided a model of good practice from which much could be learned

References

Barrett, D., and Beckett, W. (1996). Health Promoting Itself: Reaching out to Children who Sell Sex to Survive. *British Journal of Nursing*, Vol. 5; No. 18: pp 1128–1135.

Barrett, D. (1995). *Child Prostitution*. Highlight Series, No. 135. National Children's Bureau.

Barrett, D. (1997). *Child Prostitution in Britain: Dilemmas and Practical Responses*. London: The Children's Society.

Bellis, M.A., Syed, Q., Peachey, T.J., and McCullagh, T.J. (1996). Estimating the Prevalence of Injecting Drug Abuse in Female Prostitutes Working in Merseyside, paper presented at 7th International Conference on the Reduction of Drug Related Harm. Hobart, Australia.

Bloor, M., and Wood, F. (1997). *Issues in Problem Drug Use and the Addictions*. London: Jessica Kingsley.

Cameron, S., Peacock, W., Trotter, G. (1993). Reaching Out. *Nursing Times*, Vol. 89; No. 7: pp 34–36.

Casey, M., Day, S., Ward., H., and Ziersch, A. (1995). *Sexual Health Services for Prostitutes in the UK*. London: EUROPAP UK.

Crosby, S. (1997). *Getting High on the Beat: Towards a Contextual Understanding of Drug Use Among Prostitutes in City Centre Manchester*. M.Sc. Dissertation. Liverpool: Liverpool John Moores University,.

Dearling, A. (Ed.) (1998). Drugs in Europe: Special Issue. *Social Work in Europe*, Vol. 5; No. 2. Lyme Regis: Russell House Publishing.

Edwards, S. (1991). *Prostitution – Whose Problem?* Report prepared for Wolverhampton Safer Cities. Wolverhampton: Wolverhampton Safer Cities.

Edwards, S., and Armstrong, G. (1988). Policing Prostitution: A Profile of the SOS. *Police Journal*, July–September.

English Collective of Prostitutes (1992). *Prostitute Women and AIDS: Resisting the Virus of Repression*. London: Crossroads Books.

Faugier, J. (1996). *Prostitutes and Unwanted Pregnancies*, Reducing Teenage Pregnancy Symposium: Translating Research into Practice, 8th November 1996, University of Central Lancashire, Preston.

Faugier, J. and Cranfield, S. (1993). *Making the Connection: Health Care Needs of Drug Using Prostitutes*. Manchester: Department of Nursing, Manchester University.

Faugier J., Hayes, C., and Butterworth, C.A. (1992). *Drug Using Prostitutes, Their Health Care Needs, and Their Clients*. Manchester, Department of Nursing, University of Manchester.

Green, J. (1992). *It's No Game: Responding to the Needs of Young Women at Risk or Involved in Prostitution*. Leicester: National Youth Agency.

Hartnoll, R., and Power, R. (1989). Why Most of Britain's Drug Users are not Looking for Help. *Druglink*, Vol. 4; No. 2: pp 8–9.

Home Office Police Research Group (1998). *New Heroin Outbreaks Amongst Young People in England and Wales*. The Home Office.

Jacquet, C. (1992). Help on the Street. *Nursing Times*, Vol. 88, pp 24–26.

Kinnell, H. (1989). Prostitutes, Their Clients and Risks of HIV Infection in Birmingham, Occasional paper. Birmingham: Department of Public Health and Medicine, University of Birmingham.

Lee, M., and O'Brien, R. (1995). *The Game's Up – Redefining Child Prostitution*. London: The Children's Society.

Maher, L. (1995). *Hidden in the Light: Occupational Norms Among Crack-Using Street Level Sexworkers*, paper presented at the British Criminology Meetings. Loughborough, 18–21 July.

McCullagh, J. (1996). *Female Prostitution in Merseyside*, Reducing Teenage Pregnancy Symposium: Translating Research into Practice, 8th November 1996, University of Central Lancashire, Preston.

McKeganey, N., and Barnard, M. (1996). *Sex Work on the Streets: Prostitutes and their Clients*. Buckingham: Open University Press.

McKeganey, N., and Barnard, M. (1992). *AIDS, Drugs and Sexual Risk – Lives in the Balance*. Milton Keynes: Open University Press.

O'Neill, M. (1991). Routes into Prostitution: Poverty, Homelessness, and/or Leaving Care, paper given at the First National Conference on Prostitution, held at Nottingham Polytechnic, 21 November.

Parker, H., Measham, F., and Aldridge, J. (1995). Drug Futures: Changing Patterns of Drug Use Amongst English Youth. *ISDD Research Monograph Seven*. London: ISDD.

Philpot, C.R., Harcourt, C.L., and Edwards, J.M. (1989). Drug Use by Prostitutes in Sydney. *British Journal of Addiction*, Vol. 84: pp 499–505.

Rowntree, J. (1997). *Young People and Drugs*. York: Joseph Rowntree Foundation.

Scambler, G., and Scambler, A. (1995). *Health Issues for Sex Workers in London*. Report produced for King Edward's Hospital Fund for London. London: UCL Medical School.

Scoda (1998). *Drugs: A Plan for the Next Century*. London: Scoda.

Synn Stern, L. (1992). Self-injecting Education for Street Level Sex Workers. In O'Hare, P.A., et al. (Eds.). *The Reduction of Drug-related Harm*. London: Tavistock/Routledge.

Taylor, A. (1993). *Women Drug Users: An Ethnography of a Female Injecting Community*. Oxford: Clarendon Press.

Thompson, A. (1995). Abuse by Another Name. *Community Care*, 19–25 October 1995: pp 16–18.

Townsend, P. (1979). *Poverty in the UK: A Survey of Household Resource and Standards of Living*. London: Penguin.

Wolfson, D., and Murray, J. (Eds.) (1986). *Women and Dependency*. London.

Chapter 13

Drugs, Young People and the Internet

Alan Dearling

Words and phrases in bold appear in the short glossary of terms included at the end of the section.

Why the Internet?

I'm definitely not a computer or **Internet** expert. This contribution is derived from my own induction into using the net, and my personal decision to use it to help me in my work as a researcher and writer. In the past two years, I have found that Internet access enabled me to:

- Use **search engines** and web **browsers** to conduct subject searches and locate sites of potential interest.
- **Download** and print out information and documents.
- Use the **hyperlinks** included on **web sites** to visit other sites.
- Identify the names and special interests of researchers/staff and then **e-mail** them individually.
- Conduct bibliographic research trawls in library and agency resource sites.
- Receive messages and indeed large documents through my own e-mail address/ post box (this can speed up editing and other aspects of publishing and writing).
- Leave messages on **noticeboards** for future visitors and the **webmaster**.
- Get in touch with, or keep in touch with other researchers and collaborators (I'm presently compiling a book with over sixty Australians, and in 1998 I used it extensively to put together a special issue of the *Social Work in Europe* journal).

It is a particularly effective communications tool in the drugs field and probably offers more opportunities than in some other specialist fields of study. As one gains expertise in using the net for making contacts and searching for information, it becomes apparent that 'drugs' is a subject area which has a better geographical spread of sites, compared to some other topic areas such as 'policing', where there are a lot of sites and information, but the vast majority of reference material emanates from North America.

There are a lot of people involved in, or interested in drugs. They are a world-wide community. They have a large presence on the Web and they include: traffickers and dealers; enforcement agencies; national and international agencies responsible for documenting the epidemiological and social effects of drugs;

agencies using intervention and prevention strategies; researchers and research agencies; individual users; campaigning groups, both pro- and anti-, all, or particular, forms of drug use. Many of them also make use of the net to give, receive and exchange information and opinion.

The focus of this contribution is on three areas in which researchers, managers and workers may find that the Internet has something to offer with regard to drugs:

- The Internet is increasingly a global means of 'communication' between individuals and groups of people who are trying to make contact with like-minded individuals or seek information. Users contact each other by e-mail if they know the specific address they want to reach, and use previously identified web site addresses and search engines to **surf** for web sites, as yet undiscovered. They can leave noticeboard messages or messages on e-mail located at the web site.

- It is frequently referred to as 'the information super highway' and this is not inaccurate. Research agencies, state quangos and campaigning groups all operate web sites offering information; opinion; and hyperlinks to other related or relevant sites. This information will be an increasing source of education, as the web continues to grow. Young and old people alike can get access to all sites, unless access has been barred by the **service provider** or network users. And, obviously, this includes practice and management material on responses to drug use, whether at the control, prevention or harm reduction end of the response spectrum;

- The Internet also exists as a research community in its own right and research itself can be conducted using the net.

Among a number of Internet topics not covered here are: newsgroups (see an interesting article by Mann and Sutton in the *British Journal of Criminology* vol. 38 no.2, Spring 1998, about crime and criminal research on the net); building web sites; and choosing **browsers**.

Young People and Drugs

Drug use is frequently characterised as a youthful pursuit. It has historic and contemporary links with the music and counter-cultural scenes stretching from the 'beat' scene of reefers and cool jazz in the fifties; through the hippy and free festival times of Timothy Leary, Ram Dass, Ken Kesey's *Electric Kool-Aid Acid Test* (documented in Wolfe, 1968), Oz, and Hunter Thompson's *Fear and Loathing in Las Vegas* in the sixties and early seventies; and more recently the inner urban housing estates of contemporary Europe with Welsh's *Trainspotting*, and the raves, parties and dance floors of everywhere from Berlin to Ibitha, Goa and Manchester, and the international sound systems of Exodus Collective, (e-mail at: 101370.336@compuserve.com), Desert Storm, Dubious, Zion Train (their wide ranging site includes drugs info: http://www.cityscape.co.uk/users/cs23/ziontrain/index/html) and Spiral Tribe (e.g., try the Freedom Network web site at: http://www.freedomnet.demon.co.uk). In May 1998, the Exodus Collective from Luton have even been invited to work with the government's Social Exclusion Unit members to look at worthwhile responses to drugs, housing and employment problems (reported in the Big Issue, May 11–7, 1998).

The young people of the late 1990s are part of a generation who have experience of both illicit and illegal drugs AND computers throughout adolescence, and sometimes even earlier. Arguably, both are part of the social and recreational world of young people. The very fact that the **cyber cafe** has become a focus for social life in many parts of the UK, and elsewhere, may place the Internet into the same category as the video film and the arcade game – a source of amusement and information. For many younger users the net is their newspaper, their source of party info. and other listings, and it's interactive! There are even sites dedicated to maintaining Internet freedom. (Many servers including America On-Line, Compuserve and Demon are 'policing' what you can and can't view/use on net sites. If they stop you making full use of the site, they deem it 'unstable'; see. Campaign for Internet Freedom: http://www.netfreedom.org/)

Young people use computers with **modems** to visit Internet web sites which offer information about drugs for a variety of reasons, including:

- To find out sources for supplying drugs.
- To learn about the range and diversity of drugs (legal and illegal) and their effects.
- To exchange opinions on, and campaign (often for the legalisation of particular drugs).
- To find information on making drugs, growing plants which have hallucinogenic effects, testing the quality of drugs and avoiding detection.
- To explore the wider range of cultural and counter-cultural sites, for instance, about direct action, environmental protest or music festivals (these may include drugs-related material, or hyperlinks to other more specific sites).

For those working with young people in social welfare and those who need to research aspects of their social behaviour, the Internet can be an invaluable resource. However, it may actually exacerbate the tendency to stereotype youthful behaviour as 'incorrigible' and 'deviant'. In the context of drugs use, it is salutary to note that the focus of nearly all drugs information both in the media and from many drugs' monitoring organisations focuses on youthful use of soft and hard drugs which is seen as 'problematic' or at least a 'nuisance'. Only rarely does one see reference to prescribed medicines, alcohol or tobacco in the same pieces of writing or research.

One of the greatest worries with the use of the world wide web by young people is that they will be subjected to the social and peer pressure of the net as a sub-cultural environment. At street level, the Dutch have based their policy of de-criminalising soft drugs on the tactic of separating the markets for soft and hard drugs (see Trimbos Institute Fact Sheet 7 at: http://www.trimbos.nl/indexuk.html).

But many web sites include information about *all* drugs, and the attractive, experimental lifestyles which appear to be inextricably linked. For example, the Urban75 web site from Brixton states:

> *These pages aren't intended to be the definitive drugs information service, but as a straight talking, bullshit free resource for those interested in finding out more about drugs...We're not interested in boasting about how cool drugs are or how many pills you can take in a night, neither are we going to deliver any moral lectures or tell you that drugs are the work of Satan – we're just interested in giving people the facts and letting them make up their own minds.* (Urban75 at: http://www.urban75.com)

In a very real sense, the Internet is a double-edged sword in relation to drugs education strategies with young people. Nearly anyone paying to be **on-line** with a server is allocated an amount of web space for the creation of their own **web page**. The more youthful organisations in the UK and elsewhere have seized this opportunity to share information and offer services, many aimed at young Internet users. As Mann and Swann (1998) have said the Net's aim is the,

> *exchange and dissemination of information regardless of boundaries and professional hierarchies and to offer support for deviancy.*

In Amsterdam's coffee shops, since 1996 it has been illegal to sell soft drugs and alcohol on the same premises, or indeed to sell to under 18s. But in the virtual world of the web pages, there's no age bar to obtaining material about the whole spectrum of drugs (accurate and inaccurate), or even invitations to grow plants with hallucinogenic properties. Similarly, it provides opportunities for anyone to buy kits to test products for psychedelic properties. For instance, at the Conscious Dreams site (http://www.neturl.nl/codreams) there is information about the *E-Z Test for Ecstasy and other Psychedelic Drugs*, which is on sale in their Amsterdam shop. Using a pinhead sample from a pill or whatever, the user can then determine with some degree of precision, the elements of MDMA, LSD etc. contained in the specimen. Tongue-in-cheek, the site offers the disclaimer:

> *This product is meant for entertainment purposes only.*

Also of interest is the site established by the late Nicholas Saunders (now run by the Green Party Drugs Group) in a move to encourage self-help drug testing and legalisation of more drugs: http://www.ecstasy.org

The site has already been visited by over three million people internationally.

Other sites offering alternative cultural views on drugs are:

Hyperreal at: http://www.hyperreal.com/

Paranoia at: http://www.paranoia.com/drugs

New Scientist Planet Science at: http://www.marijuana.newscientist.com/

Stop the Drug War Coalition at: http://www.stopthedrugwar.org/globalcoalition

Rebel Inc. at: http://www.canongate.co.uk/rebelinc/

Drug Use and the Responses

To some extent, the 'level' of the perceived 'problem' is one of social construction. Keith Hellawell, the UK Anti-Drugs Co-ordinator, has been appointed as Drugs Czar to head up Labour's 'war on drugs'. The government strategy announced on April 27th 1998 (see at the ISDD web site listed later) has four elements:

1. to help young people to resist drugs,
2. to protect communities from drug-related anti-social behaviour,
3. to offer treatment to people with drug problems, and
4. to stifle the availability of drugs. A Cabinet sub-committee chaired by Ann Taylor has been established to co-ordinate the efforts.

But the strategy, and the hard line stance being taken by Jack Straw as Home Secretary, and the Labour administration, seems to offer no differentiation between the types of drugs being used or the social context of their use. This may serve to emasculate the message for harm reduction. Even more worrying, or nonsensical, depending upon your point of view, is the unwillingness of successive governments to review the 1971 Misuse of Drugs Act. Some would argue change for ideological reasons and others for pragmatic. Strangely it has been left to the Police Federation to set up an inquiry, now accredited as the Royal Commission on drugs in the UK, under Viscount Runciman, (Jenkins, 1997). See the main government site on statutory legislation at: http://www.open.gov.uk/ from where you can also reach the Home Office and other government sites.

There is also widespread concern that the reaction is one of 'moralising panic', designed to allay public concern, but thereby demonising the many, who:

each weekend, at least half a million young people – typically they are employed, law abiding and middle class – take ecstasy. It may be the biggest drugs experiment in history. (Davies, 1997)

Or even more Machiavellian, and contestable, would be the view of Alan Lodge and others who are participants in the counter-cultural as well as being social commentators. Lodge suggests,

every meeting designed to work out a solution (about drugs) has been used by police merely as an intelligence-gathering exercise. (quoted in Davies *op cit.*)

Alan Lodge, better known as Tash, has been compiling words and photos about the festival and counter-cultural scene of young people in the UK for over twenty five years and has a very developed web site at: http://www.gn.apc.org/tash

The site includes hyperlinks to many other related sites.

The European Monitoring Centre for Drugs and Drug Addiction (EMCDDA) is the central agency charged by the EU with collecting reliable drugs information, and it also co-ordinates the REITOX network, *'the human and computer at the heart of the collection and exchange of data on drugs in Europe'.* (EMCDDA, 1997) (This very important site is a 'must' for researchers and also provides hyperlinks to the REITOX network and beyond at: http://www.emcdda.org)

The EMCDDA defines the purpose of 'harm reduction' strategies within drug control policy as to:

- Increase the safety of communities from drug related crime.
- Reduce the acceptability and availability of drugs to young people.
- Reduce the health risks and other damage related to drug misuse.

Researchers looking for comparative information and statistics about prevalence of drug use and state interventions will find much of use to them at the EMCDDA site. They will also realise that whilst there certainly is greater co-ordination in the collection of data, policy formulation and strategic intervention in drugs it is one of the world's most politicised footballs. Another extremely useful site with links to most of the UK drug agencies working both in prevention and enforcement is: Institute for Study of Drug Dependence at: http://www.isdd.co.uk/menu.html

Also worth a visit are: Aventinus (still under construction) at: http://www.dcs.shef.ac.uk/research/groups/nlp/funded/aventinus.html European University Institute at Florence, which offers some useful research on-line at: http://www.iue.it/

At the level of *trafficking*, most governments in the first and second world economies are willing to be seen to be acting in accord against drug producing and transit countries. However, the economic reliance of those countries on drug income has to be weighed carefully against the social disruption caused by the drug producers and traffickers working out of those countries. It is a complex and difficult problem, where peasants cultivate drugs in countries like Colombia and Peru, but as little as one-tenth of the income goes to them, while the rest goes to foster traffickers' extravagant lifestyles, corruption, torture, warfare and murder. (Clutterbuck, 1995) In Morocco, the authorities are more concerned about the economic costs and potential losses involved in agricultural alternatives to growing kif (cannabis). Nash (1997) says,

> *the local agricultural authorities (in Morocco) concede that kif is twice as profitable as alternatives such as wheat and that hefty subsidies will be necessary to persuade farmers to grow alternative crops.*

For more information on strategies to prevent production and distribution (and other aspects) there are many world wide sites, including:
The Lindesmith Research Center at: http://www.lindesmith.org
Electronic Frontier Foundation has hyperlinks to most government sites around the world at: http://www.eff.org/govt.html
National Institute for Drug Abuse at: http://www.nida.nih.gov/
United Nations International Drug Control Program in Vienna at: http://www.undcp.org/index.html
United Nations Crime and Justice Network at: http://www.ifs.univie.ac.at/~uncjin/uncijn.html
World Health Organisation at: http://www.who.ch
Interpol at: http://193.123.144/interpol-pr/
Europol conference page at: http://www.infowar.com/papers/conf_011498a.html-ssi

Association of European Police Colleges at: http://www.aepc.net/
International Foundation for Drug Policy and Human Rights in the Netherlands
at: http://www.drutext.nl/right.htm (This hosts material from the *International
Journal of Drug Policy* and has many links to relevant sites, including the Release
organisation in the UK).

Two other, more young people specific, aspects of drugs are where the pattern
of use is:

- Seen as a *nuisance* or causes anti-social and criminal behaviour, which leads
  to a wide range of international, state and regional responses.
- A *health concern*, in which case responses may be determined by legislation,
  but open to the vagaries of funding, resources and the vagaries of local
  interpretation.

Many of the sites already mentioned include useful information and examples
or practical interventions. But, don't expect a high degree of harmonisation of
responses across national boundaries. Neither the pattern of drug use, or, indeed
personal Internet use, is uniform world wide. For instance:

The proportion of world wide web users as a proportion of the total population	
US	15%
Finland	12%
Sweden	12%
UK	7%
Japan	4%
Austria	3%
Italy	2%
Spain	2%

(Source: International Data Corporation: *World Fact Book*, 1997)

One can surmise that this figure is rapidly changing and that younger people
are more likely over-represented amongst those who are on-line.

In terms of patterns of drug use (in the last twelve months) amongst what the
EMCDDA refers to in their 1997 *Annual Report* as 'younger adults' (approximately
18–40), the UK comes top with 13% saying that they have used cannabis as
against only 3% in Finland. Yet Spain has the highest response at 3.2% for use
of cocaine. In school surveys of 15–16 year olds, the questioners asked respondents
whether they had ever used drugs. The results showed that 3–7% said they had
used cannabis in Finland, Sweden, Greece, Luxembourg and Portugal; this rose
to between 15–22% in Belgium, Netherlands, France and Spain, and 37% in
Ireland and the UK. In Sweden and Greece, solvents are the most commonly
abused drugs amongst 15–16 year olds.

There are a number of web sites which offer information for young people (and professionals) to look at; four are listed below. Site visitors can either just browse information about drugs and their likely effects, or can choose screen options to move on to particular sections of information, whether it is 'raves and dance drugs' or 'counselling' or 'your opinion'. Crew 2000, who offer training on the safer organisation of raves and similar are at: http://www.electricfrog.co.uk/crew2000

Lifeline (Manchester) are one of the most reputable drugs advice agencies in the UK. They say:

> *Lifeline's view on drug use is 'agnostic', we neither believe that it is an intrinsically bad or good thing to do...our corporate moral commitment is to tell the truth about drugs and drug users.*

Lifeline at: http://www.lifeline.demon.co.uk

See also:

Tacade at: http://www.tacade.com

Youthnet/The Page at: http://www.org.uk/

Surveys and Research

The actual use of the Internet as a survey tool for research data on drugs issues is relatively new. Not related to young people, but nevertheless of interest, is Ross Coomber's research (Coomber, 1997b) with 80 dealers in 14 countries on whether they 'cut' drugs they sold with other substances. The findings bore out Coomber's earlier UK research (Coomber, 1997a) where 31 dealers in South-east London were questioned about their practices, with specific reference to dilution/adulteration. As Coomber (1997b) concludes,

> *...what takes place in the drugs world is in fact often mundane and logically predictable – as a rule, dealers do not want to harm people, either because they are not that way inclined or because they want to preserve their business or both.*

So, in this instance, the Internet research study directly contradicted the popular image of drugs being adulterated with glycerine or worse on a regular basis, (for instance, Welsh, *Trainspotting* and the BBC drama series, *Looking after Jo-Jo*). At Sociological Research Online, you will find Coomber's very detailed report, *Using the Internet for Survey Research* (1997c) which provides useful information on how the Internet can be used to obtain research results, in confidence, from hard-to-reach groups in society. Sociological Research Online at: http://www.socresonline.org.uk

Other research which has come to my notice on the Internet could be conducted for a variety of purposes, some not legal! At the Drugtext site, already listed, there are forms to fill in regarding a variety of drugs, price, quality, location purchased. And at the Drug Price Report site which I found at: http://www.paranoia.com/drugs/price.report/w_index.html
the results of a drug survey conducted inside and outside of the US can be obtained.

An example entry is:
    Luton, Jan 1997
    Marijuana: skunk crossed with haze: £20-25 1/8 oz; £140 per oz.
    Quality: A. Mind-blowing, especially through a water or electric pipe.
    Availability: D; grown local, so only available in season.

In Conclusion

This is very much an introductory guide to the uses which can be made by researchers, managers and staff in the broad range of social welfare organisations. I am grateful to the participants at the Luton drugs conference and Gary Hayes at the ISDD for their useful suggestions about Internet use and interesting sites.

Hopefully, this contribution has also given some insight into how young people may choose to use the Internet for themselves. It is a quickly evolving field, so be warned, you may have to play detective and go surfing for some of the sites mentioned as they can move location and server rather often. It is also very easy to type in some of the e-mail and web site addresses wrongly, which is continual source of frustration for web users. Finally, sites and servers can also go off-line or fail to respond.

Two tips

One: for those looking for information on a particular topic is to try and choose **key words** for conducting **searches**, which accurately describe what you are looking for. You can link them together into a phrase using + signs between words. For instance 'drugs+counter+culture+uk'. Upper and lower case do not matter, but avoid inserting spaces or omitting punctuation at your peril!
Two: Not all search engines are linked coherently to web sites. I use a website at: http://www.dogpile.com/

This performs a useful (and free service) which allows the search to be conducted across about five search engine platforms at a time. This can save a great deal of time, moving from one search engine site to the next performing the same search. http://www.hotbot.com/Ses/index/html is another site where Hotbot and a whole range of other search engines can be located. Happy hunting!

For drugs workers, the police, social services or counselling agencies, it is obvious that there is already a great deal of information available on the net. For different people and agencies this means that using the Internet and the world wide web:

- Can be used to inform strategic planning and practice.
- May provide information on drugs use.
- Speeds up the transfer of information between e-mail users.
- Will allow the researcher to obtain varying opinions on the effects of drugs and interventions to limit harm or reduce use.
- Can be a means of offering drugs information and education to young people.
- To contact individuals and users as part of field research.

Note

This is a slightly revised version of the paper that the author presented at the national conference hosted by Luton University, entitled: *Young People, Drugs and Community Safety*.

Glossary

browsers: are the programs used, such as 'Explorer', 'Netscape' and 'Mosaic', for examining and downloading documents on the web.

cyber café: are physical cafes located throughout the UK and in Europe which do offer coffee and drinks, but also sell use of personal computers linked to the Internet. Charges per hour can be quite reasonable. Many also offer on-line training.

download: is to save information from the on-screen web site to the hard drive or another drive on the user's computer.

e-mail: electronic mail systems allow computer users who have a modem to send messages and even large file attachments to other e-mail sites world wide. An e-mail address usually consists of: the user's identity title@server's title.domain.country. Some e-mail companies offer free e-mail addresses, such as Bigfoot and Microsoft's Hotmail (available at http://www.hotmail.com). Users can then collect their mail from any location in the world from their personal mail box, but they usually have to compose and read e-mail while being on-line..

hyperlinks: on many web pages there are words and other web page titles usually emboldened in different colours. When clicked on, using a mouse, these links take the user to a totally different site elsewhere on the web. Many web sites offer reciprocal links to other sites which they are fraternal with.

Internet: this is the world wide network of computer networks which literally links together all sorts of information systems. To go onto the net you must have a computer equipped with a modem and have made a connection through a service provider, which gives access to the network, through a routing system, usually charged at local rate on the telephone, plus a charge to the service provider.

key words: when making a search or surfing, these are the words you choose to use on which the search is based.

modems: are pieces of hardware equipment which allow your computer to connect with other computers over the telephone line.

noticeboards: are the computer equivalents of noticeboards in an office. At many web sites there are noticeboards on which visitors to the site can leave a message.

on-line: this means to log on via the modem telephone link.

search engines: each search engine is owned and serviced by a separate company. They provide the means whereby users can search for sites using key words. This is often referred to as surfing. Yahoo, Altavista and Lycos are three currently popular search engines.

searches: are made using key words through the search engines.

service provider (also known as Internet Service Providers (ISPs)): these provide users with access to the net and world wide web facilities, usually on a pay-as-you-use basis. At the time of writing there are a growing number of service providers offering free web access, (such as Freeserve); many of the new ones are linked to national and international chain stores. Their service only costs the telephone connection costs, but sometimes there may be a cost of wading through more adverts on the opening screens and elsewhere in the home pages, and slower connection times.

surf: the popular word to describe searching across the web for interesting information and sites.

web master: the rather fantastical name for the person who runs a particular web site.

web page: a page, or more properly a site, of information which may include graphics and sound set up by an individual or organisation. Many are very intricate and can take minutes to load on to your screen. Either be patient or look elsewhere.

web sites: the same as a web page.

References

Cassidy, J. (1998). Government Asks Ravers for Advice on Policy. In *The Big Issue*, May 11–17.

Clutterbuck, R. (1995). *Drugs, Crime and Corruption.* Macmillan.

Coomber, R. (1997a). Vim in the Veins – Fantasy or Fact?: The Adulteration of Dangerous Drugs. *Addiction Research*, 5(3).

Coomber, R. (1997b). Dangerous Drug Adulteration – An International Survey of Drug Dealers Using the Internet and World Wide Web. *International Journal of Drug Policy*, Vol. 8: No. 2.

Coomber, R. (1997c). Using the Internet for Survey Research. *Sociological Research Online*, 2(2).

Davies, S. (1997). The War on Drugs is the Dialogue of the Deaf, *The Independent*, August 28.

Department of Trade and Industry (1998). *Moving into the Information Age.* The DTI at: http://www.dti.gov.uk/

European Monitoring Centre for Drugs and Drug Addiction (1997). *Annual Report of the Drugs Problem in the EU.* EMCDDA.

International Data Corporation (1997). *1997 World Fact Book.* International Data Corporation at: http://www.odci.gov/cia/publications/nsolo/wfb-all.htm

Jenkins, S. (1997). Hooked on an Unworkable Law. *The Times*, August 27.

Leary, T. (1965). *The Politics of Ecstasy.* Paladin.

Macintyre, B. (1997). 'Pot' Shot Fired by Jospin's Loosest Cannon. *The Times*, September 18.

Mann, D., and Sutton, M. (1998). Netcrime: More Change in the Organisation of Thieving. *British Journal of Criminology*, Vol. 38: No. 2.

Nash, E. (1997). The Grass That Heals Starts its Journey to Europe. *The Independent*, August 28.

Thompson, H. (1971). *Fear and Loathing in Las Vegas.* Rolling Stone.

Trimbos Institute. Fact Sheet 7: *Cannabis Policy (Netherlands).* Trimbos Institute.

Welsh, I. (1993). *Trainspotting.* Secker and Warburg.?

Williamson, K. (1997) *Drugs and the Party Line.* Rebel Inc.

Wolfe, T. (1968). *Electric Kool-aid Acid Test?*

Chapter 14

Drugs and Peer Education

Joan Bailey and Andrew Elvin

Introduction

In his satirical book, *Coping with Parents*, Peter Corey gives useful hints for teenagers in dealing with several different types of parents. These include 'nagging parents' who spend their entire lives questioning your actions or 'keen parents who' take the business of being a parent extremely seriously...they read all available books. Too often drugs education, whether delivered by parents, teachers, police officers or even youth workers, has been in the keen or nagging mode. From 'Just say No!' to 'Heroin Screws you Up' the adult-led efforts to communicate with young people appear to have been counterproductive. And yet education continues to be a principle aim of the UK national strategies against drug misuse. Both the 'Tackling Drugs Together' initiative of 1995 and its successor 'Building a better Britain' (1998) specifically mentions education. With this in mind a peer-led drugs education project under the Prudential Youth Action Scheme (Luton) was set up in the autumn of 1996. It was a youth led specific project operated under The Safer Luton Partnership, which is a branch of the national charity Crime Concern to involve young people in educating other young people about drugs. The fact that such work exists in Luton is probably testament to two specific factors. Firstly, the opportunities through national policy initiatives such as those mentioned above, and secondly, the local credibility of a long running multi-agency partnership.

This chapter seeks to describe :

- the background need for such work in Luton
- the rationale and method of setting up such a scheme
- the development of the project by the project worker.

In short, these outline the attempts in Luton to avoid the Keen and Nagging pitfalls in delivering drugs education by a peer-led route.

Firstly, it will set the context for such work and linking the initiative to local issues and needs whilst highlighting some of the practical difficulties in undertaking such a task. Asking questions such as Why Luton? Why drugs? Why high schools? Why peer-education? Describing factors such as gaining local policy commitment, obtaining resources and securing credibility within a multi-agency environment.

Secondly, it will highlight the tasks involved in managing and developing peer-education projects in schools by hearing directly from the practitioners and peer-educators themselves.

Setting the Context

Why Luton?

Luton has one of the longest running independent multi-agency, crime prevention programmes in the UK. Established in 1989 by the local authority (Luton Borough Council), the police and local businesses, it was partly a response to the failure of Luton to receive Home Office Safer City status in the first round of such programmes in 1988. But it was also greatly influenced by the council's chief executive and police divisional commander who persuaded local politicians, from all parties, that crime in Luton was indeed a problem. Moreover, that a comprehensive approach by many agencies in partnership with the community was needed to prevent crime spiraling out of control. In short an independent multi-agency programme should be established one which the local authority should be the largest financial contributor! Over time the programme has drawn on the academic thinking from left and right realists, on situational and social crime prevention work and on other key thinking on community safety. In this sense the programme has attempted to follow principles established by writers such as Hope and Shaw (1988) who highlighted that:

> *crime within local communities is likely to be sustained by a broad range of factors – in housing, education, recreation, etc. – the agencies and organisations who are in some way responsible for, or capable of, affecting those factors, ought to join in common cause so that they are not working at cross purposes or sustaining crime inadvertently*

The programme, using Simmel's model that Tilley used to evaluate the Safer Cities and Community Safety strategies of the 1980s (1992), has transformed from stranger to servant. It has been given the opportunity to act as the 'honest broker' between agencies and between statutory authorities and the community.

In recent years the level of reported and recorded crimes has stabilised and has in some years even been reduced, often against the national trend (notably 1991). Recorded crime for the year ending April 1998 is at almost the exact same level as it was in calendar year 1989. (1989 Recorded crimes = 18,895 : 1998 = 18,968). [Although it is clear from academic research and from the British Crime Survey's, published since 1982, that recorded crimes rates are very crude in determining the true level and nature of crime it is accepted that they do at least give some picture of broad trends.]

Notwithstanding these encouraging signs, it is still clear that reported and recorded crime rates per 1,000 population in Luton are significantly higher than the average for the Bedfordshire force and certainly higher than the national average. (Comparison of annual recorded crime rates per 1,000 population Luton 125.7, Bedfordshire 95.3, England and Wales average 97.7 : source *British Crime Survey 1997* and *Bedfordshire Police Statistics*)

Therefore, crime is and remains a problem in Luton.

Why drugs?

The issues of crime, community safety and drug misuse surfaced as areas of activity for the programme for five reasons:

- Through local research and a 'crime audit' the analysis of which showed a need to increase family and community based solutions to crime. (Luton University Berridge and Wells : unpublished). The steering committee of the programme decided that, through anecdotal evidence primarily from the police, that youth offending in particular was related to growing problematic drug misuse. As such drug misuse became one of the five issues for action by the programme.
- Through publication and adoption of the government strategy *Tackling Drugs Together* in Bedfordshire.
- Through reference to earlier studies (principally the Parliamentary All Party Penal Affairs Group report 1983: *The Prevention of Crime among Young People,* p 84–87) which established concern over a link between offending and growing problematic drug misuse.
- Through apparent successes of drug misuse projects within the broader organisation of Crime Concern which had given opportunities to investigate at first hand good practice in this field. (Principally, Wisecrack and Cascade).
- Through the securing of resources for drugs education linked to community safety in the town. (Single Regeneration Budget and Drugs Challenge Fund)

This action, albeit, with reference to the Parliamentary Report, being a decade too late, was justified by later research commissioned by the Bedfordshire Drug Action Team in 1997. This showed that:

- Bedfordshire recorded the highest number and proportion of drug users in Anglia and Oxfordshire in 1996/97. (Regional Drug Misuse Database Unit)
- In Bedfordshire, a survey showed that 55% of young people aged 16–17 had used an illegal drug compared to a national figure of 46% for 16–19 year olds. (*Drug Misuse in Britain*, ISDD 1996)
- In Bedfordshire, particularly Luton, the incidence of the use of heroin was very high and increasing among young people, and disproportionately amongst some ethnic minority groups.

Why high schools?

The decision to focus work on the high schools was made because: -

- The government's strategy *Tackling Drugs Together* 1995, with it's tripartite focus on crime, young people and public health, gave an opportunity to deliver some key aims locally. These were to discourage young people from taking drugs, to develop effective public education strategies focusing particularly on young people which could lead to a future reduction in problematic drug misuse and the incidence of drug related crime. In this sense the programme was accepting concepts of primary and secondary prevention. That is, to minimise the incidence of drug misuse and to reduce the number of people dependent on drugs.

- It was felt that the best way to achieve this was by education and raising awareness in the most effective way with the groups most at risk.
- There was some local anecdotal evidence, born out later by the Health Authority research, that increasing numbers of younger teenagers (12–15) were involved in problematic drug misuse. Increasingly these young people were still within school and family environments.
- There was, at the time, research which showed that interaction in established networks would prove to be effective. For example Mark Smith (1994) argues that local educators should engage with local networks (in this case high school pupils) in order to build ways of working which connect with local understandings. (although this applied to professional workers the programme felt that it could equally apply to volunteer peer-educators)
- There was acceptance of the argument that Dawson and Davis (1995) highlighted that all drugs initiatives involve a leap of faith, although some leaps are more plausible than others.

Why peer-education?

A clear decision was made to move away from teacher-led drugs education, despite the push from the government's *Tackling Drugs Together* initiative to do so, because of findings raised by the following research:

- Plant and Plant (1992) suggested that by the teenage years, peer pressure from friends overtakes other influences within the establishment of adults in relation to styles of illicit drug misuse amongst older students.
- McGurk and Hurry (1995) in their evaluation of Project Charlie (a teacher led drugs education programme with younger children) showed that Project Charlie children do not differ from their peers in their attitudes, their intentions to use drugs and their actual use of drugs but that the most successful attempts to influence children's attitudes and behaviour concerning substance misuse have taught them social skills and enabled them to resist peer pressure as well as informing about drugs.
- Dorn and Murji (1992) highlighted that a successful approach to drug prevention gave opportunities for young people to become involved in service to others rather than in simply seeking sensation.
- Forster and Pike (1995 p 147) make clear that the developmental stages of children and young people are critical in relation to promoting health, as for example peer group influences tend to override parental and educational guidance at some stages of adolescence.

Developing Peer-led Drug Education Projects

Peer Education in schools is not a new concept. Indeed, it is a model that was used extensively by schools during periods of teacher shortage. It has, however, been heralded as a positive model for involving young people in personal, social and health education.

In projects of this nature 'peer' means a person who is of similar age and who has a similar background and lifestyle. This gives the project greater credibility which may stem from being person based (age, sex and/or ethnic origin), experience based (experience as perceived by audience, for example drug misuse, contact with the criminal justice system or bereavement) and/or message based (what the peer educator is saying and the way they are saying it).

By training young people to be peer educators it is possible to ensure that accurate information, rather than potentially dangerous myths cascade down through informal channels of communication. A well placed peer can challenge behaviours and attitudes in ways that adults cannot. They can work with groups and individuals in both formal and informal settings.

The success of a peer education project in a school relies entirely on a well planned and supported programme. There are several key areas that need to be considered and taken on board in the developing and managing of peer education projects.

Setting up the project

When deciding who is actually going to do the work it is necessary to determine whether this will be an inter agency approach or not. There are three main roles to be covered:

1. **The expert** – someone who knows something about the topic to be discussed
2. **The facilitator** – someone who knows something about peer education, has a knowledge on non-formal education techniques and can work effectively with young people.
3. **The organiser** – someone who can organise the times, dates, places, access to young people, policy etc.

Although it is possible for one person to possess or assume all these roles it may be necessary to involve other agencies. (Source: Alcohol Advisory Service – Coventry and Warwickshire, *Peer Education – A Manual*)

Once the person or persons have been selected to develop the project, it is imperative that certain areas are covered. These will determine the success of the peer education project. The areas include:

- project needs
- recruitment of peer educators
- training peer educators
- support for peer educators
- evaluation

Projects needs

Given the complexity of administrative systems in schools it would be advisable to work on a small scale, possibly a pilot programme. The project should be evaluated before moving on to involve more young people.

It is important that several key areas are put into place, these being:

- support from the LEA/finance
- commitment from staff and senior management to the peer education approach
- credibility in the eyes of the staff and especially in the young people involved
- integration into the school programme
- clear planning with clear aims and objectives
- clear and specified content, identified in the training sessions with peer tutors
- explanation available for others that may be involved or interested e.g. parents, other teachers, schools.
- to be able to obtain feedback from participants and young people on the receiving end, and to have the mechanisms to respond
- ability to have fun
- certain key resources, time allocation for planning and delivery

(Source:- Allison Rummey, West Sussex Health Authority and Daniel's – *A Peer Led Drug Education Manual*)

Recruitment of peer educators

Peer educators will be recruited through one of two ways in a school environment. They will either volunteer or they will be picked by a teacher or workers.

Volunteers will have to be provided with an attractive presentation, whilst still specifying the commitment required, the expectations on volunteers and possible rewards.

The advantages of volunteers is that they are likely to be committed due to the fact that they are there because they want to be. Additionally there is opportunity for everyone to volunteer should they want to.

Some of the disadvantages, however, could be that there is no control over the skills they bring. If over subscribed how will you select individuals?. People may volunteer for different reasons than the one you want and possibly you may need to be a bit of a sales person to pull them in.

Young people who are hand picked will have certain advantages. These being:

- The use of young people who are confident and will be able to work with other young people and make the project successful.
- Young people are committed for their personal development or interest in the subject.
- Time worries are reduced because volunteers are able and already skilled.

However there are several disadvantages that can occur due to this method. These include:

• Project could become exclusive, elitist and possibly alienating.

• Young people who are academically less able may miss out on an opportunity to blossom through peer education, where they could possibly benefit more from the project than those perceived to be more able.

There are issues regarding who picks the young people, and a lot of trust may be placed in the workers judgement and lack of prejudice. Teachers will often select differently to youth workers. (Source – Alcohol Advisory Service – Coventry and Warwickshire – *Peer Education Manual*)

Training peer educators

The success of the project will be determined greatly by the quality of training offered. It is essential to equip the peer educators with the skills and knowledge to deliver peer education whilst giving them every opportunity to explore theirs and others attitudes towards the issue of substance use and misuse.

Highly successful programmes already well established and recognised to be models of good practice include the peer education programme in Solihull called Cascade, and Wisecrack in Scotland. Cascade, which has been running since 1992, states their key objective as one that 'keeps young people safe and reduces the harm from drugs by giving young people access to correct information, accurate messages concerning the risks of drugs and support to make their own informed choice'. They have attracted interest in their project both across the UK and world wide.

At the core of these and many other projects is the need to ensure that young people are clear about the approach they are taking. In successful projects the Harm Prevention and Reduction models have been the foundations of what the peer education messages are based on. This fits in very well with the Government's strategy as laid out in the White Paper *Tackling Drugs Together* regarding education and prevention. Prevention is understood to be twofold, with primary prevention stopping young people from taking or experimenting with drugs in the first place and secondary prevention the treatment and rehabilitation to help those who are misusing drugs.

This was also highlighted in Pamela McAllister's Paper, (*Drugs and Crime, Reducing the Harm to the Community – A Plan for Neighbourhood Action* 1993).

In addition to the core skills required, (presentation skills, use of resources, variety of training methods, use of drama, video, posters and leaflets) peer educators working within their schools must know their schools policy on drug prevention. For those schools who have yet to put these in place peer educators can negotiate being part of this process.

Peer educators must have clear guidelines about confidentiality and all the successful peer education projects run one or more sessions on this topic with potential peer educators.

The Health Advisory Service Review (1996), *Children and Young People: Substance Misuse Services*, said 'effective education programmes share certain features', and listed them as:

- use of peer educators
- use of active learning models
- effective use of training of the teachers
- encourage individual responsibility
- involve young people in planning and implementing programmes

By completion of the training programme, usually over four to six weeks the ideal peer educator should be able to:

- communicate effectively through discussion and leadership
- work effectively as a team
- be a good listener
- respond effectively to groups and individuals
- have knowledge of support systems for peers with problems
- reproduce exercises from the training
- command respect from their peers
- have a good and correct knowledge of the facts surrounding the topic
- have an understanding of many of the issues that the topic throws up

It is not expected that each peer educator should possess every one of the skills listed and peer educators will often work in pairs learning from each other.

Support for peer educators

Volunteers will quickly lose interest and move on if they are not provided with enough adult support. Some of the things that should be put in place include:

- opportunities for group and or individual support
- contact number with times you are available
- alternative adult for support purposes
- meeting expenses incurred as part of the work
- social events

Additionally, recognition that the skills acquired are transferable and will be able to be adapted in other aspects of the young persons life into adulthood. It is important to recognise achievement and encourage young people to use their experiences as part of records of achievement within their schools, on portfolios and CVs.

- Certificates should be produced which should list particular aspects of training undergone.
- Young people should be encouraged to promote themselves in school newsletters, local newspapers and other media when opportunities arise.
- For those young people working on schemes like the Duke of Edinburgh Award or SGNVQ accreditation parts of the training and delivery of peer education may meet particular criteria.

- Opportunities to develop further, possibly outside of school and after they leave school.
- Extension of skills to move into counselling as in the Cascade project and Youth Awareness Programme (YAP) .

Evaluation

Evaluation, whether internally or externally, is an integral part of any peer education project. Evaluation will either take on board the process or the outcome of the project. In peer education projects it is agreed that outcome is difficult to achieve and most successful projects will evaluate the process.

It is important that the aims and objectives of the project are clearly laid out as this will provide the skeleton for evaluation.

Cascade evaluated their project through questionnaires given to participants after the events, and through structured events with those involved.

The evaluation sheets provided important evidence for quality control and provided suggestions for changes to the programme.

Wisecrack evaluated initially using a qualitative method at the end of their sessions. The feedback was positive, and where suggestions were made these were taken back to the peer educators to develop solutions. Wisecrack felt that there was a need to provide more quantitative data and viewed this as a priority objective in their operational plan.

Conclusion

In Luton the model has been used in youth and community groups as well as schools. This extension of the work allows the inclusion of young people in the programme who may otherwise be excluded. These have included non-school attendees, drug users, ex-users and those that are homeless or working on the streets. The central drugs prevention unit, offering a foreword on the evaluation of the YAP project, said 'the involvement of ex-drug users is a crucial part of providing credible drug information to young people, both drug users and non-users'.

This model has worked successfully because the co-ordinator has endeavoured to identify good practice across the country, adapt these to meet the clientele in Luton and develop the projects as part of a holistic programme to address drug education. The programme is not delivered in isolation and forms an integral part of the life skills programme in each of the high schools that the project co-ordinator is working in.

An external evaluation carried out by Luton University focused on two peer education projects, one school based and one community based. The evaluation found that both projects were successful in meeting their specific objectives and have made a positive contribution to raising drug awareness. In addition the research carried out a base line study to evaluate retention knowledge. Young people were able to retain 95% of the knowledge they received from the peer educators 3 months later. (Porteous, 1998)

Finally, young people, the driving force that will take the project forward should be consulted at all stages. Their ideas and concerns should always be heard. The ultimate goal is to equip young people with the skills and knowledge to not only take the project forward but to lead it. Those tasked with the setting up, delivery and support of peer education projects must be committed and have the interest of young people at heart. If good quality training and support are not provided we as professionals will have set young people up to fail.

References

Alcohol and Advisory Services (Coventry and Warwickshire) (1997). *Peer education – A Manual.*

Bedfordshire Drug Action Team (1997). A Commissioned Study, Brisby *et al.*, unpublished.

Berridge, D., and Wells, M. (1995). *Social Indicators and Recorded Crime in Luton*, Faculty of Health Care and Social Studies, University of Luton (unpublished).

Cascade (1997). *Peer Led Drugs Education Project*, Annual Review.

Corey, P. (1989). *Coping with Parents*. Scholastic Ltd.

Dorn, N., and Murji, K., (1992). *Drugs Prevention: A Review of the English Language Literature.* London: Institute for the Study of Drug Dependence.

Forster, K., and Pike, J. (1995). *Health Promotion for All.* Churchill & Livingston.

Government green paper (1994). *Tackling Drugs Together: A Consultation Strategy for England 1995 –1998.*

Hope, T., and Shaw, M. (1988). *Community Approaches to Reducing Crime in Communities and Crime Reduction.* London: HMSO.

Jack, B., and Clements, I. (1997). *Peer-led Drug Education.* Daniel's Publishing.

McAllister, P. (1997). *Drugs and Crime – Reducing the Harm to the Community – A Plan for Neighbourhood Action.*

McGurk, P., and Hurry, J. (1995). *Project Charlie: An evaluation of a Life Skills Drug Education Programme for Primary Schools.* Home Office Drugs Prevention Initiative, Paper 1.

Parliamentary All-party Penal Affairs Group (1983). *The Prevention of Crime Amongst Young People.*

Parker, H., Bury, C., and Egginton, R. (1998). *New Heroin Outbreaks Amongst Young People in England and Wales.* Crime Detection and Prevention Series, Paper 92.

Plant, M., and Plant, M. (1992). *Risk Takers: Alcohol, Drugs, Sex and Youth.* Tavistock and Routledge.

Porteous, D. (1998). *Luton Youth Action, An evaluation of Two Drug Prevention Projects.* Luton University.

Rummey, A. (1998). *West Sussex Model of Peer Education.* West Sussex Health Promotion.

Shiner, M., and Newburn, T. (1996). *Young People, Drugs and Peer Education: An Evaluation of the Youth Awareness Programme (YAP).* Home Office Drugs prevention Initiative Paper 13.

Smith, M. (1994). *Local Education.* Open University Press.

Tilley, N. (1992). *Safer Cities and Community Safety Strategies.* Police Research Group. Crime Prevention Series, Paper 38. Home Office.

Tyler, T., and Marlow, A. (1998). *An Audit of the Distribution of Crime and Offending within the Borough of Luton.* Vauxhall Centre for the Study of Crime, Luton University .

Wisecrack (1995). *Peer-led Drugs Education Project*, Annual Review.

Chapter 15

Casing the Joint: An Evaluation of Two Drugs Education Projects

David Porteous

Introduction

In 1995 the Conservative Government published a white paper, *Tackling Drugs Together*, setting out its strategy for dealing with drug misuse in England. This required that 105 Drug Action Teams (DATs) be established across the country with a remit to develop plans and co-ordinate actions to tackle three sets of problems: drug related crime, young people's misuse of drugs and the health risks associated with drugs. The DATs comprised senior officers from local statutory agencies and are supported by multi-agency Drug Reference Groups (DRGs) whose membership includes front-line workers with knowledge and experience of drug issues and problems.

This chapter discusses the findings from an evaluation of two drug prevention projects supported by one area Drug Action Team in partnership with a local youth initiative promoting young people's involvement in social and community affairs. Across the area, the projects fell into two groups, those that were school and those that were community based, and one from each of these groups is assessed here. The first involved year 12 (lower sixth form) students delivering drugs education lessons to pupils in years 7 and 8 (ages 11–13). The second involved unemployed young people, aged 16–25, in an eleven week arts project to design, produce and disseminate photographs conveying images of drug use and misuse.

The evaluation was focused on the question, to what extent did the projects **inform choices** about drug use amongst participants and beneficiaries? Thus the emphasis was not so much on whether the projects actually brought about a reduction in drug use as with their success or otherwise in raising the awareness of young people involved, this being the more modest aim set for them. As well as seeking to establish whether the projects **worked** in this sense, the research also aimed to identify why this was the case and how they and/or other similar projects could be improved upon.

Methodology

The methodology adopted for this study reflected the fact that the evaluation was only commissioned towards the end of the two projects. In the school based project, the peer educators had received their training and delivered classes to the target groups in years seven and eight by the time the researcher met with them. The photography course was complete. Although a core group of project members continued to use the six photographs produced as a drug awareness tool in community events, many of the participants in the course had ceased to be involved. For this reason, 'before and after' assessments of participants' and recipients' awareness of issues around drugs misuse were for the most part not possible and the evaluation was largely retrospective.

For both projects, a focus group was held with project managers and participants. At the school, the researcher met with five of the team of peer educators, all students in the first year of the sixth form and the Youth Initiative Co-ordinator. The photography project group included the project leaders, the professional photographer who had led the artistic component of the course and five of the participants on the course. Both group discussions covered:

- participants' motivation for being involved in the project
- its structure and content
- what they liked and disliked about different aspects of the project
- what they would do differently
- how information about drugs misuse delivered through the project compared with that they had encountered in other arenas such as the media
- what they had gained from the project
- other project outcomes.

Finally, the groups were asked what they would do if they were in the position of the newly appointed UK Anti-Drugs Co-ordinator.

The group discussions provided a comprehensive picture of how the two projects had been organised and delivered and what they had aimed to achieve. However, whilst participants in both groups were asked for and offered evidence of success in meeting their aims, it was necessary to obtain further information to support these claims. To some extent, both groups had a vested interest in 'talking up' their achievements. Put another way, their commitment and involvement in the projects meant that they would be predisposed to see them in positive terms.

Information to assess the two projects' success in raising awareness and promoting informed choices about drugs misuse was obtained in a number of ways. For the school based project, the researcher observed the peer educators' delivering a session to other students in the sixth form. This was the first time they had led a class with contemporaries and was therefore quite different from their experience earlier in the project of working with younger children. Nonetheless the exercise provided some useful insights. The second source of evidence came through the administration of a follow up quiz to a group of year seven (11-year-old) pupils who had taken part in a peer educators' lesson some months previously. They had completed the quiz in the earlier session and this exercise was intended to test whether they had retained the information.

Evidence of the photography project's impact was derived from evaluative materials collected during the course of the project by one of the managers including:

- participation rates during the course
- 'graffiti sheets' completed by participants at the end of sessions
- a record of the ways in which the photographs produced during the project had been publicised and utilised for drugs awareness events elsewhere
- outcomes for project participants following the course.

In addition, the researcher participated in a workshop presentation by members of the project at a conference organised by the area DRG. This exemplified how the photographs could be used as a drugs awareness tool.

Finally, we considered the content and impact of the two projects with reference to similar ones undertaken elsewhere and evaluated as part of the Drugs Prevention Initiative, a programme of preventative projects commissioned as part of the former government's drugs strategy.

The peer education project
Aims and structure

The school in which the project was based is a voluntary assisted secondary school which provides secondary and sixth form education to around 1500 pupils and students. The peer education project was one of nine school based initiatives co-ordinated by the local youth initiative although only one other of these projects was focused on drugs, the remainder being concerned with issues such as bullying, counselling, mentoring, alcohol use and smoking. Both alcohol and tobacco use and misuse were also included in the 'drugs' education delivered for this project.

The project was led by the Youth Initiative Co-ordinator and supported within the school by the Head of Personal, Social and Health Education. The aim of the project was

> to enhance school pupils' awareness and knowledge of issues relating to drug misuse.

This was to be achieved through the following objectives:

- The recruitment of peer educators from year 12.
- The training and support of the peer educators to deliver drugs education lessons.
- The delivery of drugs education lessons to pupils in years seven and eight.

Recruitment of peer educators to the project followed a presentation to the entire year 11 cohort by the Youth Initiative co-ordinator. Eighteen interested students then attended a meeting with the co-ordinator who outlined what the project would involve. Following this meeting, they each received a letter inviting them to a training day, on which seven students enrolled.

The training day commenced with some ice breakers and the agreement of a group contract. Role play exercises and games were used as a means to learn about and discuss various aspects of and facts about drug use and misuse, utilising the same materials as would be used by the peer educators themselves. The training also covered the development of lesson plans and presentation skills and the students each gave a presentation. Issues of confidentiality were explained and discussed.

The peer educators then met once a week with the co-ordinator to develop the teaching materials and lesson plans. This involved a study of the content of the Personal, Social and Health Education curriculum to identify how and when drugs were taught, and of the school guidelines on what should be covered so as to ensure that curricular aims would be met. Learning resources including video were provided by the Youth Action Co-ordinator from which the students selected those that they would use.

In the actual delivery of lessons, the peer educators used the following techniques: role play exercises, games, debates, mock trials, brain storming exercises, quizzes, attitude surveys and videos. They also provided spoken and written information on drugs in more traditional form. Lessons were delivered at the planned point in the PSHE timetable (one hour per week) to tutor groups in years seven and eight. The team worked in groups of two or three per lesson. Form tutors were present throughout the lessons and sometimes contributed to the class. An evaluative element was built in towards the end of the lessons so that feedback from pupils could be collected.

Focus group findings

When asked to say what had motivated them to take part in the project, the peer educators' initial response was refreshingly honest – 'we were asked to'. However, whilst this suggests that some pressure was at first required to encourage their involvement, there were other reasons. Two students intend to pursue a career in teaching and saw this as a useful opportunity to test their ambitions. Other members of the group saw it as an opportunity to gain confidence in public speaking and to enhance their CV for when they applied to university.

The group were asked to critically reflect on the three main components of the project:

- The training day was seen very positively because it had demonstrated to the students how their own lessons might work. The participative nature of the exercises were said to be enjoyable and interesting and this meant that they absorbed the information. On the down side, it was described as a long and tiring day, and the latter parts of the day had to be rushed somewhat. The group agreed that the training would be better delivered in two half days if possible.

- In the preparation of lesson plans, students emphasised that they were aiming to compliment the existing curriculum, not to undermine or replace it. To illustrate this, one pupil provided some of her own lesson plans together with the teacher's initial lesson plans.

- The most successful lessons, according to the students, were those in which pupils had taken an active part since this made them fun and enjoyable. Giving very technical information about drugs on the other hand did not work well as the pupils found it difficult to understand and became bored.

Comparing what they had learnt through the project with information they had received elsewhere, the peer educators observed that in the media it is harder drugs which are focused on and that the effects are overly dramatised and even celebrated and promoted by, for example, pop stars. Similarly, they felt that although their parents may have mentioned the dangers of drugs, more everyday or commonplace problems such as those associated with smoking tobacco had in general not been discussed at home. On what they had learnt previously in school, the group said that they could not remember what they had been taught and that their experience was of having information 'pumped into you'.

The peer educators felt that they had gained the following through their participation in the project:

- transferable skills – presentation, preparation etc.
- confidence in public speaking
- knowledge about drugs and their harmful effects
- an understanding of how the media distorts issues around drugs
- confidence in working with students because of a better understanding of the issues
- the experience of being responsible for a class of 30 pupils
- a feeling of being valued by, and of working with, teachers
- an appreciation of how hard it is to be a teacher
- seeing teachers' point of view

They also cited a number of other beneficiaries:

- teachers – who had been able to observe the lessons being given by someone younger as well as participating in them
- pupils – who had 'been taught stuff without realising it'. The students reported that some pupils had requested further peer education at the end of the lessons and had provided positive feedback generally
- their parents, younger brothers and sisters – who had learnt more about drugs.

Asked what they would do if they were in the position of the UK Anti-drugs Co-ordinator, the students argued that there should be a co-ordinated approach to drugs education with all schools having the same structures and that more peer education should be promoted because students (and younger teachers) are in general more 'streetwise'. In terms of information about drugs, they felt that it is important to move away from the 'Just Say No' approach to one which explained how and why drug use should be avoided, including information about the short and long term health risks and about the harmful effects of tobacco and alcohol as well as harder drugs. Harm reduction should be the aim, they argued, whereby the dangers, including the legal implications of taking drugs, are made clear, but it is left to recipients to reach their own judgments and conclusions.

The 'should cannabis be legalised' debate

The researcher had the opportunity to observe the peer educators in action when they presided over a debate amongst their contemporaries in the first year of the sixth form. The session commenced with a presentation of the 'facts about cannabis' by the peer educators which described amongst other things how the drug is consumed, what the known effects of consumption are and the Dutch system, where cannabis is decriminalised. The group then divided into 'for' and 'against' sub groups in which they developed their arguments supported by information from the peer educators. Lastly, the two groups came back together for the debate, led by nominated representatives, and a final vote.

There were a number of problems with the session. First of all it was clear that the peer educators had not prepared sufficiently as a group. This meant that they were unclear of their respective roles and, when doing the presentation, were reading the content of the overhead slides for the first time, giving the impression that they had no more knowledge of the facts about cannabis than the audience. The large sixth form group (approximately 60 students) were very boisterous and the peer educators were reliant on the teachers present to maintain order. In this environment, the debate did tend to deteriorate into a slanging match amongst some of the louder (male) participants and it was difficult for others to hear the arguments presented.

In defence of the peer educators, this was the first session which they had run with their contemporaries and they were understandably intimidated and nervous. The group was, in retrospect, probably too large for them to manage, and they were left somewhat in the lurch because the Youth Action Co-ordinator had been asked to cover for an absent teacher.

Notwithstanding the difficulties, the session did generate quite a lot of discussion. When, at the end of the debate, we asked the students whether they had learnt anything new, some participants said that it had made them think about familiar issues in a different light. Certainly it was an enjoyable occasion, except for the peer educators. And whilst before the groups divided to develop their arguments, 90% of them indicated that they thought cannabis should be legalised, the 'against' team presented the most convincing case and the final vote was evenly split.

Quiz results

A second exercise which provided evidence of the impact of peer education was a quiz on the effects of smoking administered to one class of pupils in year seven. The quiz contained ten questions and the pupils completed it twice, once at the beginning of a lesson on smoking delivered by peer educators in December and then again as part of a separate PSHE lesson in May. The mean average score achieved by pupils for the first quiz was 5.5 (out of 10) and the mode average (the most frequent score), 7. When they completed the same quiz five months later, the pupils' mean average score was 9 and the mode average 10. Although ideally an independent researcher would oversee such a before and after test and with a larger sample of pupils, these results suggest that this group of pupils had both absorbed and remembered the information they received.

Evaluation

To what extent can the peer education project be said to have succeeded in achieving its aims and objectives? On the latter, there is no doubt. A team of committed students were recruited as peer educators, they received ongoing training and support and developed the confidence and knowledge to successfully deliver drugs education lessons in accordance with curricular and school expectations to full classes of pupils in years seven and eight. The objectives of the project were therefore met. What is more difficult to ascertain is the degree to which the experience of being taught by the peer educators enhanced the younger pupils' knowledge and awareness of drugs over and above that which they would have gained through the delivery of these lessons by teachers.

On the one hand, we would need a different and more comprehensive research methodology to the one adopted here to properly address this question. One appropriate method would be to have before and after assessments of two groups of pupils' experience of drugs education – one group receiving a lesson from a teacher, the other receiving a lesson from the peer educators. (N.B. The DAT and Youth Action co-ordinators had, in fact, planned this form of evaluation, but a lack of resources and time restricted the scope and nature of the research.) On the other hand, there is quite a large body of evidence to suggest that this model of delivering drugs education was successful, namely:

- The peer educators own reflections on the project. They had found the process rewarding in terms of enjoyment and the new skills they had required, they reported positive feedback from both teachers and pupils and they argued forcefully that peer education worked because as students they had been able to involve pupils more easily than older teachers could.
- The fact that the project was sustained, which supports the above claims.
- The positive results of the before and after quiz, described above.
- The generation of lively and provocative discussion in the admittedly difficult debate observed by the researcher and described above.

In addition, we may note that, apart from the benefits of the project for the young people on the receiving end of the peer educators' work, the students themselves gained in several ways, most notably through enhanced confidence, the acquisition of new skills and an understanding of the teaching process. It is clear that their curriculum vitae will be enriched by their participation on the project as they had hoped.

An evaluation of a peer education project sponsored through the Drugs Prevention Initiative provides further insights which we can assess this project against. Shiner and Newburn's (1996) study considered the effectiveness of the London Borough of Newham's Youth Awareness Programme. Under this programme, drugs education workshops were delivered by young people with direct experience of drug misuse to other young people (aged 12–16) in schools and youth clubs. Notwithstanding the differences between this project and our school based project, Shiner and Newburn's conclusions are instructive.

The authors hypothesise that central to the success of peer education as a model is the notion of credibility which they suggest has three dimensions:

1. Person-based credibility, arising from perceived (and often shared) personal characteristics, in particular, age.
2. Experience-based credibility, arising from a perceived (and possibly shared) experience, for example drug use.
3. Message-based credibility, arising from what is being said and the way it is said…realistic messages about health risks and the minimisation of harm.
(Shiner and Newburn, 1996, p 52)

A 'complicated balance' of these three dimensions to credibility, Shiner and Newburn argue, 'is crucial' (ibid. p 60). Moreover, whilst given the right balance, 'peer education is potentially an influential and effective approach to drugs education' (ibid. p 69), other factors, notably the extent to which recipients are questioning their own drug using behaviour at the point when the education workshops (or classes) are held, will also come into play.

At our school, the peer educators, even if they had experience of drug use, were not drawing on such experiences as part of the drugs education lessons. Indeed, in this context it would probably have been quite inappropriate to do so. However, from the foregoing discussion it should be evident that the notions of person-based and message-based credibility were important. Their person-based credibility derived from their age and from the fact that they were fellow pupils at the school or, perhaps more significantly, from the fact that they were not teachers. The message-based credibility derived from their rejection of the 'just say no' approach to drugs education. Their more open-ended approach is the same as the one adopted by the peer educators in Newham. Shiner and Newburn's research suggests that this kind of message is appropriate because it recognises that young people critically evaluate information which they receive. A quote from one of the young people they interviewed makes the point:

> *They (YAP) don't speak down to you, like 'don't take drugs and you don't do that', like a parent would. They talk to you not down at you, do you, know what I mean and that's about it really, it's really good. (A teacher would say) 'Right, sit down there, I'm telling you you're not going to take drugs'…They look down at you, just treat you like little kids. (YAP) talked to you like an adult, like what you are and what you should be treated like, yeah* (ibid. p 61).

Interestingly, another of these researchers' findings was that young people were less likely to find peer educators credible if they were of the same age because they would be deemed to have only similar experiences to their own. Although there were other problems with the 'legalise cannabis' debate discussed above, the peer educators' apprehension about the session and the slightly irreverent reception they received would tend to support this finding.

The photography project

This was a community based arts project which, through funding from the National Lottery Arts for Everyone programme, set up an eleven week photography course targeted at unemployed young people aged 16–25. The course aimed to produce between six and ten photographic posters on the theme of substance misuse (including illicit drugs, solvents, alcohol and tobacco) for dissemination in the media and at community events. Although the arts project has subsequently continued to exist, the principal focus of the evaluation was with the process and outcomes of the photography course rather than the broader initiative.

Aims, structure and membership

The project was initially conceived by a group of friends at a local arts centre with an interest in using art as a medium for drugs education and diversion from drugs. From the outset they sought and obtained financial and staff support from the area DAT, the local Youth Initiative Action and from a local drugs advice, information and treatment agency.

The project's aims as set out in its application to the National Lottery were:

> *to provide training and facilities, introducing local young people to arts experiences, supporting independent cultural expression, building skills and motivating personal development, through the production of peer-aimed images.*

In meeting this aim, a number of subsidiary objectives were identified:

- To run a photography course focused on the production of posters depicting substance use and misuse.
- To target young people disenfranchised from arts activities.
- To disseminate the posters in the media and to use them as a drugs awareness tool at community events.

In its application the project leaders established targets of 20 young people being involved in the course and six to ten photographic posters being produced.

Following its successful application for funding, the project distributed application forms to approximately 50 local organisations including statutory agencies, local community centres, community groups, a foyer for young homeless people, libraries, health centres and drug and alcohol advice services. A total of 208 application forms were handed out and 26 forms were completed and returned.

The course ran for a period of eleven weeks. The first two sessions, held at the foyer and co-ordinated by the local drugs agency workers were focused on substance misuse and harm reduction. They involved participants in brainstorming activities, exchanging stories of substance use and discussion of the social context in which young people use drugs.

All but one of the remaining sessions were held at the local Arts Centre where there is a darkroom. Participants were engaged in the production of the photographic posters. This involved designing the images, makeup, set and costume design and modelling. A professional photographer co-ordinated the process and was responsible for developing the photographs. The other element of the course was a group visit in week four to the 'Sensation' exhibition at the Royal Academy of Arts, which was intended to introduce participants to contemporary art focused on topical social issues.

Of the 26 young people who originally applied to enrol on the photography course, 11 actually attended one or more sessions of whom four attended eight or more times. A further 13 young people who did not actually complete applications joined the project of whom four attended six times or more. For the total of 24 participants, the average attendance was 4.2 sessions. However, this somewhat distorts the reality of participation which is that there was a core group of eight young people involved throughout and a slightly higher number who were involved on a more sporadic basis – indeed seven only attended one of the eleven sessions. The mean average attendance per week was 9 and the mode average ten. The implications of these varying participation rates are discussed below.

Since several of the project participants did not complete application forms, the age, gender, ethnicity and economic status of the whole group could not be established from this source. However, statistics provided by one of the project leaders showed that there were 13 female participants and 11 males whose ages ranged from 16 to 25 (with one exception, a 40-year-old husband of one participant who was invited to support his spouse who became ill midway through the project). 19 participants were white British, three were Bangladeshi, one Indian and one South African. The majority of participants were unemployed when the course started.

Focus group findings

Participants in the project who attended the focus group discussion said that they were motivated to join because it was free, because it involved photography and was 'hands on' training, because it was an opportunity to develop skills and because there is generally very little for unemployed young people to do otherwise. No mention was made of the drugs awareness component of the course and this was echoed in the reasons given by the 26 young people who had completed application forms. Here the most commonly cited reasons were that the course would help them get a job, meet new people, develop new skills and in particular skills in photography and artistic expression.

Asked what they liked about the project, participants mentioned the relaxed atmosphere, the fact that participation was voluntary – one could be more or less involved in different activities according to one's interest, the process of contributing, exchanging and interpreting ideas, the opportunity to express one's creativity, the experiential nature of the course and the fact that it was fun. The visit to the Sensation exhibition was described as thought provoking as well as enjoyable.

'Graffiti' sheets completed by participants in the earlier weeks of the course echo these sentiments as this sample of comments illustrate:

> *Hearing everyone's own personal views about drugs.*
>
> *Ideas of what can be achieved, listening to other people's experiences, achievements and ideas.*
>
> *Working together with others, having lots to laugh about, good mixture of humour. Looking forward to the dressing up and photography next week.*

Few dislikes were given either in the focus group discussion or the evaluative graffiti sheets. The rather sporadic attendance to the course was identified as problematic although a number of reasons were suggested for this – people were getting jobs, sorting out benefits etc. – and it was felt that the flexible nature of the project (which operated like a drop-in) had been a positive aspect so that it did not matter if you were unable to attend all the sessions. The relatively low attendance of young people from ethnic minorities was seen as disappointing though minority community groups and centres had been targeted at the recruitment stage.

Participants identified a number of ways in which the project could be improved. Lengthening the project would be beneficial, it was felt, in order to increase participants' involvement in the photographic process and especially the development stage. Another possibility which the project leaders in particular had explored was of providing some means by which participants' involvement could be recognised, such as records of achievement, certificates of attendance etc. A systematic evaluation of sessions (which had been discontinued midway through the course), and of the project as a whole, was seen as important although potentially off-putting – hence the discontinuation. Finally, participants were agreed that more spacious and warmer premises would be desirable.

Comparing the drugs component of the project with other arenas in which drugs are discussed or focused upon, participants stated that the project had not adopted a yes/no approach but rather had enabled them to think about issues. They described the media presentation of drugs issues as one of scaremongering in creating panic and fear, as feeding people with views from which they either walk away or do not consider critically, as depicting young people in general as a problem and as ignoring the range of reasons why people take drugs including enjoyment.

Participants said they had gained from the project in the following ways:

- it had been an experiential, learning process;
- it had involved commitment in terms of time and effort;
- it had provided satisfaction and enjoyment – 'a natural high' as one person put it;

- the participants had achieved things of which they were proud;
- it had been a way of getting one's voice heard;
- it had generated thought amongst participants about the effects of drugs;
- it provided a way of reaching young people – especially those who do not see, hear or listen to existing messages.

Finally, asked what they would do in the position of the UK Anti-Drugs Co-ordinator, participants identified a range of actions although there was not universal agreement on all of them. For a start, it was felt that a different, more independent 'drugs czar' should have been appointed, perhaps an ex-user. Once in place that person should:

- Insist that all GPs have drug (e.g. methadone) prescribing services.
- Increase resources for addicts ensuring safe and accessible treatment.
- Give more power to user groups in relation to policy, advice and information.
- In prisons
  - identify the scale of existing problems
  - provide clean works to injecting users
  - run more rehabilitation and diversion programmes and reward users who come off drugs.
- Provide more community based day-care.
- Be responsive to the different needs of different kinds of users.
- Educate and empower young people based on harm reduction, not 'just say no'.
- Decriminalise and then legalise cannabis to prevent people from exploitation from dealers 'pushing' them onto harder drugs.
- Start drugs education in schools earlier.
- Provide drug testing facilities at drugs agencies and dance/music events;
- Provide more for young people to do, especially diversionary activities involving the arts.

Workshop at the area DRG Drugs Conference

Having created six photographic posters depicting images of substance use and abuse, project members were subsequently involved in their dissemination through a number of avenues. These included:

- an article in Amateur Photography magazine
- an interview on a local BBC radio station
- participation in a 'National Youth Week' conference
- participation in a local authority 'Listen to Youth' Forum
- the involvement of participants as photographers at community events
- exhibitions at a local Youth Centre and at a university conference on 'Young people, drugs and community safety'

As part of the evaluation, we witnessed the project leaders and participants leading a workshop at a conference organised by the area DRG. This engaged delegates in a brainstorming exercise to identify the positive and negative effects of two substances, heroin and solvents, as depicted in two of the photographs produced during the course. The posters proved a useful mechanism for generating discussion amongst the group, who included police officers, a local magistrate and drugs and youth workers working in different contexts and agencies. Feedback on the presentation included one observation that the project team had managed to 'wake up the dinosaurs'. Another participant commented that it 'was a very interesting set of photographs, presenting a unique insight into the minds of the individuals who created them.'

Evaluation

As with the school based project, the evaluation suggests that the photography project successfully achieved its stated aims and objectives. The course, incorporating drugs awareness sessions as well as active participation in the creation of photographic posters depicting substance use and misuse was delivered as intended. Group discussions with a small number of participants and written comments from other participants, in the form of evaluative 'graffiti' sheets, suggest that they enjoyed the course and that they gained confidence and developed skills through the process. A majority of participants were unemployed and their reasons for participation included learning new skills in arts and photography – three participants have moved into further training or work within the arts following the course. 24 young people took part in the project altogether, although attendance was sporadic and only a core group of eight participated fully throughout. Six posters were produced and these have been used as a resource for drugs awareness. The project has captured some interest in the media and some participants have represented the project as photographers or otherwise at conferences and community events.

The relatively low attendance on the project of half of the participants should be viewed as more of a cause for consideration than concern. There appears to be several reasons for this. Some people found work, were actively seeking work, or were sorting out benefit problems. It may be that the participative nature of the project limited the number of people who could be actively involved throughout and the project leaders acknowledged that the waiting time between photographic shoots caused some people to drop out. No doubt some people attended the course once and decided it was not for them.

The project leaders acknowledged that the drop out rate was disappointing and had discussed how the problem might be addressed in future. One idea considered was to introduce some formal recognition of participants' achievements such as a certificate of attendance. However, they also feared that this would overly formalise the course and put off some participants for whom the relatively relaxed and informal environment was an attraction. A second suggestion was to incorporate a weekly debriefing session within the course so as to allow participants to feedback concerns and suggest changes or additions. Sustaining such an evaluative element throughout the project is to be recommended and it would also be useful to try to find out why people who leave the course have chosen to do so (notwithstanding the difficulties associated with tracking down young, mobile, busy people).

To what extent can the project be said to have informed young people's choices about drugs? Although this was not the explicit aim in the application to the National Lottery, the project clearly sought to do so; for participants, by focusing the photography course around substance use, and more generally by disseminating the photographs and both providing and using them as a resource or tool in drug awareness events. In the process of delivering the course, the project also sought to divert young people at risk of substance misuse away from use by providing them with an opportunity to channel their activities in positive ways.

One indicator of the project's impact in this regard is the participants' own use. Many of the young people on the project were acknowledged drug users. Nonetheless, participants refrained from drug use whilst attending the course sessions and at least two participants, both heroin addicts, said they had or were attempting to stop using having been involved in the project.

A second indicator is the interest and use that has been made of the photographic posters produced by the project. This suggests that materials are viewed as a valuable drug awareness resource by other organisations. And as noted above, the workshop presentation at the area DRG conference demonstrated how the posters could be used to generate discussion about different kinds of substance abuse.

In their examination of six DPI funded diversionary projects, Davis and Dawson (1996) identify ten key features of successful projects. The projects were all similar to the one considered here in that they aimed to divert young people away from drug use by 'engaging young people in leisure, recreation or other community-oriented activities.' (Davis and Dawson, 1996, p 2) Where they varied were in the age of the client group, the type of activity and the extent to which the projects carried an explicit drugs prevention message. Not all the points listed by the authors are relevant here as they refer to projects working with young children. However, those that are relevant are worth quoting in full as they provide a useful benchmark against which to assess the photography course.

The greatest success is achieved when a highly desirable, highly rewarding activity incorporates explicit drugs prevention messages from the outset. Young people will tend to accept a message delivered by credible figures, through a medium which they identify.

The activity on offer must excite the passion of young people, for example music, sport or computer technology. It is even more effective if it has some prospect of a permanent place in their lives, even offering eventual employment.

Project workers need to gain credibility through relevant skills and local knowledge. Essential qualities are:

- *an envied level of talent and skill in the activity on offer*
- *local experience and knowledge, giving them an understanding of current pressures on young people*

Project workers need to be confident in their ability to transmit drugs prevention messages. Workers, especially volunteers, may lack the necessary confidence. But hastily-delivered training on drugs issues is unlikely to be effective.

Where the potential exists to adapt an attractive medium to drugs prevention work, it is vital to give thought to:

- *whom the project is aimed at*
- *the means by which messages will be transmitted*

Bolting on a drugs element to an inappropriate medium does not work. Sometimes it weakens an otherwise perfectly viable project. (ibid.)

Measured against these success factors, this course seems to have been effective. Those participants who took part in the focus group discussion had found it to be rewarding both in terms of the new skills they had developed and the opportunity to express their thoughts about substance misuse in a creative manner. Some participants, including drug users, said that they would not have otherwise become involved in drug-related programmes. The fact that the project led to the production of actual posters meant that there was a tangible outcome to people's involvement (although this was clearly not the case for those who dropped out), and contributed to participants' sense of ownership of the project. There is evidence that the course contributed to positive outcomes for some young people in terms of training and employment.

The project team included a professional photographer whose knowledge and skill were appreciated by participants and his involvement gave credence to the course. The project leaders were experienced drugs advice and counselling workers. Their approach enabled participants to express their views on drugs freely and openly and this was appreciated by young people who were critical of the 'just say No' approach to drugs awareness that they associated with mainstream media coverage. The project leaders commitment to the project is evident in the fact that unpaid work has continued beyond the duration of the course. It is also worth noting that the project was underpinned by the support of a local drugs agency and the Drugs Action Team.

Conclusion

In its recently published ten year strategy for tackling drugs misuse in the UK, New Labour's first stated aim is 'to help young people resist drug misuse in order to achieve their full potential in society.' (Government White Paper 1998, p 3) 'Prevention should start early,' the document reads, 'with broad life-skills approaches at primary school, and built on over time with appropriate programmes for young people as they grow older via youth work, peer approaches, training and wider community support.' (ibid. p 13) Both of the projects evaluated in this study would be likely candidates for inclusion in the programme of action outlined by the Government which includes drugs education in schools, reducing the cultural acceptability of drugs, promoting 'positive activities' and intervening with at-risk groups of young people. (ibid. p 15).

Judging the effectiveness of such projects is no easy task. Certainly we will resist what Davis and Dawson call the 'leap of faith' required for claims to be made about their impact on actual drug and substance use (*op. cit.* p 7). We should also acknowledge that more rigorous evaluation than that conducted here is necessary. The use of control groups would be especially valuable. Nevertheless, given that raising drugs awareness is a central plank of government policy, the study does suggest some elements of good practice.

First is the emphasis upon harm reduction. Both projects' participants and leaders argued against 'just say No' messages in favour of a 'just look at the facts and way up the consequences' approach. Underpinning this is a belief that young people will critically evaluate information about drugs and that providing comprehensive, accurate information should therefore be the priority. The other more tacit assumption is that drug use is already prevalent amongst young people and that drugs education should be based on a recognition of this fact rather than on an 'ideal' of a drugs free society.

Following on from this, the use of techniques and materials appropriate to the client group again characterised both projects. The photography course was an effective medium through which participants could explore and discuss issues around substance misuse in a way which engaged their interest and allowed them to develop other skills. Some participants, including drug users, said that they would not have otherwise become involved in drug-related programmes. The peer educators selected study tools which actively involved younger pupils and made the process enjoyable for them, whilst remaining focused on the existing curriculum.

The third related point concerns the 'credibility' of the messengers. The role of the local Youth Initiative Co-ordinator in providing ongoing training and support to the peer educators in the school project was crucial, as was the support offered by teachers. Yet the age and status of the educators was what apparently mattered most. In the other project, the professional photographer's role was very important in ensuring a tangible, high quality outcome to the group's work. Alongside this the open, non judgmental stance of the drugs and youth workers seems to have fostered a sense of ownership amongst participants.

The overall message from this study is that drugs education should be delivered objectively, in an accessible manner, by people with the whom the audience can identify and respect. It is a message which chimes with the findings from previous evaluations and which should advance the government's objective of raising awareness. But if more young people know more about drugs, will fewer take them? Now there's a question.

References

Davis G., and Dawson N. (1996). *Using Diversion To Communicate Drugs Prevention Messages To Young People: An Examination of Six Projects*. London: Home Office.

Drugs Prevention Initiative (1996). *Programme of Work 1995–1999*. London: Home Office.

Government White Paper (1998). *Tackling Drugs To Build A Better Britain; The Government's 10 Year Strategy for Tackling Drugs Misuse*. London: The Stationery Office Limited.

Shiner M., and Newburn T. (1996). *Young People, Drugs And Peer Education: An Evaluation of the Youth Awareness Progamme*. London: Home Office.